A gift from the
Friends of the
La Jolla Library

About *The Way Into...*

The Way Into... is a major series that provides an accessible and highly usable "guided tour" of the Jewish faith and people, its history and beliefs—in total, a basic introduction to Judaism for adults that will enable them to understand and interact with sacred texts.

The Authors

Each book in the series is written by a leading contemporary teacher and thinker. While each of the authors brings his or her own individual style of teaching to the series, every volume's approach is the same: to help you to learn, in a life-affecting way, about important concepts in Judaism.

The Concepts

Each volume in *The Way Into...* Series explores one important concept in Judaism, including its history, its basic vocabulary, and what it means to Judaism and to us. In the Jewish tradition of study, the reader is helped to interact directly with sacred texts.

The topics to be covered in *The Way Into...* Series:

Torah
Jewish Prayer
Encountering God in Judaism
Jewish Mystical Tradition
Covenant and Commandment
Holiness and Chosenness (*Kedushah*)
Time
Judaism and the Environment
Zion
Tikkun Olam (Repairing the World)
Money and Ownership
Women and Men
The Relationship between Jews and Non-Jews
The Varieties of Jewishness

The Way Into

the Varieties of Jewishness

Sylvia Barack Fishman, PhD

דרך למוד דרך למוד דרך למוד
דרך למוד
דרך למוד

JEWISH LIGHTS Publishing
Woodstock, Vermont

The Way Into the Varieties of Jewishness

2007 First Printing
© 2007 by Sylvia Barack Fishman

Library of Congress Cataloging-in-Publication Data
Fishman, Sylvia Barack, 1942–
The way into the varieties of Jewishness / Sylvia Barack Fishman.
p. cm. — (The way into—)
Includes bibliographical references and index.
ISBN-13: 978-1-58023-030-8 (hardcover)
ISBN-10: 1-58023-030-X (hardcover)
1. Judaism—History. 2. Jews—History. 3. Jews—Identity. I. Title.
BM155.3.F57 2007
296.09—dc22

2006029730

10 9 8 7 6 5 4 3 2 1

The publisher gratefully acknowledges the contribution of Rabbi
Sheldon Zimmerman to the creation of this series. In his lifelong
work of bringing a greater appreciation of Judaism to all people, he
saw the need for *The Way Into...* and inspired us to act on it.

Manufactured in the United States of America
Jacket Design: Glenn Suokko and Jenny Buono
Text Design: Glenn Suokko
❀ Printed on recycled paper

Published by Jewish Lights Publishing
A Division of LongHill Partners, Inc.
Sunset Farm Offices, Route 4, P.O. Box 237
Woodstock, VT 05091
Tel: (802) 457-4000   Fax: (802) 457-4004
www.jewishlights.com

In loving memory of my parents,
Rabbi Nathan Abraham and Lillian Astrachan Barack

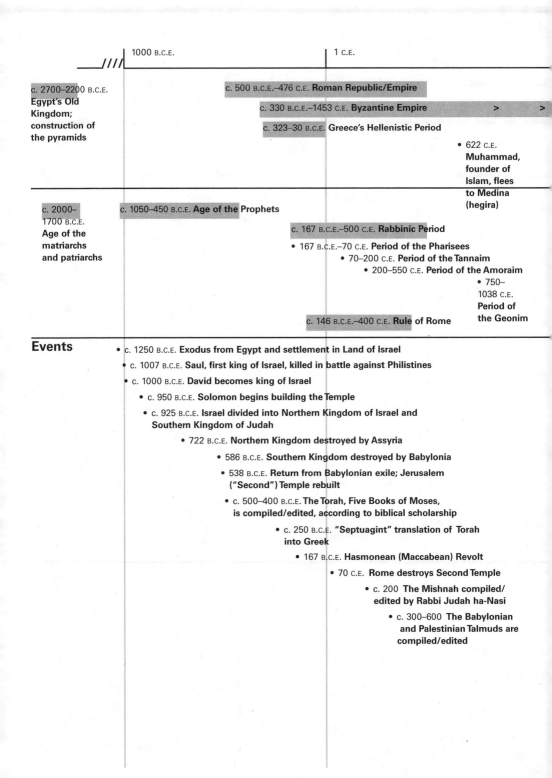

1000 B.C.E.	1 C.E.

c. 2700–2200 B.C.E.
Egypt's Old Kingdom; construction of the pyramids

c. 500 B.C.E.–476 C.E. **Roman Republic/Empire**

c. 330 B.C.E.–1453 C.E. **Byzantine Empire** > >

c. 323–30 B.C.E. **Greece's Hellenistic Period**

• 622 C.E. **Muhammad, founder of Islam, flees to Medina (hegira)**

c. 2000–1700 B.C.E.
Age of the matriarchs and patriarchs

c. 1050–450 B.C.E. **Age of the Prophets**

c. 167 B.C.E.–500 C.E. **Rabbinic Period**

• 167 B.C.E.–70 C.E. **Period of the Pharisees**

• 70–200 C.E. **Period of the Tannaim**

• 200–550 C.E. **Period of the Amoraim**

• 750–1038 C.E. **Period of the Geonim**

c. 146 B.C.E.–400 C.E. **Rule of Rome**

Events

• c. 1250 B.C.E. **Exodus from Egypt and settlement in Land of Israel**

• c. 1007 B.C.E. **Saul, first king of Israel, killed in battle against Philistines**

• c. 1000 B.C.E. **David becomes king of Israel**

• c. 950 B.C.E. **Solomon begins building the Temple**

• c. 925 B.C.E. **Israel divided into Northern Kingdom of Israel and Southern Kingdom of Judah**

• 722 B.C.E. **Northern Kingdom destroyed by Assyria**

• 586 B.C.E. **Southern Kingdom destroyed by Babylonia**

• 538 B.C.E. **Return from Babylonian exile; Jerusalem ("Second") Temple rebuilt**

• c. 500–400 B.C.E. **The Torah, Five Books of Moses, is compiled/edited, according to biblical scholarship**

• c. 250 B.C.E. **"Septuagint" translation of Torah into Greek**

• 167 B.C.E. **Hasmonean (Maccabean) Revolt**

• 70 C.E. **Rome destroys Second Temple**

• c. 200 **The Mishnah compiled/edited by Rabbi Judah ha-Nasi**

• c. 300–600 **The Babylonian and Palestinian Talmuds are compiled/edited**

1000 C.E.   2000 C.E.

- c. 1040–1105 **Rashi, French Bible and Talmud scholar and creator of line-by-line commentary on the Torah**
  - 1178 **Maimonides (1135–1204) completes his code of Jewish law, the** *Mishneh Torah*
    - c. 1295 *The Zohar,* **Kabbalistic work of mystical teaching, composed**
      - 1492 **Jews expelled from Spain**
        - 1565 **Joseph Caro publishes** *Shulchan Arukh,* **the standard code of Jewish law and practice**
          - 1654 **First Jewish settlement in North America at New Amsterdam**
            - 1700–1760 **Israel Baal Shem Tov, founder of Hasidism**
              - 1729–1786 **Moses Mendelssohn, "Father of the Jewish Enlightenment"**
                - 1801–1888 **Samson Raphael Hirsch, founder of "Modern Orthodoxy"**
                  - 1836 **Yeshiva University founded**
                    - 1873; 1875 **Reform Judaism in U.S. establishes Union of American Hebrew Congregations and Hebrew Union College**
                      - 1887 **Conservative Judaism's Jewish Theological Seminary founded**
                        - 1897 **Theodor Herzl convenes First Zionist Congress**
                          - 1933–1945 **The Holocaust (Shoah)**
                            - 1935 **Mordecai Kaplan establishes the Jewish Reconstructionist Foundation**
                              - 1948 **Birth of the State of Israel**

Contents

Acknowledgments

Writing this book was much like touring a vast continent, deciding which locales to visit and which to regretfully pass over, in order to create an itinerary that reflects the diversity of the land as a whole. It was an exhilarating trip, opening up new vistas, and creating a desire for longer stays and detours into neglected regions. I hope that reading this book accomplishes similar goals for readers as writing it did for me.

My thanks go first to Jewish Lights Publishing's publisher, Stuart M. Matlins, who suggested the concept and has been unfailingly supportive; to Alys R. Yablon Wylen, my skilled and thoughtful editor; and to Emily Wichland, who expedited the book's publication in numerous ways. I am indebted to my friends and colleagues, expert travel guides who generously discussed the journey and read individual chapters: Shaye Cohen on "Ancient Jews, Homelands, and Exiles"; Jonathan Decter on "The Wandering Jews"; Eugene Sheppard on "Emancipating into Modernity"; and Jonathan Sarna on the chapters on contemporary American Judaisms. Their comments improved these chapters, and any remaining infelicities are my own responsibility.

As always, I am grateful to Brandeis University, to my colleagues in the Near Eastern and Judaic Studies Department, to the lively staff of the Cohen Center for Modern Jewish Studies, and to the Hadassah-Brandeis Institute, especially for enabling Hillary Hampton, Rachel Werner, and Sarah Krevsky to help me gather materials.

Last but never least, substantive thanks go to my husband, Phil, an avid reader of Jewish history who has been interested in this intellectual journey long before I started writing it. Our ongoing discussions about various dimensions of the Jewish experience have been immensely helpful, and he remains my best critical reader. Thanks too to my children and grandchildren, and our conversations about the ways they creatively make Jewishness central in their busy lives. This book is dedicated to the blessed memory of my parents, Rabbi Nathan and Lillian Barack, who served diverse Jewish and non-Jewish communities with inclusive love and dedication—but still made our Shabbat home a joyous anchor for life.

Introduction

"Inside every Jew there is a mob of Jews," writes Philip Roth.[1] Observers of the American Jewish community sometimes comment that when William James wrote his famous commentary on *The Varieties of Religious Experience*[2] at the turn of the twentieth century, he would have needed several more volumes to deal with all the varieties represented by the Jews.

Contemporary American Jews are often perceived as being uniquely divided into a plethora of groups. Some of those divisions have to do with Judaism as a religious faith: More than half of American Jews describe themselves as associated with (although not necessarily members of) wings of American Judaism, such as Orthodox, Traditional, Conservative, Reform, Reconstructionist, Renewal, or Secular Jewish Humanist congregations. Other divisions are based on geography and culture, as Jews bring traditions from their roots in North American, Israeli, European, Latin and South American, Australian, Middle Eastern, North African, Asian, former Soviet, and other Jewish communities. Still other divisions have to do with Jewish peoplehood, or secular cultural experiences that seem unconnected to religiosity: Jews who relate to their Jewishness primarily through Zionism, or Jewish social action, or Jewish intellectualism, or Jewish culture. Not least, gender provides an important—and often under-recognized—division: The Jewish experiences of many women vary significantly from those of men, and gender can play a crucial role in the ways in which people identify as Jews.

Jewish humor plays up this dividedness. One common joke describes a Jew on a desert island building two synagogues—one where he worships and the other that he "wouldn't set foot into!"

The many varieties of the contemporary American Jewish experience are often bewildering to the casual observer. The primary purpose of this book is to describe the historical emergence and development of the diverse ways in which Jews today connect to their Jewishness. This book is not a comprehensive history of all the times and places in which Jews lived. Rather, *The Way Into the Varieties of Jewishness* highlights some significant and striking diversities of Jewish experiences in earlier times and portrays the broad spectrum of contemporary American modes of Jewishness.

Although observers generally recognize that Jewish societies and ideas of Jewishness today take many forms, homogeneous stereotypes about the past often prevail. Historical Jewish communities are sometimes imagined to have been monolithic. However, scholarship increasingly shows that from biblical through modern times Jews have existed in diverse contexts and have responded to the challenges presented by those contexts in diverse ways.

Thus, this book begins with an exploration of the shifting and sometimes coexisting forms of early Jewishness reflected in ancient texts. Chapter 1 discusses some of the biblical narratives that became part of Jewish memory and draws on archaeologists' and historians' views of the Israelite tribes that established themselves in the hill countries of what became the ancient Land of Israel. There were many sources of diversity in ancient forms of Jewishness: Pagan culture and cultic rites are repeatedly denounced by the literary prophets, so it seems clear that they had a lingering impact that was difficult to eradicate. During the period prior to the Babylonian exile, biblical texts chronicle internal power struggles in Israelite societies; promonarchy and antimonarchy factions (the dissension among kings, priests, and prophets); the emergence of Judaean and Northern Israelite kingdoms with their own separate religious centers. Later there were culture wars between Hellenizers and Hasmoneans, Pietists, Pharisees, Sadduccees, Essenes, and Early Christians. Exilic experience varied Jewishness even further, and very early in the history of the Jewish people. The earliest Diaspora communities were established in the territories of Babylonia, Persia, and Egypt a mere six hundred years after the Israelites came to Canaan, and six hundred years after that more sweeping Diasporas brought Jews to far-flung locations across the Roman Empire. The first chapter ends with the standardization of rabbinic forms of Judaism in those communities that transmitted Jewishness to succeeding generations.

Chapter 2 follows the evolutions of what would become Sephardi and Ashkenazi varieties of Jewishness in medieval and Renaissance societies, spotlighting rich cultural developments on the Iberian Peninsula, as well as in France, Germany, and Italy. Attitudes and behaviors diverged as Jews migrated and responded either to relatively benign environments or to bitter persecutions at the hands of their Muslim and Christian host cultures. Although social transformations were building and thrusting the Jews, embedded within their diverse host cultures, forward toward cataclysmic transformations, in the gradual historical shift toward modernity, premodern communities in the sixteenth and seventeenth centuries arguably provided contemporary Jews with coherent, normative models of rabbinic Judaism. In many areas during this period Jewish life was centralized under cohesive Jewish communal control. Chapter 2 examines the social characteristics that typified these communities and looks at them as a backdrop for understanding the oncoming changes.

Chapter 3 explores religious decentralization and secularization. Emancipation and differing types of Jewish Enlightenments, in conjunction with sweeping secularizing social movements, plus economic, political, and historical changes, transformed Jewish life and made Jewishness more profoundly diverse than ever before.

The "brutal bargain" of adapting to Christian "civilized" behavior played itself out very differently in differing locales. In Germany, the emerging Reform movement wrestled with Western values, understood new sources of information (including scientific thought), and adopted lifestyles that influenced all forms of modern Judaism, whether through adaptation or resistance. In addition to the Reform movement, several groups were precipitated by the challenges posed by these Jewish reformers: two types of Orthodoxy, one that embraces and one that emphatically rejects Western culture, and an intellectually liberal but ritually traditional group of Positivist-Historical thinkers, whose brand of Judaism foreshadowed what would later become Conservative Judaism. Since Eastern European Jews tended not to reform their religious Judaism, but rather to secularize their lives and outlooks, chapter 3 also sketches out the diverse types of secular Jewish experiences that emerged during this period, from socialists of both the nonsectarian and the Jewish varieties; to nationalistic nonsectarian and Jewish Zionistic nationalists, to individualistic artists and intellectuals.

The next four chapters comprise this book's major focus on the contemporary American forms of Jewishness that evolved and developed in late nineteenth- and twentieth-century America. Initially, the differences between these movements were not clearly demarcated, and several key leaders shifted from one movement to another. Along the way religious and social issues galvanized and sometimes split adherents. These chapters show how an emphasis on boundary demarcation was at least partially motivated by the express purpose of defining particular forms of religious Judaism as coherent and separate from competing modes of Jewishness.

Chapter 8 spotlights the spiritual journeys of "Jews by Choice," tracing Jewish attitudes toward conversion historically and in contemporary America. Original research shows that Jews by Choice are not a monolithic group—any more than any other group of Jews is a monolithic group—but rather fall within one of three very different approaches to Jews and Judaism.

Gender is an important tool for analysis throughout the book and has been "mainstreamed" into every chapter. As we analyze the lives and identities of Jews over the centuries, the social and religious experiences of Jewish women are discussed, together with a consideration of how changes in women's religious lives have affected the Jewish community.

Finally, the Conclusion suggests that interactions between contemporary American Jewish religious experiences have produced, across the board, American experiential hybrids that share American commonalities, making them distinctive historically and in the world today. This concluding chapter incorporates ideas from the social sciences and argues that the creation of ethnic capital is critical for the transmission of Jewish culture to the next generation. The challenge of valuing Jewish distinctiveness in a country that prizes pluralism—but in subtle ways undermines it—is faced by all forms of Jewishness, but most especially by those that downplay particularism. Although vociferous discussions about boundaries proliferate among America's Jewish leadership, the Conclusion suggests that an emphasis on boundaries is misguided. Instead, we see that working to enrich the nucleus of Jewish life—distinctive Jewish culture—provides the richest promise for transmitting the varieties of Jewishness from today to tomorrow.

1

Ancient Jews, Homeland, and Exiles

For much of their recorded history, Jews described themselves as members of a social group with three interwoven strands of identification: a common ancestry and thus a distinctive ethnicity, a distinctive religion, and a common culture. These ethnic, religious, and cultural strands of Jewish identity were disentangled in the modern period, often rewoven in different ways, and frequently isolated from one another. Some modernizing Jews declared that Judaism was only a religion, or only a peoplehood, or only a culture. This chapter, however, sets the stage by looking back at descriptions of the earliest periods of recorded Jewish history, when Jewish ethnicity, religion, and culture first came together and developed.

Geography plays one key role: Early Jewish identity was linked to nationhood and the place where Jewishness was formed. That land-linked Jewishness eventually evolved into a religious culture that could sustain a sense of peoplehood, even for Jews located far away from the homeland that forged their Jewishness. The position of the "Other" plays the second key role, as Second Temple historian Shaye Cohen points out. When Judaism developed a sense of a boundaried "league" that defined membership and was capable of formally incorporating newcomers, the term "Judaean" took on the "religious" and "cultural" meanings of the word *Jew*.[1]

This chapter asks three questions:

1. How can we think about Jewish identity when looking at the early Jews, from their Israelite beginnings until the end of the Second Temple and the emergence of rabbinic Judaism?
2. What were the major components of the early Jewish belief system before its development through centuries of Diaspora existence?
3. How have these early Jews and early Jewish teachings influenced diverse forms of Jewishness historically and today?

In answering these questions, we turn to several kinds of sources, including ancient Jewish texts, the research of contemporary scholars, and changing understandings of Jewish memories in historical Jewish literature. Picturing the complex, multifaceted Judaisms of the past takes differing forms depending not only on what is being perceived, but also on who is perceiving it.

Memories Out of Biblical Texts

For centuries, "memories" of the earliest Jewish experiences have been shaped by narratives in the Hebrew Bible. As Yosef Hayim Yerushalmi famously suggests, history and memory are not the same thing. Collective memories are transmitted by a social group through "conscious efforts and institutions." For many ethnic groups in antiquity, this transmission took place through oral materials, folklore, or mythology, but these methods "will only partially apply to so literate and obstinately bookish a people" as the Jews—a people who, Yerushalmi notes, were repeatedly commanded in their texts "to remember!" Nor is modern historiography, the type of scientific study of historical periods that has been developing since the early nineteenth century, an unerring tool.

Historical research is only one way of getting at the realities of the past, "superior in some obvious respects, deficient and perhaps even inferior in others."[2] We too begin by attempting to understand the relationship between biblical and early rabbinic Jewishness and diverse forms of Jewishness over centuries and in our own time.

Biblical narratives describing the beginnings of the Jewish experience are part of the cultural toolkit not only of people raised in the Jewish tradition, but also, with differing interpretations and adaptations, of those raised in Christian and Islamic traditions as well. Although the God of creation and history hovers over much of the action and becomes an active character on occasion, secular individuals as well have found much in the Hebrew Bible to intrigue and move them. When Bill Moyers invited men and women from diverse ethnoreligious backgrounds to reflect on the family narratives of Genesis in a National Public Television series, their conversations were enriched by their own experiences and perceptions, and also by the experiences and perceptions of the religious cultures with which they had interacted.

The interpersonal and familial narratives of Genesis have gripped the interest and imagination of readers for centuries, not only because they have been perceived as part of a holy book, but because they dramatically capture universal human themes: Abraham leaves his home and his own culture to pursue an unknown future. Infertile Sarah is mocked by her fertile handmaiden, Hagar, disrupting the established balance of domestic power. Abraham agrees that God's commands must supersede his own human affections, almost sacrificing his son to demonstrate his devotion to the Divine. Rebecca and Isaac play opposing favorites with their twins and fuel an enduring enmity and struggle for political dominance. The wandering Jacob lays his head on a stone in the wilderness and sees a ladder that stretches from earth to heaven. Rachel and Leah—the original "big love" sister team—

are married to the same man, competing for his affections; Jacob loves his beautiful but infertile younger wife, but continues to impregnate her sister, while simultaneously breeding livestock for his own flocks. Indeed, both inside and outside the tent, the means of production—wells, treaties, husbandry, and agriculture—and reproduction—wives, fertility, and infertility, frequently take center stage.

Perhaps the most broadly influential Hebrew Bible saga, the Exodus, includes many powerful narrative episodes: depictions of the bitter enslavement of the Jews in Egypt; the moral awakening to the suffering of others of the palace-sheltered Moses; the three women—Jocebed, Miriam, and Pharaoh's daughter—who collaborate to foil a male tyrant's murderous plans; God's call to action out of the bush that burns but is not consumed; Moses and Aaron's enterprise of speaking truth to power; and the flight of the slaves through the sea, which parts for them, and into the wilderness. Not only Jews, but many different religious, ethnic, and political groups over time have perceived the stories of their personal and political liberations through the stories, words, images, and symbols of the Exodus drama.

For Jews, the story of their enslavement, liberation, and their delayed conquest of a promised homeland is the informing narrative of the birth of their nation. Many nations have birth stories, and there are common thematic, symbolic, and plot elements concerning the heroes of many national birth stories. The biblical Exodus, however, is distinguished by the personality assigned to the slaves who become the people of Israel, over and above the personality of the hero: "Israel is a protagonist whose moves and struggles determine the map."[3] Indeed, even the life of Moses is keyed closely to the story of the nation. He is born as one of the babies almost obliterated by an infanticidal Pharaoh, and he remains behind, barred from the Promised Land, like others of his generation (albeit for differing reasons).

The Jews as a nation have a complicated personality and a nuanced character development (and regression). The nation-people's heart is as murky and deceptive as the heart of any human being. No wonder this people upstages their liberator!

> The nation—particularly in Exodus and Numbers—is not an abstract detached concept but rather a grand character with a distinct voice (represented at times in a singular mode) who moans and groans, is euphoric at times, complains frequently, and rebels against Moses and God time and time again. Israel has a life story, a biography of sorts. It was conceived in the days of Abraham; its miraculous birth took place with the Exodus, the parting of the Red Sea; then came a long period of childhood and restless adolescence in the wilderness; and finally adulthood was approached with the conquest of Canaan.[4]

This obsession with Israel's "reason for being is exceptional in the ancient Near East," literary scholar Ilana Pardes concludes. Thus, the Exodus story has "its own logic and plan that have no relation to the concerns of modern historical writing," anthropologist Carol Meyers observes. "Like the Hebrew Bible as a whole, Exodus is meant to teach, not to record."[5]

These narratives, while psychologically and spiritually gripping, reveal little about the beginnings and development of Israelite life in ancient Canaan. For that information, contemporary readers draw not only on biblical texts, but also on information researched by archaeologists and historians of the Ancient Near East. These scientific findings do not displace biblical narratives and rabbinic discussions about what the Bible, laws, and ceremonies meant to Jews throughout the centuries, because they serve different purposes. Anthropological and historical study reveals the evolution of early Jewish peoplehood, the placement of early Jewish culture among the other cultures of the Ancient Near East, and many other aspects of the development of the Jewish experience barely addressed in biblical and rabbinic texts.

Even "dispassionate" scholars, however, bring to their task interpretive frameworks that contextualize how they "read" the Jewishness of the past. For example, biblical and other texts describe power struggles in early Jewish societies between the social groups identified with the monarchy, the priestly classes, the prophets, and later the Rabbis. How do contemporary readers feel about these leaders who at different times wanted to consolidate their power and standardize Jewish behaviors—but disagreed with each other about which domain should be preeminent? The way in which readers perceive varieties of early Jewishness depends to some extent on how they feel about power of the state (monarchy), or about organized religion and prescribed religious rituals (priestly classes, and later the Rabbis), or about the superiority of one belief system over another (prophets). Some contemporary American readers, for example, may read through the lens of mistrust of government power. Some feminist readers yearn back toward their concept of a benign, prepatriarchal womanist pagan society. "New Age" readers prefer a pluralistic celebration of diverse religious cultures to the biblical struggle to impose monotheism.

In the views of various readers, the Davidic unification of the Israelite tribes and the conquest of surrounding peoples and their lands becomes colonialism; patriarchal and prophetic insistence on one Creator who guides history becomes the deicide of the Queen of the Universe; Pharisaic insistence on ritual pieties distorts the spirit of religion; prophetic disdain for idol worship becomes intolerance and cultural imperialism; the God of Job is seen as a bully.

Some interpretive issues, affecting how readers today can understand past Jewishness, emerged with the advent of modern secular thought. Baruch Spinoza, in his *Tractacus Theologico-Politicus* (1670), rejected the Mosaic authorship of the Torah

(Pentateuch). Julius Wellhausen, creator of the school of higher biblical criticism, argued in his *Prolegomena to the History of Ancient Israel* (1878) not only that the Torah was a collection of diverse texts, but also that much of it was composed about a hundred years after the destruction of the First Temple. Today, most Bible scholars assume diverse authorship of parts of the Hebrew Bible, but dispute the dating of various parts, especially the relative antiquity of laws and rituals or universalistic moral teachings.

Given the fact that Israelite cultures, with their cultic animal sacrifices and other ancient mores, were so different than later Judaisms, scholars argue over the appropriateness of using the term *Jews* or *Jewishness* to talk about them. Biblical scholar Marc Brettler argues for the term *early Jews,* suggesting that the diversity of ancient Jewish culture made remarkable continuities possible. Jewishness evolved, and strategies that had previously been sidelined or in the background moved up to the foreground of Jewish religious life. Some that had been central, conversely, were marginalized or eliminated.[6]

The Early Jews: Hill Country Tribes and Ancient Israelites

Social scientists and historians, relying on archeological evidence and those biblical narratives that are supported (or at least not contradicted) by outside sources, describe ancient Israelites who reinvented themselves repeatedly in response to changing conditions. The shaping of the early Jews into a distinctive ethnic group was powerfully affected by their coming together into a political unit, itself premised on their acquiring their own geographical space. Around the beginning of the Iron Age (1200 B.C.E.), Israelite tribes abandoned the scattered towns they had inhabited during the late Bronze Age and established numerous permanent villages along Canaan's hilly spine, just west of the Jordan River Valley, in the previously sparsely inhabited areas of Judaea in the south, north-ward through Samaria, and up to the Galilee. The establishment of a coherent Israelite area of settlement was a response to "a social or even a political revolution." The ancient Israelites may have sought an environment in which they could worship their particular notion of God in their own peculiar way. In their new homes they created a kind of frontier society where they could break away ideologically as well as physically from the far more powerful Canaanite and Egyptian civilizations.[7]

Under these new conditions, the activities of both male and female Israelites shifted. Meyers suggests that women occupied a more central role, as they often do in a frontier agricultural-domestic economy.[8] Archaeological evidence as well as biblical texts attest to the diverse activities of these economically independent Israelite tribal households, in which most items needed for family members were produced within the tribal unit. Although gender roles were clearly defined and women irrefutably occupied subordinate religious status, they were in many ways the economic centers of the extended household. They also seem to have had some standing in their domestic communities. Biblical texts such as Proverbs 1:8, some sections of which are thought by scholars to be quite ancient, "part of the earliest Israelite traditions," urge sons to listen not only to their "father's instruction" but also to their "mother's teaching"—a stipulation that is not matched by surrounding cognate cultures. Similarly, biblical law (Exodus 21:15) prescribes punishments for the son who "strikes his father or his mother," in contrast to other Semitic law codes, such as Hammurabi's code no. 195, which stipulates consequences only for one who strikes his father.[9]

Nevertheless, the power structure in ancient Israelite tribal households was patrilineal and patriarchal, as it had been among the Canaanites who preceded them in the hill country. Ancient Israelites were exhorted to be endogamous, according to numerous biblical texts, but the biblical record itself indicates that marriage across ethnic lines was not common. Narratives recount male Israelites marrying non-Israelite women, sometimes with negative consequences, but often with no ill effect. Biblical scholars remind us that women generally took on the religious culture of their husband's tribe.[10] Indeed, numerous stories present non-Israelite women who become agents of God's will as they interact with Israelite men: Tamar (Genesis 38), Rahab (Joshua 2), Yael (Judges 4–5), and Ruth arise, some as literal "mothers in Israel" and others who substantively believe in the Jewish God and aid the causes of Israelite men.

Located in the center of the Middle Eastern Fertile Crescent that gave rise to a succession of conquering empires spreading pervasive and sometimes overlapping cultural attitudes and artifacts, the Israelite tribes themselves gradually became a nation. Through their evolution, they called themselves by different kinds of names that refer to aspects of social organization: *people, nation, assembly, covenanted people, congregation, league,* and *b'nai yisrael,* literally "children of Israel," most often translated into English as "Israelites." As Meyers suggests, this "expansion of a family term" had powerful significance," and "the expression of national identity through the language of family bonds" persisted. Meyers and other scholars argue that at least some of the family groupings and tribes had a sense of being part of a larger political unit even before the monarchic period.[11]

Kings and Kingdoms

For many centuries the geographical component of early Jewish identity was dominant, albeit often threatened. During the first two hundred years after their emerging as a definable political entity in previously Canaanite hill country, Israelite tribal societies, led by chieftains called *Judges* in biblical narratives, struggled against powerful attacks by Philistines, as well as Canaanites, Sidonians,

Hivites, Ammonites, Moabites, and nomadic tribes like Amalek and Midian. As tribal units clustered together, the early Jews were at a distinct disadvantage. Their most powerful enemies were monarchies. Kings could tax their subjects and create standing armies and strong, centralized regimes. However, the tribal nature of Israelite societies engendered a powerful mistrust of kings, especially among some segments of society who feared that power would be taken from them in a monarchical system.

Promonarchy and antimonarchy sentiments are expressed in biblical texts as differing visions of the Jewish experience. Despite a grassroots appeal for "a king to govern us, like other nations" (1 Samuel 8:5), Samuel at first presents monarchies as antithetical to the worship of the one God: People who serve kings, these texts suggest, backslide into a kind of slavery that limits their ability to serve God. In later narratives, conflict between the king, as a political authority, and religious authorities, such as prophets and priests, flares up repeatedly. While very far from a separation of church and state in the modern sense, struggles for political power kept the leadership of the early Jews bimodal—kings versus prophets, and sometimes trimodal—kings versus priests versus prophets.

Biblical accounts of the making of Jewish nations have been the subject of scholarly debates not directly relevant to the scope of our discussion. However, these narratives describe how political diversity was exacerbated in struggles around monarchy, as the political authority of kingship precipitated Israelite factionalism. Monarchists wanted political unity with the tribes united under a king, but the biblical Samuel warned of heavy tax burdens and other oppressions. Saul was anointed king by Samuel after Philistine armies captured the Ark of the Covenant and destroyed the Temple in the Ephraimite capital of Shiloh. Saul was an effective leader in wars against the Philistines, but his authority was undermined by recurring conflict with Samuel, who, according to biblical texts, deeply regretted his choice. After Saul's death, seven years of civil war broke out. David became the unifying king of all the tribes of Israel (around 1000 B.C.E.), and the Israelites entered a period of military conquest and national expansion.

Under David's leadership, Israelite armies reportedly created a powerful kingdom that stretched from Dan in the North past Beersheba in the South, and that was buffered by extensive subjugated states and conquered territories. Not least, David captured Jerusalem from the Jebusites and made it the capital of the Israelite kingdom. For decades, the Israelite kingdom appears to have been one of the strongest empires in the western region of the Fertile Crescent. Although factionalism briefly erupted both before and after David died, his son Solomon became king around the year 970 B.C.E., got rid of his enemies, built the First Temple in Jerusalem, established heavy taxation to support his various cultural and architectural projects, and ruled over an increasingly prosperous kingdom for decades.[12] Jewishness at this time was deeply linked to an agricultural lifestyle: One of the earliest extant Hebrew archaeological findings dates back to the Solomonic period, about 950 B.C.E. The Gezer Calendar, inscribed on a limestone tablet, lists the agricultural activities of the year, including sowing, harvesting, prunings, and gathering various crops.[13]

Jewishness was also linked to the building of the Temple, a place where early Jewish worship could be centralized. Premonarchical Jews had been used to offering sacrifices at local altars. Indeed, meat was probably consumed primarily in conjunction with cultic sacrifices. Additionally, prescriptions for sacrifices occurring during the rounds of daily life would have made it onerous for people living in outlying areas to have to travel to Jerusalem in order to fulfill these obligations. The priestly class pressed for religious unity under their jurisdiction. Biblical passages reflecting the priestly point of view characterize sacrifices performed elsewhere as sinful and displeasing to God. Descriptions of the crowded masses of people who flocked to the Temple environs during the three harvest festivals indicate that, at least for those occasions, pilgrimages were common. However, the priestly biblical exhortations to cease sacrifices elsewhere make it just as clear that this activity continued during the Temple period as well. And yet, as biblical scholar Yehezkiel Kaufman notes, many of the major literary prophets do not seem concerned about these extracurricular altars, as long as they are not part of idolatrous cults. The prophets, instead, are concerned about ideological unity and squelching the idol worship that emerged seemingly "under every leafy tree." They discredited idolatrous worship—perhaps mischaracterizing the literalness with which pagans regarded their deities.[14]

Divided Jewish Nations

After Solomon's death the monarchy was split into two kingdoms, with Reheboam, son of Solomon, ruling over Judaea, and Jereboam, a man who had earlier attempted a rebellion against Solomon and had fled to Egypt when it failed, in the North. Jereboam established two putatively Israelite temples in Dan and Beth-El, where pagan temples had previously existed. The two Jewish kingdoms battled each other for decades, and their fraternal warfare diminished their power over peoples they had previously conquered. A stele (pillar) inscribed by Mesha, king of Moab, in 850 B.C.E., for example, says:

> As for Omri, king of Israel, he humbled Moab for many days, for Chemosh was angry with his land. And his son followed him and he also said, "I will humble Moab." In my time he spoke, but I have triumphed over him and over his house, while Israel hath perished forever.

With this kind of motivation, Judaea and Israel made peace with and became allies of each other. They existed side by side for two hundred years, with Judaea ruled by the Davidic dynasty, and Israel remaining independent, with a turnover of nine different rulers, as Assyria gathered strength to the North.[15]

Jews have never lived in a vacuum, either in the ancient or the modern world. Jews as a people and Jewishness as a religious culture have been affected by—and have affected—the peoples and cultures around them. The first citation from nonbiblical sources referring to the ancient Israelites comes from a period when city-states around Israel were able to develop because the biblical Philistines had weakened the power of the Egyptian empire. Although Egypt regained power from time to time, its position was effectively eclipsed in the ensuing centuries. Assyria and Babylonia were engaged in a power struggle in the Mesopotamian region at about the time when Northern Israel's King Ahab—husband of the notorious Queen Jezebel—made an alliance with Assyria's enemies. Ahab gambled and lost; Northern Israel was defeated by Assyria and became a vassal state, paying huge amounts of taxes. A rebellion by Northern Israel was put down around 720 B.C.E., and the capital, Samaria, was destroyed.

Those inhabitants of Northern Israel who were not butchered were dragged off into exile, scattered widely, to become the "ten lost tribes," their fate the subject of legend and speculation. The Assyrians had a policy of "forced population transfers, mixing together defeated peoples from various places so that their ethnic identities would disappear, leaving only an identity as Assyrians."[16] It is likely that these Northern Israelites, for the most part, followed the Assyrian agenda and disappeared from history simply through assimilation and intermarriage into the larger body politic. The disappearance of that segment of the early Jewish people is significant, because it demonstrates that the continuity of Jews and Jewish culture was in no way a forgone conclusion. For the Northern Israelites, like so many other captive peoples at this time, the elements did not come together to make it possible for them to survive.

Diaspora Judaism, and a Chance to Return

Meanwhile, Babylonia rose into ascendancy, defeating Assyria in 612 B.C.E. Judaea rebelled against Babylonian authority in 597 B.C.E., precipitating the exile of King Zedekiah of Judaea and some of his supporters (586 B.C.E.). Subsequently, Babylonia destroyed the Temple in Jerusalem and exiled more extensive numbers of Jews to Babylonia. Although some of these Judaeans were brought or made their way to other cities, they generally lived in social networks that were large enough for them to sustain a distinctive culture and were usually ruled by authorities who were only interested in destroying their political independence, not their cultural distinctiveness. The Babylonian empire itself was defeated by the Persians in 539 B.C.E. Persian King Cyrus established a political entity called Yehud, located in Judaea, and allowed the Jews to return in 538 B.C.E.

As many have noted, a good number of those Jews who wept so copiously along the "waters of Babylon," and lamented their inability to "sing on foreign soil," remained in Babylon, where they apparently felt reasonably comfortable. Some relocated to Persia. One group returned with Ezra and Nehemiah to rejoin those Judaeans who had remained in their own land, to rebuild the Temple, and to reconstruct the Jewish religious society. As Brettler comments, the Babylonian exile was short but defining, "a watershed period." The time before it is called "the pre-exilic period" and the time after "the postexilic period."[17]

Thus, Judaea, where the tribe of Judah had originally settled, became once again the core location of the surviving Jews and provided the name that would eventually identify them among other ancient peoples: Judaeans. Based on the Hebrew term *Yehudi* (*Ioudaios* in Greek), *Judaean* was understood both by the ancient Israelites and by their neighbors as an ethnic-geographical identity, much like the term *Egyptian* or *Thracian*.[18] As Diaspora communities of Judaeans multiplied and grew, ethnic aspects of being a Judaean grew more prominent, but did not completely eclipse the importance of geography. A Judaean, even in exile, was a person who came from Judaea.[19]

Characteristics of Early Jewishness

What do we know about pre-exilic Judaism? Some modern scholars draw a sharp distinction between the religious practice of the Jewish people prior to the destruction of the First Temple and the practice as it developed during the Second Temple period and beyond. Indeed, the former, which emphasized the Temple cult, is frequently referred to as *Israelite religion,* and the latter, which gave more emphasis to canonical religious texts and personal ritual, is usually referred to as *Judaism* and, particularly in its later development, as *rabbinic Judaism.* While this distinction certainly has merit, it is important to realize that the differences can be exaggerated and that there are many deep connections between the ancient practice of the religion and the Judaisms that we experience today.

A more nuanced approach pays attention to core practices and attitudes that were important in varieties of early Judaism as well. Even to early Israelite religion, such values and behaviors as the Sabbath, circumcision, avoidance of pork, prohibitions against intermarrying with certain tribes, and the enterprise of reinterpreting biblical materials are integral. Ritual practices, including both prescriptive and proscriptive injunctions, reinforced boundaries between the Israelites and their neighbors. Creating and maintaining boundaries between the Israelites and the Philistines seems to have been a key goal.

In biblical texts, as Ronald Hendel points out, "the term 'uncircumcised' is often used as a synonym for 'Philistine'" (Judges

15:18; 1 Samuel 14:6, 31:4; 2 Samuel 1:20). Circumcision was practiced by most of the cultures surrounding Israel—but not by the Philistines. Invaders from the Greek Aegean region who entered the eastern Mediterranean shortly after 1200 B.C.E. (when the Israelite tribes were establishing themselves in the hill countries of southern Canaan), the Philistines had superior technology and quickly achieved political and military dominance. The narratives of Samson, Saul, and David focus on the conflict between the Israelite tribes and the Philistines. Israelite wars with the Philistines were an important contributing factor to the emergence of the early Jewish monarchy and nation. Patterns of differentiation similar to circumcision are seen in terms of Israelite avoidance of pork:

> The earliest trace of these food laws in Israelite culture comes from the era of Philistine hegemony, the same period when circumcision seems to have become an ethnic boundary marker. Recent archaeological excavations of early Israelite and Philistine sites show a remarkable contrast in the presence and absence of pig bones.... The Philistine preference for pork was apparently imported from their Aegean homeland. It was arguably the catalyst for the explicit avoidance of this food in early Israelite culture.[20]

No less than circumcision and the avoidance of pork, the observance of the Sabbath created boundaries between the early Jews and the peoples around them. Recent scholarship suggests that the division of time into weeks, the placement of the Sabbath at the conclusion of each week, and the concept of a day of rest that applies culturewide were all Israelite inventions. By the seventh century B.C.E. an extant Hebrew inscription referring to the Sabbath exists, and it is mentioned frequently in the writings of eighth-century-B.C.E. prophets. It is discussed in ways that tie it closely to circumcision and the food laws, underscoring its usefulness as a pre-exilic boundary-marking institution, as Hendel suggests:

> One of the distinctive ritual marks in biblical time is the Sabbath. It is, like circumcision, a "sign of the covenant" (Exodus 31:12–17), and, like the food laws, it is a matter of holiness. God commands: "You shall keep the Sabbath, for it is holy to you" (31:14; similarly 20:8–11). Just as God rested on the seventh day of creation, Israel shall rest every seventh day.[21]

These rituals helped to create boundaries and to maintain Jewish distinctiveness. Later, Jews attached the outsider status of the "uncircumcised" people to the Assyrians and the Babylonians, and still later to the Greeks. Greek and Roman descriptions, in turn, mock the Jews for observing the Sabbath. It seemed bizarre to their Greek and Roman detractors that any people could be so lazy as to cease working one full day a week—and to extend these privileges even to women, slaves, and animals! The Sabbath is also a particularly interesting core practice because it is unseen anywhere else in the ancient world and seems to have been a unique conception of the early Jews. Circumcision, not surprisingly, was horrific to Greek and Roman observers because to them it was tantamount to the mutilation of the male body. The avoidance of pork simply seemed ridiculous—why would any nation want to avoid a particular food group, especially one with so many culinary applications?

Democratization and a Tradition of Sacred Interpretation

Less well recognized is the antiquity of biblical interpretation. Biblical interpretation, "once seen typically as the hallmark of the

Rabbis," was already under way in the pre-exilic era, as Marc
Brettler notes. The scholarship of Nahum Sarna, Michael Fishbane,
Brettler, and others demonstrates that "most of what existed in
Hellenistic Judaism had earlier antecedents."[22]

Some of this early interpretive activity, which dramatically
affected conceptions of Jewishness, took place around what Bruce
Halpern calls "an elite redefinition of traditional culture"[23] in the
seventh through sixth centuries B.C.E., when many scholars believe
the book of Deuteronomy was written. The process was set in
motion by the prophet Hosea, who already in the mid-eighth century B.C.E. contrasted ritual ceremonies, especially frequent animal
sacrifices, with ethical behaviors and social concerns growing out
of a passionate love of God. Hosea was particularly scornful of
Northern Israel's shrines, which had been taken over from pagan
usage and, he charged, were still permeated with pagan attitudes,
atmosphere, and cultic activity. Hosea's exhortations urged the
early Jews to put aside their earlier relaxed attitude toward what
we might call religious pluralism and to purify their religious
activities of the dangers and seductions of "native practice," which
was "reinterpreted as a foreign assault on Israel's cultural boundaries." Although Hosea preached in the North, and they were
located in the Southern Kingdom of Judah, some argue that Kings
Hezekiah and Josiah (2 Kings 18 and 23) were influenced by these
critiques when they purified Jewish behaviors under their own
jurisdiction.[24]

"The new course of Judaism as a religion of interior choice
and commitment" is what the revolutionary biblical book of
Deuteronomy proposed, according to Ronald Hendel and other
biblical scholars. Since many twenty-first-century readers tend to
think of obeying the law and spirituality as opposing, rather than
complementary concepts, it is important to understand that for seventh through sixth century B.C.E. interpretive reformers, this new
emphasis on observing the law was innovative because it stressed

individual commitment, rather than cultic ritual, which was the older form of worship:

> The object is to love God and to obey the law that God has planted in our hearts. Priests, prophets, and other religious intermediaries are rarely mentioned; rituals are mere reminders of God's gracious laws. God is transcendent and One, not a multiplicity of local phenomena, as might be gathered by the multiplicity of shrines.

The articulation *par excellence* of this new, inward-looking, law-oriented Judaism, suggests Ronald Hendel, is *Shema Yisrael* and the following passages, which became the cornerstone of biblical and later of rabbinic Judaism. Hendel writes, "This is classic Jewish spirituality, nurtured by Deuteronomy and transmitted through the centuries."[25]

The placement of this formulation as Moses's farewell address is extremely significant, since it was the covenant engineered by Moses, rather than that of Abraham, that became the cornerstone of covenantal Judaism:

> And Moses went up to God. The Lord called to him from the mountain saying, "Thus shall you say to the house of Jacob and declare to the children of Israel: 'You have seen what I have done to the Egyptians, how I bore you on eagles' wings and brought you to Me. Now then, if you will obey Me faithfully and keep My covenant, you shall be My treasured possession among all the peoples. Indeed, all the earth is mine, but you shall be to Me a kingdom of priests and a holy nation.' These are the words that you shall speak to the children of Israel."
>
> ... All the people answered as one, saying, "All that the Lord has spoken we will do!" (Exodus 19:3–8)

In the passage above, just before the giving of the Ten Commandments, the idea of Jews being "a kingdom of priests and a holy nation" is introduced. The Deuteronomic passages reinforce the idea of individual and national responsibility for fulfilling the terms of the covenant. Tellingly, it presents the ideal that the priesthood should not be limited to an aristocratic or secretive caste, as was common in antiquity. Instead, the highest level of spirituality was considered within Judaism to be a universally available attainment, at least for Jews. The simultaneous democratic—and elitist—implications of these words are evident in a presentation of Jewishness that emphasizes a privileged status earned through merit rather than birth.

The interpretations that shifted the emphasis from Jews bringing animals to priests for cultic sacrifice to the "kingdom of priests" who maintain their place within the covenant by loving God and following God's laws both narrowed and spiritualized the concept of Jewishness. Placing these interpretations at key moments in the life of Moses, the monolithic covenant-negotiator of Jewish peoplehood, sacralized the very activity of biblical interpretation. Hendel argues sweepingly: "Deuteronomy begins a process that will become central in rabbinic Judaism: attributing all revisions and interpretations of biblical law and religion to the original revelation at Sinai."[26] When contemporary Jews speak of *Torah mi Sinai,* the idea that rabbinic law derives its authority from Sinai, they are referring to this concept.

Religious texts also became central as a replacement for prophecy as a result of early exilic experiences, suggests Brettler. The words of Ezra and Nehemiah constantly refer to biblical texts, as they exhort the returning exiles toward behaviors that conform more closely with divine specifications. In their attempts to ensure allegiance to God's laws, these two leaders sometimes made standards even more rigorous, as in Ezra's expansion of prohibited intermarriage to include the "peoples of the land," rather than merely the original prohibited tribes. One of their innovations fore-shadowed contemporary congregational protocol:

> The entire people assembled as one man in the square before the Water Gate, and they asked Ezra the scribe to bring the scroll of the Teaching of Moses with which the Lord had charged Israel.... Ezra opened the scroll in the sight of all the people ... as he opened it, all the people stood up.... They read from the scroll of the Teaching of God, translating it and giving the sense; so they understood the reading. (Nehemiah 8:1–8)

Strikingly, unlike the giving of the Torah at Sinai, which addresses a male congregation, Nehemiah 8:2 specifies that women were part of the listening congregation receiving this instruction and hearing the reading from the Torah scroll. As instructions for the celebration of particular biblical holidays were read, the assembled men and women listened and followed those instructions. The Torah and holy books became understood as a way of knowing what God wanted Jewish men and women to do.[27]

Jewish Encounters with Western Cultures

Geographical changes have had a profound impact on Jewish religious culture. Ancient Judaism was constructed in the ancient Land of Israel. Jews began as politically and culturally linked tribes, became a nation, and briefly a military empire. Early Jewishness was forged at a time when centralizing Jewish life was a priority. Sacrificial rites, especially at the Jerusalem Temple, were core experiences of Jewishness for centuries. However, Diaspora communities that were not directly connected to Temple worship became a fact of life very early in Jewish history. With Jews living in Babylon, Persia, Egypt, and elsewhere, alternative forms of worship emerged, worship that emphasized prayer rather than animal sacrifice. What came to be known as rabbinic Judaism developed as Jewish life became more and more decentralized, and increasing numbers of Jews lived away from the Zion that they considered their spiritual center. With the canonization of the Hebrew Bible and an increasing succession of exiles, textual interpretation expanded exponentially in the Land of Israel as well as in Diaspora communities.

Persian rule over Jewish populations lasted from 539 until 334 B.C.E., when Alexander the Great conquered the region. Although Alexander himself didn't pay much attention to the province of Judaea, this conquest set in motion sociopolitical and cultural trends that transformed Jewishness in many ways. For two centuries Jews who remained in the homeland interacted with the Hellenic influences of Ptolemaic Egypt and Seleucid Syria. At the turn of the Common Era, Rome ruled Jewish life, and Greco-Roman culture, as well as politics, continued to have enormous power.

Hellenizers, Hasmoneans, and Jewish Pietists

Greek culture permeated Jewish life both in the Land of Israel and in Diaspora communities such as Alexandria.[28] Greek influence was social, cultural, linguistic, and educational. Affluent, upper-class Jews were much more interested in taking on Hellenistic mores than were the rural peasants or lower-class urban Jews. As a result, the conflict between forces for and against the Hellenization of Jewish life in the Land of Israel was partially a class struggle. Jason, a Hellenizing high priest, established two Greek educational institutions, a gymnasium and an *ephebeion,* and called a Greek city in Jerusalem, Antioch-at-Jerusalem. Although the influence of Greek culture was not necessarily lethal to Jewish cultural transmission, in certain circles the clear intent was to obliterate distinctive Judaic practices and to replace them with Hellenistic values and behaviors. Jason's successor, Menelaus—whose accession to the high priesthood triggered an internal civil war—took his enthusiasm for the Hellenization of Palestinian Jewry very far indeed and may have been instrumental in encouraging Antiochus Epiphanes to crack down and suppress Judaic piety in 167 B.C.E.

Harsh laws were passed, making Jewish observances illegal. A group of Pietists, or Hassideans (in Hebrew, *Hasidim*), rebelled against this attempted eradication of Jewish religious practices, and they were supported by the lower-class masses of people in Jerusalem and its environs. These Pietists are first heard of in connection with this persecution. They were committed to the revival of Jewish rituals and customs and getting rid of pagan customs in Jewish environments. The Pietists were notable in their willingness to die as religious martyrs rather than compromise their Jewish practices in any way.

The book of Maccabees describes the arrival of Syrian-Greek troops in Modi'in (west of Jerusalem) with the demand that the Jews sacrifice a pig to Greek gods. In the narrative, the priest Mattathias stabs a Jewish traitor, who offers to comply with idolatrous worship, and shouts to the crowd, "Follow me, all of you who are for God's law, and stand by the covenant" (1 Maccabees 2:27). A military struggle ensues, reportedly for twenty-five years, much of it along the coastal plain area that is now Tel Aviv. During the fighting, many Jews moved back from the countryside to Jerusalem for safety. In 142 B.C.E., during the reign of the Seleucid King Demetrius, the Greeks signed a peace treaty with Simon, the last surviving son of Mattathias, and the Hasmonean dynasty began. Ironically, and contrary to Jewish Sunday school impressions of the period, the Hasmonean rulers were not anti-Greek in their interests or their rulership style. The goals of the Pietists were hardly upheld once the Hasmoneans came to power, and they ceased to cooperate with Hasmonean rulers.

Nevertheless, the Hasmonean victory, establishing an autonomous Jewish state, almost certainly made possible the continued existence of Jewishness. Both the upper-class Sadduccees, discussed below, and the Hasmonean leaders tended to promote Hellenistic culture. The use of the Greek language was widespread. Greek names were used for Jewish children (and sometimes to rename adults). Jews in the Land of Israel—including rabbis and other religious and communal leaders—often communicated with each other in Greek. Some ambitious Hellenizing Jews went quite far in their attempts to conform to Hellenized cultural practices. Some male Jews attempted a cosmetic/surgical reversal of their circumcisions. For many Jews of the time, however, the adoption of some aspects of Greek culture was not part of a conscious attempt to assimilate. It was part of the air they breathed—much as American culture and the English language are for Jews in America and around the world today.

Some of the later Hasmonean rulers devoted themselves to territorial expansion—an activity at which they were extraordinarily successful. Not only did they conquer substantial territories, unmatched since the days of David and Solomon, they implemented mass conversions of many of the people they conquered, forcing the men to be circumcised and to take on the religious and social laws of the Judaeans. It was through one of these forced conversions that the family of Herod the Idumean became "Jewish." When Alexander Yannai (103–76 B.C.E.) ruled over the Hasmonean kingdom, he conquered even more territory, and the Jewish state stretched along the Mediterranean seacoast from the Egyptian border up to Mt. Carmel in the North. Not surprisingly, this active proselytizing drive of Hasmonean-ruled Judaism dramatically declined with the destruction of the Second Temple by the Romans. Although it was never repeated, it is important to remember that forced conversions have not been unknown in Jewish history. Pompeii's annexation of Judaea (37 B.C.E.) brought the country under the aegis of Rome, ended the Hasmonean rule, and paved the way for Herod to be named ruler of the Jews by the Romans.

Pharisees and Sadduccees

The Pharisees' approach to Jewishness, which is central to the development of rabbinic Judaism, began in the early Hasmonean period around 200–150 B.C.E. and flourished until the end of the Second Temple period. It emphasized strict adherence to ritual law, including ancestral interpretive traditions not written in the Torah, and championed Torah study as among the highest values in Judaism. The origin of the name *Pharisee* probably comes from its Hebrew meaning of separateness (*perushim* in Hebrew) and may be related to the early Pharisees' emphasis on ritual purity. The Pharisees' stress on biblical study and legal scholarship also tended to separate them from the common folk, who frequently were illiterate (the so-called *am ha'aretz,* literally "people of the land").

The Pharisees were not, however, the population with the greatest economic status and power. Furthermore, Pharisaic emphasis on prayer, the "devotion of the heart," was available to every person attempting to communicate with God. This relatively democratic ideal of every individual having the capacity to speak directly to God was in marked contrast to the type of prayer that took place in the context of animal sacrifice, which required priestly facilitation. Thus, despite what one could regard as their spiritual elitism, the Pharisees, as Josephus attests, enjoyed widespread popularity and affection among the masses.

Their fierce opponents, the Sadduccees, included a large proportion of the priests and aristocrats. The Sadduccees dominated Temple worship and frequently were members of the Sanhedrin (the supreme Jewish council and tribunal of the Second Temple period). The Sadduccees were a socioeconomic elite, and active leaders, who at times may have been more numerous, especially in positions of power, than the Pharisees whom they opposed. The Sadduccees championed the fundamental correctness of religious law exactly as it was written in the Torah, and opposed the authority of interpretive traditions outside the Torah, because interpretations could lead to change. The immediate influence of the Sadduccees ended with the Roman destruction of the Second Temple and upper-class Jerusalem culture, partially because the sociopolitical base of their power was eradicated. However, similar fundamentalist ideas emerged once again a thousand years later in the teachings of the Karaites, who also rejected the authority of accumulated rabbinic interpretation and exegesis. Medieval Jews, including some well-known rabbis, sometimes conflated the two groups, even though they were neither identical nor directly related to each other.

The apparent popularity of the Pharisees among the common people may have been related to their downplaying of the inherited privileges associated with the Temple priesthood in favor of study and prayer. In this vein, the Pharisees emphasized two new institutions in Jewish life: the study hall (*beit midrash*) and prayer hall (*beit knesset*, or synagogue). Some scholars suggest that these institutions themselves may have been Judaic adaptations of Greek schools and gathering places.[29]

Pharisaic leaders did not have the honorific title of *Rabbi*, preferring to be simply referred to by their birth names, such as Shimon Ben Shetach (the Pharisee leader at the time of the Hasmonean king Alexander Yannai, 103–76 B.C.E.), Hillel, and Shammai (leading Pharisees during the late Second Temple period). It was only around the time of the destruction of the Temple that the honorific *Rabbi* for Pharisee scholars came into common usage. Following the destruction of the Second Temple in 70 C.E., the Rabbis of the Mishnah and Talmud considered themselves the direct inheritors of the tradition of Moses. Thus, in a very real and concrete sense, the Pharisees may be considered to be the founders of rabbinic Judaism. Certainly, their emphasis on the responsibility of the individual to Jewish law made possible the decentralized versions of Jewishness that evolved as Diaspora Judaisms became dominant. Leading Pharisees at this time included Rabbi Gamliel (the teacher of the Apostle Paul), Rabbi Yochanan Ben Zakkai (the founder of the Academy at Yavneh), and Rabbi Akiva (a major contributor to the Mishnah).

With the Second Temple gone, Palestinian Jewish life almost decimated by brutal Roman attacks, and Jews enslaved in Rome and exiled to diverse locations, Hellenism declined in Jewish eyes as an alluring culture. It may be that Rabbis in the Pharisaic tradition no longer had the same fear of the seductions of Greek language and culture. Persecution had created very effective boundaries between Jews and Greco-Roman culture, and some Rabbis made use of its cultures and idioms. The Talmud reports that Judah ha-Nasi said, "Why talk Syriac in Palestine? Talk either Hebrew or Greek" (*Sotah* 49b). In the first century C.E., Rabban Gamliel had five hundred students of Greek wisdom in addition to his five hundred students of Torah (*Sotah* 49b). Both Gamliel and Judah ha-Nasi were *nesiim*, official representatives of the Roman government, however, and since they had official connections with Rome, one cannot extrapolate and be sure from their actions that other Rabbis shared their comfort level with Greek study.

The Essenes

Toward the end of the Hasmonean revolt, the Essenes, a small ascetic sect, took up residence south of Jerusalem, near the Dead Sea region. They were monastic, celibate, communitarian groups of men, probably about four thousand, who supported themselves by manual labor, including agriculture. They ate meals communally, underwent communal baptisms, and were exceedingly punctilious about religious ritual observances. Men wishing to join the group underwent a period of probation before entering on a permanent basis. One way in which the Essenes demarcated themselves from other Jews was in their rejection of the Jewish lunar calendar. Instead, during the later era of the Second Temple, the Essenes advocated a calendar based on the solar year. They most probably rejected the authority of the Jerusalem Temple priesthood as well. Their lifestyles and beliefs have been further elucidated by careful analysis of the Qumran sects described in the Dead Sea Scrolls, discovered in 1947.

Rabbinic Judaism and the Written "Oral" Law

Rabbinic Judaism dominated and standardized Jewish practice according to halakhic discussions in the "Oral Law" (*Torah she'b'al peh*), legal conversations embedded in narrative materials, which had been passed down orally. According to Jewish tradition, rabbinic conversations interpreting biblical laws wrestled with ideas that had been originally transmitted along with the Torah to Moses. Rabbinic conversations that were compiled and edited into their final written form into the Mishnah (about 200 C.E.) and the Gemara (about 600 C.E.) recorded hundreds of years' worth of scholarly dialogues and the frequently conflicting understandings of Rabbis who lived in different times and places.

The Mishnah, edited under the auspices of Rabbi Judah ha-Nasi, summarizes (frequently tersely) much of Jewish law in six orders (or *sedarim*). Though it was completed about 130 years after the destruction of the Second Temple, the Mishnah may include sections that go back to various periods of the Second Temple. Indeed, some of the laws and traditions discussed in the Mishnah are attributed to the earliest periods of the Second Temple, including the time of Ezra and the period of the Great Assembly (*Knesset Hagedola*). The Rabbis quoted in the Mishnah are referred to as *Tanaim* (singular *Tana*).

Following the conclusion of the Mishnah, various scholarly schools were formed whose main purpose was the discussion and elucidation of the sometimes terse and frequently cryptic mishnaic rules. The scholars who engaged in this later activity were referred to as *Amoraim* (singular *Amora*). Their schools were primarily in the Galilean region of Northern Palaestina (Roman province)—the section of the homeland into which most Jews had relocated by this time—and in Babylonia particularly in the Babylonian cities of Sura and Pumbedita. Collections of these scholarly discussions of the Mishnah—commonly called the Gemara—were produced in both Palestine and Babylon and are known as the Palestinian or Jerusalem Talmud (*Talmud Yerushalmi*) and the Babylonian Talmud (*Talmud Bavli*). Since frequently published editions of the Gemara almost always include the accompanying mishnaic text, it is common usage to refer to both the Mishnah and the Gemara collectively as the Talmud. Significantly, with the discussions of the Gemara, the ascendancy of diasporic Jewish culture had officially begun.

The Jews of Babylonia enjoyed more physical comfort than the impoverished Palestinian Jews, who had relocated into small communities in the Galilee after the destruction of Jerusalem and were often outnumbered by early Christian communities. Although persecutions flared up sporadically, for long periods of time Babylonian Jews were relatively unmolested by their Zoroastrian hosts, and they lived with far greater self-sufficiency and cultural separation than the Hellenized Palestinian Jews. Additionally, the Babylonian Jews were generally much more affluent than the Palestinian Jews. All these factors had an impact on the interpretations found in the Babylonian as compared to the Palestinian Talmud.[30] They also had an impact on the fate of these two versions of the Oral Law. During the Gaonic period that immediately followed, centered in Babylon, the Babylonian Talmud was adapted as the ultimate authority and source for Jewish law. Due perhaps to the great authority and prestige of the Gaonic leaders, its acceptance spread from Babylon throughout the Jewish Diaspora.

Magic, Messianism, and Early Christians

As we have seen, by the end of the Second Temple period Jewish life was rife with religious and ideological experimentation and change. Numerous splinter groups had emerged, only to disappear. Of all the diverse forms of Jewishness extant at that time, the two that survived into modern times were rabbinic Judaism and Christianity. The same concepts of universalistic and yet specific covenantedness that urged reform in Deuteronomy and Hosea, and that were developed in Pharisaic and then rabbinic Judaism, were cherished but given a different meaning by the early Christians. Early Christianity, which began as a purely Jewish sect, was redirected around 60 C.E. under Paul of Tarsus (who began life as Saul the Jew) as a universalistic and evangelical model of the concept of a holy nation no longer bound by the ethnic boundaries of the early Jews. In time, the overwhelming majority of Christians began their lives in religious traditions other than Judaism. "You shall be My treasured possession among all the peoples," a phrase that captures the essence of the "chosenness" of Israel, has had overwhelming implications in the religious and secular history both of the Jews and the wider world.

The Jesus movement was connected to the Galilean countryside, especially in villages near the Sea of Galilee. Jesus preached primarily in an environment in which an interest in magic was thriving, and many of the stories preserved in the Gospels emphasize Jesus as a faith healer and wonder-working personage. The area of Jesus's primary initial influence was probably far less swayed by Hellenism's sophistications than major urban areas like Jerusalem, and so was a more fertile area for ideas of magic and messianism. The early Christians, like the Essenes, often formed ritualized groups for eating and discussing matters together. Also like the Essenes, they were interested in speculation on the coming apocalypse and on eschatological teachings. Nor were the early Christians the only Jews interested in messianism. Rabbi Akiva supported a revolt against the Romans led by Simon Bar Kochba, considered by some (including Rabbi Akiva) to be the messiah. The revolt, of course, was savagely put down by the Romans in 135 B.C.E. Indeed, the creation of innovative groups with spiritualist preoccupations in a time of cataclysmic change seems to be a recurring motif in Jewish history.

For Jews, the favored relationship is conditioned on loyalty to the covenant. Jesus and his first followers were Jews, and early Christianity was in many ways very similar to forms of Judaism. Jewish Christians seem to have continued frequenting synagogues well into the second century C.E. Most Jewish converts to Christianity continued their Judaic practices for some time. In some second-century Palestinian cities, Jews and non-Jews lived side by side. However, while Jewish groups have viewed their covenant with God as an eternal condition with behavioral obligations attached, Christians came to view the "Old Testament" covenant as abrogated and replaced with a new, primarily belief-based covenant with Christianity. The way to salvation was through belief in Christ alone. As Cohen points out, Paul preached that Christ superseded the law when dealing with non-Jews who became Christian.

> Though he found fault with gentile Christians who wished
> to *begin* observing the Law, he never found fault with Jews
> (or Jewish Christians) who wished to *continue* observing
> the Law. He condemned Jewish Christians who sought to
> impose the Law on gentile Christians, but he never attacked
> observance per se.[31]

Early Christianity became distinguished from Jewishness in steps. Some scholars place the completion of the process early, others as late as during the reign of the Emperor Constantine, who converted to Christianity in 312 C.E. From the Jewish side of the widening divide, Christians were regarded as *minim* (heretical sects). Eric Meyers suggests that Christian rejections of Jewish approaches challenged the Rabbis' "multi-vocal, elastic understanding of the truth of the Oral Torah" and precipitated some circumscribing of permitted opinions. Nevertheless,

> as opposed to orthodox Christianity, as it began to develop by the end of the 2nd century C.E., rabbinic Judaism never developed a set of dogmas, but neither was it quite as open as it seems or as some have claimed it to be. Those whom the rabbis included within their circles were allowed extraordinary freedom of expression and interpretation. Those who were excluded were suppressed.[32]

In the meantime, from the Christian side, whatever tolerance Paul had shown toward Jewish law came to reflect negatively on Paul himself. The sincerity of Paul was the subject of fierce—and tragically symbolic—arguments by the Church fathers. Augustine, for example, argued that "in Paul's time it was still theologically permissible for a Jew (and a Jewish Christian) to continue observing the law." However, Jerome could find no good in Judaism, even in the early days when Christianity emerged from Jewish society. Cohen comments, "Jerome believed that the arrival of Christ rendered the Law not only *mortua* (dead) but also *mortifera* (lethal). Christianity was *bonum* (good), Judaism and paganism alike were *mala* (bad)."[33]

With the separation of Christianity from Judaism, the stage was set for the two-thousand-year sojourn of Jews in Diaspora communities. The very concepts that Christian and later Islamic religious traditions had borrowed from diverse Jewish cultures were often demonized and used as a rationale for persecution.

Nevertheless, the history of Jewishness in Diaspora communities, as we shall see in chapter 2, was rich and diverse. Somber notes and dark days alternated with astonishing cultural creativity and resourcefulness. Biblical and rabbinic texts and Jewish religious civilization traveled with the Jews and sustained their further development for centuries, often under very difficult circumstances. As modernity emerged, rationalists and reformers rejected many of the details of rabbinic Jewish life and the substance of much that is contained in talmudic discussions. However, taken in the context of their own time, the Rabbis of the first centuries of the Common Era were astonishingly creative, even revolutionary in much of their thinking, as they brought old traditions forward and crafted a "portable" Judaism[34] that could be moved and adapted to the often-convoluted wanderings of the Jewish people.

Mirror, Mirror: Early Jewishness and Later Jews

For more than two thousand years, Jews read the Bible and saw themselves. They identified with biblical characters as though they moved among them. Rabbis living in Spain, Italy, France, and Morocco from the eleventh through the fifteenth centuries looked at Esther's plight in the Persian court, for example, and intuited the insight of modern scholars that this is a narrative about living in the Diaspora. But they thought of Esther, as they thought of other biblical characters, as though she were living not in an ancient Persian harem but in their own courts. Esther reminded them of Jews in the courts of Spain and other European countries, and also of the ways in which religious persecution impinged on their own families and lives.

The brilliant poet, philosopher, astronomer, and physician Abraham Ibn Ezra, who left Spain in 1140, possibly after his son converted to Islam, emphasized that Esther was taken against her will, grammatically analyzing the Hebrew verbs to prove his point.

Abraham Saba, exiled from Spain to Morocco (mid-fifteenth–early-sixteenth centuries), was tormented by what he saw as the rape of Esther, reminding him of the martyrdom of many of his coreligionists. "Why," he asked with palpable anger and disbelief, "did Mordecai not risk his life to take her to some deserted place to hide until the danger would pass, or even take her to another kingdom?.... Why did Mordecai not do one of those things that the simplest Jews in Portugal did?" Other medieval exegetes held Esther up as a model and a consummate politician who should be emulated by Jewish men. Interpreted as the epitome of the clever courtier who understands how a subject should approach a ruler in order to accomplish difficult goals, she is praised in detail as a *medinit,* an excellent statesman.[35]

When Polish Jews, reeling under the Chmielnicki massacres (1648), read the story of Jacob driven out of his own home because his brother Esau threatened to kill him, they similarly saw reflections of themselves. Their biblical patriarch was essentially a "dweller of the tents," a peaceful man. Jacob tricked his father, his brother, and his father-in-law only because these actions were necessary for his sustenance and survival. Such actions resonated with Polish Jews who were forced to live by their wits in a hostile environment. They sang *Al tirah avdi Yaakov,* God's biblical consolation, "Do not fear, my servant Jacob," when the Sabbath ended and they faced the unknown worries of the weekday world. They thought of how the biblical patriarch was renamed *Israel* and became the father of wandering Jews who had to make their way by their wits, who sometimes had little more than a stone to rest their heads on—but who nevertheless saw a wonderful ladder reaching from the earth to the stars. So strong was the identification that when they were asked how Jacob spent his days, the rabbis said he was enrolled in a rabbinical seminary, *Yeshivat Shem b'Ever.* Oppressed European Jews sang the words "David, King of Israel, lives and endures" and yearned for a time when Jewish life would not seem threatened. The image of David, triumphant after years of trial, seemed like a promise for the future.

German reformers in the eighteenth and nineteenth centuries responded deeply to the words of Isaiah, Jeremiah, Amos, and Micah, prophets who, preaching from about the eighth to sixth century B.C.E., emphasized ethical behavior over formalistic ritual. This classic "priest versus prophet" conflict became a major influence and justification for the reformers' claim that their approach was more authentic than the rules and regulations of rabbinic Judaism. The description of Israel—rather unique even in the Hebrew Bible—as a "kingdom of priests and a holy nation," contains tremendous tension between the universalistic and particularistic implications. As Reform Jewish thinkers articulated the "mission" of the Jewish people, some found inspiration in the idea that as "a kingdom of priests," Israel's role might be to preach God's message to the world. By contrast, other Jewish movements emphasized the Jewish people's role as a "holy nation" where *holy* connotes a degree of separation and insulation and removal from the larger world.

Similarly, the Reform movement made ideological use of the powerful schism between the Pharisees and the Sadduccees in the late Second Temple period, which revolved around the Pharisaic/rabbinic insistence on an oral halakhic tradition, with roots they said dated back to the giving of the Torah at Sinai. The Sadduccees, as we have seen, rejected the authority of ongoing rabbinic discussions. As we have noted, the interpreting Rabbis eventually won this ideological battle and created what we now know as normative rabbinic Judaism. Reform ideology echoed this conflict. Interestingly, both Orthodox and Reform Jews approved of the interpretive impulse and claimed to be the spiritual inheritors of the Pharisees, not the Sadduccees.

One may also say that the biblical message of radical societal change and redemption (along with the centrality of the Land of

Israel) led directly to such modern movements as secular and religious Zionism, secular concepts of *tikkun olam* (repairing of the ills of the world), and even to the extraordinary involvement of many East European Jews in the socialist and Marxist movements of the twentieth century. The continuing conscious influence of prophetic and other biblical voices for universalistic morality can be seen in the recent statement of Ruth Messinger, a woman who has helped to change world reaction to the genocide in Darfur through her work as executive director of the American Jewish World Service: "We put into action the biblical maxim to not stand idly by when another's blood is being shed."[36]

The mystical-ecstatic visions of Moses and, especially, those of Isaiah and Ezekiel formed the basis for the mystical and kabbalistic movements that strongly influenced a number of different forms of Judaism, from the mysticism of medieval Sephardi Jewry, to premodern Polish Jewry, including the messianic mysticism of Sabbatai Tzvi and Jacob Frank, and the many strands within the Hasidic movement. These are reappearing in twenty-first-century garb in some aspects of the Jewish Renewal movement, in "New Age" Judaism, and in Kabbalah centers.

For many Jews, one powerful expression of their complex identities as a religious culture and a people is read in the book of Ruth. Ruth told her mother-in-law, Naomi, "Where you go I will go, and where you live I will live. Your people will be my people, and your God my God. Where you die I will die, and there I will be buried" (Ruth 1:16–17). Ruth, who began as triply marginalized—a convert, a woman, and an outsider from the Diaspora, articulated the interwoven motifs of religion and relationship that defined Jewish experience in all its variability. This Jew by Choice expressed a central principle of Jewishness. A Jew who could not relate to Jewish tragedies and joys was considered to be somehow cut off from his Jewish antecedents, regardless of his lineage. Ultimately, to be a Jew was to participate in the future of the Jewish people.

Thus, over time, early Jewishness became invested with the diverse Jewishness of later times and places. As biblical literary scholar James Kugel puts it, these meanings "clung" to the biblical texts, and for later readers "came to be the meaning of the text":

> Interpreters came to the conclusion that Abraham was the son of an idol-maker, that he was the first person to believe in one God, and that among his many virtues was an extraordinary generosity toward strangers. None of these things is stated outright in the Bible, though each of them is based on some slight peculiarity in the biblical text.... The shape and significance of the entire Bible came to be modified.... This *interpreted* Bible ... came to stand at the very center.[37]

The narratives of the Hebrew Bible have had diverging meanings for Jews in different times and places. These glimpses of the way biblical narratives were understood by medieval rabbis in Spain or France, by oppressed Polish Jews, or by German Reform thinkers make us even more conscious that, just as they read the Bible through the assumptions of their societies, we as contemporary readers also interpret as we read. We too are embedded in the social and cultural fabric of our times and view the past through the lens of our assumptions and values.

2

The Wandering Jews

Peoplehood and Jewish Culture in the Diaspora

Ethnographers define *peoplehood* as an ethnic group sharing a common descent, language, culture, and homeland. The "portable Jewishness" crafted by rabbinic leaders in the first two centuries of the Common Era included all four of those characteristics, although it appeared, on the surface, to have only three.

Most Jews understood themselves to have descended from Jewish lineage. Historian Jacob Katz notes that while Christian and Muslim societies only symbolically regarded themselves as linked to peoples of the past, Jews believed themselves to be quite literally and "directly descended from the ancient people of Israel." With a few important exceptions, the waxing and waning but virtually omnipresent external hostility increased that strong sense of peoplehood by reinforcing the boundaries around Jewish social networks. Scattered across many different environments, Jews perceived themselves as comprising *am Yisrael,* the people of Israel, which to them meant they were the descendents of the patriarch Jacob, whose alternate name was Israel. Jews in all communities shared a language of prayer—Hebrew—and they developed several specialized vernaculars according to location: Aramaic, Judeo-Arabic, Ladino, Judisch-Deutsch, Yiddish. The fabric of ordinary life was densely interwoven with the ongoing developments of rabbinic law, or *halakhah*. As Jews perceived their existence, daily Jewish life had a "total reliance on the distant past, for Jews traditionally regarded everything of value in Jewish religion—law, learning, and culture—as stemming from ancient times, the period of the Bible and Talmud."[1]

Only the Jewish homeland seemed, on the face of it, absent from Diaspora Jewish daily reality. The lands in which most Jews lived were not their own. Jews were understood by themselves and by the people among whom they lived as, by definition, not belonging. Both Christian and Jewish tradition viewed the Jews as an exiled people who were only, to use sociological terms, sojourners in the countries they inhabited.

The country to which the Jews did belong was their ancient homeland. As a powerful, informing myth, the Jewish homeland, *Eretz Yisrael* (Land of Israel) lived vividly in the communal imagination and helped to complete a sense of peoplehood. The prayers that Jewish men were expected to recite three times daily facing Jerusalem were punctuated with mentions of Zion; on Sabbaths and holidays an additional service recalled the sacrificial services in the great Temple. From time to time individuals or small groups of Jews made their way "up" to the sacred cities of Safed or Jerusalem. There was never a time in which the land was empty of Jews.

Although not every Jew was equally pious, the quotidian lives of most Jews were organized around home, synagogue and study hall, and some form of *kehillah,* the communal governing apparatus that enforced communal norms and often served as a liaison, representing Jews to the Christian or Muslim majority among whom they lived. The *kehillah* centralized Jewish life around community, and that physical and social communalism is one of the profoundly defining characteristics of premodern Jewishness. The *kehillah* derived much of its authority from the fact that Jews needed to be part of a religious entity. For premodern Jews, there was little prospect of existence beyond the community.[2] Persecution was a recurring motif in Jewish life, and to greater and lesser extents the xenophobia of Christian and Muslim host cultures promoted Jewish social cohesiveness, rather than individualism. Centuries before the emergence of "neutral societies"[3] that focused on the individual, people were defined by the ethnoreligious group into which they were born. Jews did not "choose" Judaism, as they are often currently said to do—instead, Jewishness was their destiny. Thus, Jewish peoplehood was defined both by internal religious culture and by external attitudes.

The Jewish Calendar and Life Cycle

Jewish culture was distinctive, organized around a Jewish lunar calendar, anchored in the fall by the solemn High Holy Days: Rosh Hashanah, the Jewish New Year, and Yom Kippur, a fast day on which God decided the fate of every individual in the world. A variety of fast days commemorating tragic events punctuated the year, the most important being the ninth day of Av, *Tisha B'av,* when Jews read the biblical book of Lamentations and recalled the destruction of Jerusalem and its Temple. The biblical agricultural festivals, which before the exile had occasioned pilgrimages to the Temple in Jerusalem, took on new layers of historical meaning, customs, and interpretations in Diaspora communities. On Passover, for example, the Rabbis decreed that one had not fulfilled one's obligation to tell the story of the Exodus from Egypt unless one explained the symbols of the Paschal sacrifice (*pesach*), the unleavened bread that recalled the unexpectedness with which the Israelites fled from Egypt (matzah), and the bitter herbs (*maror*). But what was an appropriate symbol to use for the bitter herbs? In ancient Palestine a bitter, wild lettuce with milky sap had served as a perfect symbol for life in Egypt.[4] For Jews in Europe or on the Iberian Peninsula, another plant needed to substitute. For each of them, the substitute dictated by local rabbinic authorities acquired its own authenticity.

The highlight of the Jewish calendar arrived every week in the distinctive Jewish Sabbath. One victory that rabbinic interpretations of biblical restrictions made possible was a day that brought a modicum of dignity, relaxation, and joy into difficult Jewish lives. From sundown on Friday, when candles were lit, until the lighting of the *havdalah* candle twenty-five hours later, Jews did not cook, sew, tear, write, travel, carry burdens, or engage in any biblically defined *work*. And yet, they were enabled to eat whatever comprised for them the best food of the week, drink wine, and sing together by candlelight. Married couples were expected to enjoy sexual activity as one of the Sabbath's blessings. Dressed in the finest clothes they owned, groups of men (and in certain settings, groups of women) gathered together to pray, to study, and, on particularly auspicious Sabbaths, such as the weeks before Rosh Hashanah or Passover, to hear learned lectures. Although poverty and other factors often diminished the optimum celebration of the day, this weekly occasion devoted to family, community, and God was a social reality for many and a unique communal cultural ideal. As secular Zionist thinker Ahad Ha'am (1856–1927) would say of the erosion of that vision, "More than the Jews have kept the Sabbath, the Sabbath has kept the Jews."

The laws and customs (*minhag/minhagim*) established by rabbis and Jewish societies affected every aspect of life, especially family formation, education, and social responsibilities. Jewish societies were family-oriented—prayers for boys at their circumcision and for girls as they were named in the synagogue hoped for "Torah, marriage, and good deeds." Parents generally took responsibility for arranging marriages for their children, and young couples often lived with one or the other set of parents until they were able to set up housekeeping on their own. Marriage was considered the only productive marital status for adults, as Jewish societies generally created no socially approved role for single adults (as in the Catholic clergy, for example). Sexual feelings and relations were considered necessary and important aspects of married life, for companionship and pleasure as well as for the purpose of procreation, although procreation was certainly emphasized and encouraged.

The Jewish social ideal posited that boys and men were to pray at appointed times, preferably in a *minyan,* or prayer quorum, of ten men, and to devote daily time to sacred study. Fathers were responsible for providing their sons with a Torah education, for having them learn a livelihood, and for teaching them how to swim. Girls were educated by their mothers, but occasionally also by male relatives or by tutors or in schools. For Jews in the Islamic world, it was common for communities to organize schools so that all male children received a rudimentary education. In Ashkenaz (the Hebrew term for European societies in the German Empire, France, Poland, Russia, and Eastern Europe), however, each father was responsible for paying for his own sons' education.

In each of their diverse societies, male and female Jews experienced a dramatically different religious and social existence. While men were urged to participate in public Jewish contexts, women were prohibited from doing so. Men were expected to raise their voices in group prayer services; women were silenced by the warning that their voices constituted a naked call to licentious behavior. While men were urged to study, women were urged to make it possible for men to study by raising children, taking care of domestic concerns, and often, in Ashkenazi communities, by making a living as well. Rabbinic texts did not exaggerate when they described women as "a nation unto themselves."[5]

Jewish Integration on the Iberian Peninsula

Jews lived as often-despised minorities in societies that identified and categorized people according to their religious community.

Both Christianity and Islam declared themselves to be the unique, legitimate replacements for Judaism and the Hebrew "Old" Testament. The stubbornness of the Jews in refusing to adopt either of these "replacement theologies" cast Jews as "unbelievers" or "infidels." Although the actual living situations of Jews differed dramatically from time to time and place to place, from the Middle Ages until emancipation (see chapter 3) many aspects of Jewish life were controlled by others: Feudal lords, monarchs, and Christian and Muslim governing bodies decided where Jews were allowed to live, and which means of employment they could and could not engage in. They imposed special taxes on Jewish residents. At their preference, they allowed Jews into particular geographical areas or, in Christian domains, expelled them. As Katz argues, not only did their Christian or Muslim rulers assume that they had the right to determine the details of Jewish life in this way—the Jews accepted their dependence as well.[6] At certain times and places, Jewish life was miserable indeed. Nevertheless, sometimes for hundreds of years at a stretch, Jewish culture and rich expression flourished.

Few environments can surpass the glories of the "golden" age of Iberian Jewry as an example of flourishing Jewishness. To compare the golden age of Sephardi Jewry with twentieth-century America, we would have to imagine that composer Aaron Copland, novelist Philip Roth, and filmmaker Steven Spielberg were each also rabbinic scholars who lived deeply religious lives and produced volumes of religious codes and analysis alongside their compositions, novels, and films.

Sepharad, as the Iberian Peninsula was called in Hebrew, provided a "uniquely congenial" environment for Jews after the eighth-century Arab-Berber invasion of Andalusia. (Prior to 711, the rule of Visigothic Christian rulers had tormented the six thousand Jews scattered in small communities in southern and central Spain.) Some Jews took up arms and supported the Muslim onslaught. They were well-rewarded for their pro-Muslim attitude, and for more than two hundred years the Sephardim were relatively well-treated: Jews were allowed to own and cultivate small pieces of land, to broker and distribute agricultural products, to become artisans, to practice medicine, and to engage in import-export businesses with extensive travel.

Small wonder that Moroccan and Egyptian Jews migrated to Andalusia in the eighth and ninth centuries; by the tenth century Iberia was home to approximately eighty thousand Jews. As historian Howard Sachar notes, these Sephardi Jews, as they came to be known, enjoyed "a comfortable, middle class" status, "sharing a collective security of existence all but unimaginable to their harried fellow Jews in Christian Europe." Sephardi Jews who traveled were well aware that they were living a very different variety of Jewish existence than Jews in other parts of Europe. As one Sephardi intellectual compared the relative lifestyles of his Andalusian coreligionists and the Jews of Ashkenaz:

> [The Ashkenazim] eat boiled beef, dipped in vinegar and garlic ... and as the fumes ... penetrate their minds, they then imagine that by these viands they have achieved an image of the Creator.... They have no fixed ideas except on rutting, eating and drinking.... Stay clear of them and do not come within their embrace, and ... let not your pleasant companionship be with any other than our beloved Sephardic brethren ... for [the Sephardim] have intellectual capacity, understanding, and clarity of mind.[7]

During these relatively serene centuries, the Jewish community enjoyed significant autonomy. Jews had their own communal self-government, a council of notables. They were taxed by the Muslims as a *dhimmi* (a designation for Jews, Christians, and Zoroastrians), and thus subordinate population, but they were also allowed to collect taxes for their own social, medical, and educational needs. Jewish rabbinic courts adjudicated conflicts, and Jewish jails dealt with miscreants within the community. The cohesiveness and autonomy of the Jewish community and the continuing immersion of its elite males in Judaic learning produced generations of Jews with great Jewish knowledge, daily Jewish practice, and multifaceted Jewish experiences into which they incorporated many aspects of the Arabic renaissance that surrounded them. For although Jews lived according to Jewish religious cultural dictates and were supervised by Jewish governing bodies, they were also integrated into the vibrant surrounding culture to some extent socially, but to a much greater extent intellectually, learning Arabic literary principles, Greek philosophy, mathematics, and science.

The Arabic renaissance took place in an environment in which both Jews and Muslims remained deeply steeped in their own religious cultures. The uniqueness of this duality, with its combination of autonomy and integration, is best illustrated by the bicultural interests and output of Jewish luminaries. Samuel Ibn Nagrela (d. 1056, often referred to as Shmuel haNagid), who headed the Jewish community and wrote lyrical poetry on secular subjects in Hebrew, was revered as a rabbinic authority and was also praised by Jewish and Muslim biographers as a skilled Arabic scribe. Solomon Ibn Gabirol (d. 1057) wrote three hundred poems, including both love poetry and religious poetry, some of which has been incorporated into Jewish liturgy, and a philosophical magnum opus, *The Fountain of Life,* which impressed Christian clerics. Moses Ibn Ezra (d. 1138) wrote hedonistic celebrations of life as well as liturgical poetry in his youth, and parts of today's Yom Kippur liturgy in his middle age. And Judah Halevi (d. 1141), a poetic genius who wrote great Hebrew lyrics in the classical Arabic tradition, became a practicing physician. Halevi believed that God's presence permeated the Land of Israel, and he ended his life attempting to travel there by boat, after writing the moving classic *The*

Book of the Kuzari, which extols the superiority of Judaism over other religions and secular philosophy.[8]

This productive period was disrupted when the Almohades, a fanatic group of Islamic warriors, came down from their Algerian mountain homes, conquering city after Iberian city in the 1140s and imposing harsh anti-Jewish and anti-Christian measures that lasted for decades. The eclectic cultural experiences and entrepreneurial activism of the Jews, who fled by the thousands, are reflected in the fortunes of the Maimon family and their thirteen-year-old son, Moses. Like many displaced Iberian Jews, they lived a near-nomadic existence, settling for a time in Fez, Morocco, where Moses Maimonides, now a young man, studied medicine. They then moved to Fustat (near Cairo), where the family became jewel merchants. Maimonides' skill as a physician gained him fame and financial security. Some reports say he became the royal doctor to Sultan Saladin and his family. Historically, Maimonides is known to have maintained a full private practice and written medical literature.[9] Many of Maimonides' assumptions about life were influenced by his Muslim surroundings. His medical advice seems strikingly modern in its insistence on regular exercise, fresh air, and personal hygiene.[10] However, his attitudes toward women and sexuality were also influenced by Muslim mores and make many contemporary readers uncomfortable. Although Maimonides would have characterized his approach as "moderate" rather than ascetic, he clearly mistrusted the effects of ungoverned carnal impulses.[11]

Despite his family's wanderings, Maimonides became a renowned participant in the Arabic-Jewish cultural renaissance as well as a towering Jewish thinker, influencing Jewish communities during his time and Jewish philosophy to the present day. His philosophical writings drew deeply from the cultural renaissance of Muslim intellectual life, as it was animated by the rediscovery of ancient Greek culture and the adaptation of Greek philosophy to help resolve conflicts between religion and science. At the same time, he became a Jewish communal leader, rabbi, and judge in Fustat in 1165. Among other activities, Maimonides worked to reduce enmity between the Rabbanite and Karaite Jewish communities.[12] His influence was widespread because he wrote prodigious numbers of legal responsa (letters including legal rulings to religious queries) to many communities.

Maimonides' powerful reputation as a Jewish thinker was most firmly established by his *Mishneh Torah* (Code of the Law) in 1185 and his *Guide for the Perplexed* in 1190. Their dramatic differences in spirit, subject matter, and style reflect the polyphonic cultural influences of this period of Jewish life. The *Mishneh Torah* is an utterly lucid, orderly (and somewhat dry) codification of Jewish law by minute categories, a comprehensive reference work. The *Guide for the Perplexed,* written in Arabic with Hebrew letters, is an elegant, complex—and often perplexing—work of philosophical discourse, which was translated into Hebrew and praised, critiqued, but, above all, *read,* later by Albertus Magnus, Thomas Aquinas, and Roger Bacon. At his death in 1204, Maimonides was mourned by Jews in Jerusalem as well as in Iberia and North Africa, but his influence on Jewish life and thought continued. Indeed, as Arabic-Jewish flowering drew to a close and the next chapter of Sephardi Jewish life very gradually developed in Christian Northern Spain, Maimonidean philosophy created its own schism with less philosophical Jewish approaches, and Maimonides himself was for a time in danger of being subjected to a posthumous excommunication.

Thirteenth-century Christian Spain seemed as though it might provide a beneficent home for the Jews who fled cruelly repressive Almohade Muslim rulers in Southern Spain. Sephardi Jewish communities reassembled in this seemingly sunny alternative environment. The rulers of Christian Northern Spain received Jewish immigration positively, not only because they needed population but because they felt Jews could be helpful in tasks related to commerce and urbanization. Jews were attractive to them also because they had a reputation for diligence and loyalty to rulers who accommodated Jewish lifestyles. They were allowed to settle together and to create their own communal institutions. Their livelihoods included a wide variety of artisanship—leather, soap, parchment, candles, iron, armor, textiles, silver, jewelry. They also engaged in mercantile activities, as shopkeepers, brokers, money changers and lenders (the medieval equivalent of bankers), making it possible for an economy to grow. They occupied elite levels of leadership positions, as the physicians, lawyers, notaries, advisers, and personal secretaries of kings and nobles.[13]

Some Jews of Christian Northern Spain in the thirteenth century grew wealthy by becoming "tax farmers," people who collected government taxes, along with a hearty cut for themselves. These families socialized with similarly affluent Christian elites, attending each other's life-cycle events, gambling together, and engaging in other social activities. Jews became preferred as physicians and translators among the Christian oligarchy. Some monied Jews adopted the permissive lifestyles of their social stratum, including interreligious sexual relationships, with some Jewish women serving as courtesans, and Jewish men taking Christian or Muslim concubines.[14]

The libertine lifestyle was not characteristic of most Sephardi Jews, however, and actually served as a provocation for mistrust of external culture among some segments of the Jewish population. Observing the sexual freedoms of limited segments of the Jewish population, Sephardi rabbinic leaders recommended strict supervision of Jewish women's activities. *Kol k'vudah bat melekh p'nima*, they repeated, "The glory of the king's daughter is in interior settings," interpreting a biblical phrase to support limited female access to the outside world. Those entertainments most likely to lead to sexual congress, such as drinking parties with instrumental musical entertainments or singers, were proscribed. Indeed, it is from this period and its anxieties that one source of the later prohibition against *kol ishah*, the hearing of women's voices, is found. Thus, although Jews as an ethnoreligious group enjoyed far more freedom in Sepharad at this time than they did in the lands of Ashkenaz, Jewish women's lives were generally less restricted among the Ashkenazim.[15]

Adverse reactions to the influences of outside Muslim and Christian cultures on Jewish life and thought were not limited to relaxed moral standards. The influence of classical Greek philosophy on Maimonides and his followers was troubling to many Jews. The bitter struggle between Maimonidean and non-Maimonidean modes of thought was partially one of philosophy, partially one of location, and perhaps partially one of class conflict. Chief among the points of contention was the accusation that Maimonides denied the resurrection of the body, believing instead that only the soul was immortal and returned to God as its source after death. In the 1230s, *Guide for the Perplexed* was banned in southern France, and rabbis may have participated in the burning of the book in Paris. A counter-excommunication was mounted by supporters of Maimonidean thought in Provence, with letters and emissaries of both sides traveling back and forth, gathering support. This conflict in Jewish approaches reflected a similar struggle between Christian elite thinkers like the Augustinian theologians and populists such as the peasants and their friars, including Francis of Assisi.

Although the antirationalist but moderate Moses ben Nachman—Nachmanides—managed to defend Maimonides and prevent his excommunication, the battle between self-declared "rationalists" and "anti-rationalists" continued. In 1305, Solomon ibn Adret, the chief rabbi of Barcelona, proclaimed as heretics all those who followed the Maimonidean influence (but not Maimonides himself), banning for persons under age twenty-five the study of "Greek works on science and metaphysics," which he asserted were "blasphemous nostrums" that "mock the words of the sages."[16] Many also condemned the teachings of Averroes, a philosopher contemporary to Maimonides, who espoused ideas many Jews and Christians found heretical. Eventually, those who opposed Jewish Averroeism and Maimonidean philosophy denounced those who followed it to the dark and growing forces of the Inquisition.

Nobody Expects the Spanish Inquisition

A popular comedy routine of the Monty Python troupe features a bourgeois British couple answering a knock on the door of their apartment and discovering, to their surprise, robed clerics of the Spanish Inquisition. "But we weren't expecting you," the couple protests, only to be told, "Nobody expects the Spanish Inquisition." It is almost impossible not to think of that retort when reflecting on the Jews of the Iberian Peninsula, thriving first in Muslim and then in Christian cultures, and then crushed by a tidal of wave of violence from the late fourteenth century onward. The desirability of Jewish qualities and talents, which had earned Jews supporters, gave way to forces that demonized the Jewish religion. The persecution of Iberian Jewry was not taking place in a vacuum, but was occurring all around the European arena, amid Crusades and ritual murder libels, pogroms and massacres.

Despite their virtually nonexistent Jewish military power—it was, after all, Muslims who had repeatedly warred against and taken territory from Christian rulers—Jews were vilified far more than Muslims. Routinely, the Jewish "historical" role as "antichrists" was invoked, and Jews were also routinely referred to as "devils" and "sorcerers," worthy of butchering riots. To some extent, hatred of Jews had been fanned by socioeconomic factors: The once prized role of tax collector, which Spanish Jews had sought out as a lucrative practice, had earned them the hatred of the peasantry whom they taxed. As money lenders, too, Jews were alternately sought out and hated.

But hatred of the Jews was also stoked by their very social integration. As in Nazi Germany five hundred years later, when Jewish assimilation was far more infuriating to antisemites than Jewish distinctiveness, one of the first acts of the Spanish Antipope Benedict XIII (regarded as the Pope by the kingdoms of France, Scotland, Sicily, Castille, Aragon, Navarre, and Portugal, in opposition to the Roman College of Cardinals whose chosen pope was Boniface IX) in 1412 was to ghettoize the Jews, to mark them off with special dress, to circumscribe their socioeconomic parameters, and to require them to wear special badges. Some historians show that Jewish life was generally maintained at a fairly high level during the fifteenth century. Nevertheless, one Jew of the period wrote:

> They barred us from commerce, agriculture, and crafts. They forced us to grow our beards and our hair long. Former palace dwellers were driven into wretched hovels and ill-lit huts. Instead of the rustle of silk, we were compelled to wear miserable clothing.... Hunger looked everyone in the face, and children died at their mothers' breasts from exposure and starvation.[17]

The work of the Inquisition was aided by *meshumadim*, Jews who converted to Christianity. Some converts became priests and attained fame and respect in church circles for their anti-Jewish activities. Their influence was particularly vicious because Jewish leaders were often asked to participate in disputations about the relative dogmas of Judaism and Christianity, with Christian clerics getting "inside information" from formerly Jewish apostates. Most Jews did not become quislings of this magnitude, but they did convert in vast numbers—frequently thousands at a time. Conversions increased, not surprisingly, during cataclysmic events such as anti-Jewish riots in 1391. Large numbers of the most thoroughly converted came from the most distinguished, well-educated, and affluent Sephardi Jewish families. Some elite families abandoned substantive links to Jews and Judaism even before they became formally baptized.

In hindsight, the loss of communal commitment to Jewishness among the Iberian population is sobering. Strikingly, many such Jews declared privately as well as publicly that they had "seen the light" of Christian replacement theology before they converted. Some declared that the Jews suffered like Christ because they rejected Christ. On the Iberian Peninsula, many of the elite Jews who converted not only joined the Christian faith, they also lost their attachments to Jewish peoplehood and the entire Jewish enterprise.[18]

Apostasy may have seemed the only rational choice, if we consider that to be Jewish during the prologue of church-incited anti-Jewish riots, which left thousands dead and mutilated, or during the reign of the Inquisition was to incur enormous human and social costs. The only escape from the pariah status of Jewish peoplehood and all the accompanying disadvantages was to convert to Christianity. Ironically, even conversion did not necessarily rescue Jews, since New Christians were subject to special suspicions of "backsliding," and some Christian authorities took steps to separate the New Christians from their Jewish friends and relatives. Indeed, *conversos,* Jews who converted—not full Jews—were the primary targets of the Inquisition.

Some Spanish and Portuguese *conversos* retained secret Jewish rituals and feelings of identification. Although Christians popularly referred to them as *Marranos,* that derisive name, which means "pigs," has been replaced in contemporary discussions by the designations *crypto-Jews* (secret Jews) or *anusim* (compelled ones, referring to their conversions). Crypto-Jews were far more frequent among the lower middle-class than among the upper class. In addition, as feminist historian Renee Levine Melammed has shown, a disproportionate number of those clinging to secret Judaism were women—and a disproportionate number of betraying Jewish "backsliders" were the husbands and sons of those women, who did not wish the Judaic activities of their wives and mothers to compromise their own position in a church-controlled society. In these dangerous times, where Judaism survived it was primarily Jewish women who preserved it through their adherence to home-based Jewish, familial rituals.[19]

During the fourteenth and fifteenth centuries, some Jews—and some crypto-Jews—correctly assessed the bleak future of Iberian Jewish life and set off for whichever locations were currently allowing Jewish immigration. Others, including the remaining leaders of the Spanish Jewish community, hoped that the situation would somehow improve. But attempts to separate the *conversos* from their Jewish families were often frustratingly unsuccessful to Christian leaders, who finally lost faith in conversion as a solution for their Jewish problem. In the spring of 1492, Spanish rulers Ferdinand and Isabella famously deferred to the pressure of Inquisitor General Tomas de Torquemada and issued a proclamation expelling "all Jews and Jewesses" and forbidding all Christians to communicate with, aid, or harbor Jews under "pain of death" and "pain of excommunication." In August 1492 the last professing Sephardi Jews left Spain. They joined brothers and sisters who preceded them before the official exile, settling in various corners of the Ottoman Empire, where they reassembled into new, distinctive, and often vibrant Jewish communities.

Even after they wandered to Amsterdam, Turkey, Egypt, North Africa, and the Americas, those Sephardi communities that retained ritually observant lifestyles were marked by a number of characteristics that differentiated them from the Ashkenazi European communities and from each other. Some of those differences dealt with liturgical choices and the order and melodies used in prayer services. Recipes for traditional foods (including differing foods permitted on Passover) were characteristic of the countries in which the Sephardi Jews made their homes. Other differences were deep expressions of social psychology. Jews who had lived in Spain and Portugal adopted prevalent cultural attitudes toward women's appropriate roles, which were in general fairly restricted. By contrast, from the Middle Ages onward, Ashkenazi women played an important role as brokers for Westernization; through their marketplace activities, these women helped to move European Jews toward the gradually emerging middle class.

For a substantial portion of the Sephardi population, repeated rupture had created a sophisticated, enterprising approach to existence. Sephardi Jews were often skilled merchants, and some were involved in trade across national borders. For a segment of the Sephardi population, a cosmopolitan lifestyle was a doorway to the gradual influences of modernity, and these Jews themselves played indirect roles in societal changes.

However, many of the expelled Sephardi Jews were deeply religious people, who lived according to rabbinic dictates in their new homes. In their new homes, Sephardi scholars continued with their scholarship. Indeed, the *Shulchan Arukh* ("The Arranged Table"), regarded by some Orthodox Jews as the authoritative codification of Jewish law, was written by Joseph Caro (d. 1575), who lived in the Ottoman Empire after the expulsion from Spain and eventually made his way to the city of Safed to live among the Jewish mystics. The *Shulchan Arukh* was first published in Venice in 1564–1565.[20] Additionally, Sephardi Jews in particular locales often evolved very distinctive religious customs, which had enormous authority to them. Thus, the various streams of Sephardi Jewry that flowed into Jewish communities around the world were different from Ashkenazi forms of Judaism, but were far from monolithic.

Jewish Culture in Medieval Christian Europe

Jewish life in France, England, the German Empire, Italy, Hungary, Poland, and the rest of Eastern Europe underwent repeated cycles of opening and closing narratives. Jews were expelled from England in 1290; repeatedly expelled, invited back, and again expelled in fourteenth-century French locales; and expelled from Germany in the fifteenth century.

Where Jews were allowed, Church doctrine formalized their subordination in public settings and in social relationships. Jews were not allowed to employ non-Jews or in any way be in a position of authority over a Christian, and sexual relationships between Jewish men and Christian women were forbidden. Social segregation was encouraged and sometimes enforced. Jewish dwellings were often required to be in separate areas of a city, and Jews were often compelled to wear identifying garments or badges.

Periodically, Jews were accused of sadistically killing Christian children to use their blood to make matzah (unleavened bread), the infamous "ritual blood libel," and massacres of the villages in which the accused Jews lived often followed. The Crusades, beginning in 1095 and 1146, created their own circle of hell for Jews in their path, facilitating the annihilation of Jewish populations and the confiscation of Jewish property. Nor were Jewish books safe from persecution: Encouraged by the virulent anti-Talmud beliefs of Pope Gregory IX, who asked the kings of England, France, Castille, and Portugal to seize all copies of the Talmud in 1239, authorities in some locales called rabbis to disputations about the legality of Talmud literature. These disputations, as we have noted, were often precipitated by accusations made by former Jewish converts to Catholicism. Thus, in 1240, for example, the apostate Nicholas Donan charged that the Talmud continued blasphemous statements about Jesus. He debated the veracity of this statement with four rabbis, resulting in the burning of the Talmud in Paris in 1242.

In Ashkenaz, as opposed to Sepharad, Jews were severely limited with respect to which occupations they could pursue. During the medieval period, Jews in many areas were forbidden to own or farm land. In some places they were not allowed to be artisans. Their mercantile skills, however, were critical. Because Christians were forbidden to indulge in usury, Jews who could loan money provided Christians with a medieval banking system that could fund individual and community enterprises. That pattern of Jewish-Christian interaction is familiar to many through Shakespeare's "comedy," *The Merchant of Venice*. As the play makes clear, Jews were both endured and hated for this service. Because the Catholic Church was uncomfortable with the dependence of local economics on Jewish usury, it periodically forbade Jews even from serving as money lenders—rulings that impoverished Jewish populations. The decision in 1275 of Edward I of England to outlaw Jewish money lending was followed in 1290 by the expulsion of England's Jews—when Jews ceased to be of use to the crown, they were often purged from the country as well.

This dependence on the goodwill of Christian hosts, vulnerability to outbreaks of officially and unofficially sanctioned antisemitic violence, and atmosphere of hatred of the very substance of Jewish life and belief provide the backdrop for any consideration of medieval Ashkenazi Jewish life. During the period of the Black Death (1348–1349), more Jews of Provence were killed in anti-Jewish massacres than were killed by the plague.

That having been said, our purpose is not to focus on historical persecutions, but instead to spotlight some divergent forms of Jewishness that evolved among Jews in various times and places. We have already seen that Sephardi Jews regarded the Jews of Ashkenaz as a culturally backward, parochial group. However, Ashkenazi communities were diverse and comprised their own spectrum of cultural developments.

A few representative examples from the lives of individual Ashkenazi Jews point to these sometimes surprising variations. Information about the internal experience of historical Jewish life can be gleaned from the letters, travel literature, and other written materials found in the Cairo Genizah, a kind of unwitting archive created by the tradition of not throwing out any papers or books that have God's Hebrew appellation somewhere on their surface. Because they are written materials, and much of the population was certainly illiterate, the information is most useful in looking at elite, literate classes of Jews. Although most of these documents pertain to the Jews of the Islamic world, among the hundred thousand pages rediscovered by Solomon Schechter in 1896 is a beautiful elegy by Eliezer of Worms, an eleventh-century German Talmud scholar, for his wife, Dolce, and his two daughters, who perished in the first Crusade (1196). Of his wife, he noted that "she made [him] books from her toil," "sewed together about forty Torah scrolls," "recited Psalms" and "sang hymns and prayers," "instructed women," and spent long hours in the synagogue, "coming early and staying late." Similarly, he said of his thirteen-year-old daughter Bellette that she "learnt all the prayers and melodies from her mother" and was skilled in "spinning and sewing and embroidering," and of his younger daughter, Hannah, "Each day she recited the *Shema Yisrael* and the prayer that followed it. She was six years old and could spin, sew and embroider, and entertain me by singing."[21]

In his praise for their accomplishments, it becomes clear that the Jews of Ashkenaz were not living in a vacuum. For financially solvent families, there was an expectation that girls and women would receive a Jewish education and would also acquire the same cultural graces that one found in Christian families of the same socioeconomic cohort. This expectation, and the obvious pride a Talmud scholar takes in the religious and nonreligious cultivation of the women in his family, reveals that medieval German Jewish life partook of wider cultural developments, despite the backdrop of grim persecutions. New analysis of the lives of medieval Ashkenazi women reveals that even in pious households and communities women played a key economic role in families and Jewish societies. As a result, women served as sociological brokers, guiding Ashkenazi Jewish families toward bourgeois models of behavior and values.[22]

Much of Eliezer of Worms's contributions as a halakhic thinker are preserved in the school surrounding Rashi (d. 1105), Rabbi Shlomo Yitzhaki, who was born and lived and wrote most of his life in Troyes, France. A monumental figure, Rashi is regarded by many as the greatest commentator on the Bible and especially on the Talmud in Jewish history. Rashi's commentaries are still regarded as indispensable and are his legacy to the ages; even in his own time the power of his mind was recognized, and he educated numerous students. For this discussion, he is also significant in the way his life illuminates the integration of the Jews of Troyes in the surrounding culture.[23] Like many of his Jewish neighbors, Rashi made his living by cultivating grapes. In his writings there are references to many languages, including French and German, as well, of course, as Hebrew and Aramaic. Rashi's Jewish neighbors spoke French in their daily interactions, gave their children French names, and made use of non-Jewish melodies for their lullabies. Some Jewish religious prayers were composed in the French vernacular, and there are Jewish prayer books extant with prayers in French and Hebrew, and some with prayers entirely in French. Rashi's attitudes toward female sexuality exemplify the more positive Ashkenazi view, as opposed to the cautious Sephardi rabbinical approach: His advice to his daughters on strategies to retain their husbands' sexual interest has been preserved and is quite graphic. He also seems to have educated his daughters to read and understand the Talmud and to have arranged for them to marry men who would continue to study

Talmud with them. Rashi's daughters are quoted by name as talmudic experts, and one of them became his amanuensis at the end of his life.[24]

Rashi's major significance to Ashkenazi Jewishness was his ubiquitous contribution to the understanding of sacred texts, in a society that, more than any other in human history, made their regular study by nonclerics a central social ideal. Contemporary scholarship has made it clear that most Jewish men had neither the education nor the leisure to engage in Talmud study on a regular basis. Nevertheless, study of texts was much more widespread than in surrounding cultures, and the hope that ordinary men would do so was unique to Jewish societies. Men who did engage in talmudic scholarship brought breathtaking intellectual passion to the endeavor, despite frequent danger and privation. Commentaries were written in prison and distributed from there (for example, by Rabbi Meir of Rothenberg, in 1286). Colleagues and disciples often rescued the texts of commentaries, completed them, transported them across geographical borders, and disseminated them. Consider the example of thirteenth-century German scholar Mordecai ben Hillel Ha-Kohen (d. 1298), whose liberal, pro-woman statements have gained him the admiration of contemporary Jewish feminists. His *Sefer Mordecai,* usually referred to as *The Mordecai,* had such enormous scope that it was transported in two versions, the "Rhenish," which includes the religious opinions and practices of Jews in France, England, and Germany, and the "Austrian," which encompasses those of Austria, Hungary, Bohemia, Saxony, and Moravia. Mordecai died a martyr's death in the Rindfleisch massacres, along with his wife and five children.[25] His active life, his liberal attitudes, his prolific writings documenting the diversity of Jewish behaviors, his tragic death, and the way his scholarship lived on after him and influenced further generations exemplify the accomplishments and the dangers of Ashkenazi Jewish life.

The Jewish Experience in the Transition toward Modernity

Much of Catholic Europe had been closed off to Jews by the end of the Middle Ages. Indeed, after 1519 the only remaining significant Jewish communities in German lands were located in Frankfurt and Worms. Poland had emerged as the major significant refuge for Ashkenazi Jews, absorbing immigrants from Bohemia, Moravia, Italy, and Germany. With much of the Ashkenazi Jewish population concentrated in Poland, a set of virtually uniform practices and attitudes emerged, and Jewish life was relatively cohesive for a time. German immigrants had brought Yiddish with them, which became the common language of Poland's Jews and eventually all Central and Eastern Europe's Jews. Not insignificantly, printing presses capable of producing Hebrew books appeared in Europe almost simultaneously with the extinguishing of the Spanish and German Jewish communities, greatly enhancing the portability of Jewish culture in the new centers of Jewish life: Poland, Italy, Bohemia, and Moravia for Ashkenazi Jews, and across the Ottoman Empire and increasingly the industrial cities of Western Europe for Sephardi Jews.[26]

The Renaissance, and later the beginnings of the Industrial Revolution and the emergence of a rudimentary middle class in the sixteenth and seventeenth centuries, broadened Jewish options in many places. In Italy, where communities had their own distinctive forms of Jewish attitudes and practice, the Renaissance proved a time of extraordinary opportunities—much more so than before or for hundreds of years after. Upper-class Jews and Christians interacted socially, played cards and tennis, gambled and went to masquerade balls together. Educated Jews had access to the literary flowering around them: Dante's *Divine Comedy* was transliterated into Hebrew characters, and rabbis referred to his poetry in their sermons. These sermons were often published in Hebrew but delivered in Italian. Despite clerical prohibitions against accepting Jewish students, some Italian Jews attended universities in the fifteenth and sixteenth centuries and received elaborately illuminated diplomas attesting to their completed courses of study.

The Italian states were relatively tolerant, keeping Jews isolated in the ghettos, but almost never subjecting them to real physical persecutions and massacres, as was common practice in other European countries. Partially as a result, Italian Jews acculturated to Italian mores in many regards, such as making wine part of daily meal consumption and not paying particular attention to obtaining kosher wines, as Venetian Rabbi Leon Modena testifies in his *Riti Ebraici* (Venice 1638).[27] In keeping with the relatively liberal understandings of gender roles in the Renaissance, Jewish gender roles became more fluid as well. Jewish girls were enrolled in religious schools (sometimes sitting alongside their brothers) and expected to become literate in the Hebrew of the Bible and prayers. Some Jewish women advanced beyond this, writing Hebrew and Italian religious poetry, becoming scribes and typesetters and even ritual slaughterers. More common was the role of women as Jewish philanthropists, for which they were duly honored.[28]

In other parts of Europe, the Jews' ability to take advantage of new opportunities as Europe moved out of a feudal economy and toward modern financial arrangements was made possible, ironically, by the capital they had been building and passing from generation to generation when Jewish money lending and tax collecting were their only options.[29] Jews became important economic players in Poland, Lithuania, and the German Empire partly because they had no natural competitors. The ruling class needed money to fulfill its ambitions, and whatever Christian burgher class might have emerged to fulfill that function was impoverished and decimated during the Thirty Year War. In France, where the state had its own forms of capitalism, the transition out of a feudal economy was accomplished with Jewish capitalists.[30]

One of the best descriptions of seventeenth-century Jewish life in Ashkenaz is found in the *Memoirs of Gluekl of Hameln.* Gluekl was born in the mid-1640s in Hamburg, where Jews were uneasily tolerated for the economic prosperity they brought. They were not allowed to worship, bury their dead, or govern themselves in Hamburg. Legally, all these functions were performed in the neighboring town of Altona. Gluekl was engaged by twelve and married at fourteen to Haim, a youth just a few years older than she, from the small town of Hameln. Such early matches, atypical of Christians in their locale but not uncommon among more affluent European Jews, accomplished three goals: They helped parents outmaneuver the unreliable political status of the Jews by establishing their children in life as soon as possible; they enabled parents to support the young couple emotionally; and they enhanced the eventuality of progeny. This match turned out to be suffused with love, according to Gluekl's repeated comments in the memoirs. Her husband not only treated her with affection, but also regarded her as an erudite business partner, depending on her judgments when making decisions. When he died, Gluekl, the mother of thirteen children, took over the business, traveling with jewels and other merchandise from city to city.

To make the long evening hours pass more quickly, Gluekl wrote her memoirs and reflections on life in seven volumes. Her writing displays impressive and wide-ranging knowledge of Judaic materials. She was evidently fully observant of Jewish rituals and laws, but also keenly introspective and thoughtful as she examined her life and the behavior of those around her. She was not easily intimidated. She knew how to write Hebrew letters quite well, and learned allusions to the Hebrew Bible and rabbinic materials are threaded throughout her work. Her comments on her husband's death, for example, consciously echo the books of Job and Lamentations. Like most intellectually accomplished Jewish women, she acquired her information from voracious reading of

Yiddish translations and commentaries, but probably did not have an extensive knowledge of Hebrew literature. Unlike some Jews, who could only read German transliterated into Hebrew letters, Gluekl also read German in the Gothic letters. Women like Gluekl, typical of middle- and upper-class Jewish women, were less well educated in sacred literature than men with similar talents and social status, but they were far more educated than many Christian women in the communities around them. Above all, their assumptions about life called for female energy and assertiveness, rather than a passive or docile approach to challenges.[31]

Sephardi Jews Strike Out for New Homes

While most Jews who fled the Iberian Peninsula settled in communities in the Ottoman Empire, when Jews began to move into the cities of Amsterdam, London, and Hamburg in the sixteenth and seventeenth centuries—before they were officially allowed to move there, it might be added—Sephardi Jews were among the first to take advantage of those economic opportunities. They were joined by hidden Jews who had remained behind in Spain and Portugal. Unlike the Jews who left before or during the expulsion, those Jews who stayed in Iberia practiced little, were often quite cynical about organized religion, and were cut off from the continuing evolutions of rabbinic Judaism. Many related far more to the Jewishness of biblical narratives than to ensuing developments. The halakhic Judaism of the Sephardi Jews who had left prior to or during 1492 was alien to those who did not leave until the sixteenth century. Tensions developed not only between Sephardim and Ashkenazim, but also between the two Sephardi communities—one that wished to create a controlling communal structure, and the other that resisted it.

That friction between pious and liberalized Sephardi Jews is epitomized historically in the life story of philosopher Benedict

(Baruch) Spinoza, whose father emigrated from Portugal to Amsterdam, where Baruch was born. Because of his knowledge of biblical Hebrew and Maimonidean commentaries, some historians assume that he studied with the local rabbinic scholars, but no details about his actual education have ever been found. While some have assumed that Spinoza garnered his heretical ideas from a freethinking ex-Jesuit, recent scholarship places the source of the heresy firmly within the "heterodox controversies" of the Amsterdam Jewish community itself, in which, one generation earlier, Uriel da Costa had been excommunicated for declaring that all religions were manmade and that the human soul was not eternal. Baruch Spinoza famously developed a rationalistic metaphysics in his approaches to ethics not based on organized religion. Although some of his writings indicate that he believed deeply in God as the highest good and the basis of morality, he was excommunicated by the communal authorities of the Sephardi community in 1656.[32]

Spinoza's philosophical writings had profound and continuing influence. They can be said to have foreshadowed the idea of *Wissenschaft des Judentums* (scientific study of Jewish cultures and texts), proposed more than a century later in Germany, in that he subjected religious beliefs to careful, rationalistic scrutiny. As philosopher and novelist Rebecca Goldstein observes, Spinoza gave the world modernity by arguing that "no group or religion could rightly claim infallible knowledge of the Creator's partiality to its beliefs and ways." Looking at virulent religious conflicts in his time and ours, "the conclusions he drew are still of dismaying relevance."[33]

For some Sephardi Jews, opportunities across the ocean beckoned. Dutch Brazil offered immigrants the same religious freedoms as Holland itself and attracted about two dozen Sephardi Jews in the middle of the seventeenth century. However, when Portugal conquered parts of Brazil and the Portuguese Inquisition extended its power to the New World, the Jewish community sailed north-ward to New Amsterdam, which would become, of course, New York with oncoming British victories. By the eighteenth century, Sephardim from the Antilles, Amsterdam, London, and directly from Spain and Portugal had joined them, bringing the number of Jews in the now-British colonies close to two thousand.[34] Sophisticated and enterprising people, these Sephardim were more notable for the survival skills that had been honed through the generations than they were for elaborate piety or sacred learning. They proceeded to build their lives in a colony that already resisted investing the state with the ability to engage in wholesale religious persecution.

Trauma and Messianism in Polish Jewish Life

The capitalistic skills and tradesman image of the Jews opened doors for them but produced a powerful backlash as well, often exacerbating religious intolerance and fanning the waves of anti-semitism that flared up sporadically but viciously. This was particularly true in Poland, which had served as a haven for Jews during periods of minimal Jewish presence in Western Europe. The atrocities inflicted on Polish Jewish communities during the Chmielnicki massacres (1648), for example, were profoundly disheartening to the pious Jewish population. Many were convinced that things were so bad that the messiah *must* be at hand; some even kept suitcases packed so that they could emigrate quickly to the Land of Israel when the messiah arrived. Several messianic movements united followers among both the Sephardi and Ashkenazi Jewish populations, who devoted themselves in large numbers to their putative liberators. Some historians argue that Polish Jewish suffering contributed to the emergence of Jewish messianic movements centered around charismatic personalities, such as Sabbatai Tzvi (1626–1676), who first appeared in Turkey in 1665 and was lauded by almost all Ottoman Jews, and by many Ashkenazi Jews as well, as the messiah. However, when Sabbatai Tzvi converted to Islam to save his own life, only a minority of his formerly huge number of believers followed him into apostasy. The Sabbatean heresy was followed by an even more perverse messianic movement led by Jacob Frank (1726–1791), which spiraled downward into dark, orgiastic behaviors, urging followers to conduct themselves in ways that were, by definition, the exact opposite of Jewish law. Each of these movements, in turn, imploded, leaving shaken communities behind both in Poland and in the Ottoman Empire. For both communities, the price of flirtations with messianic movements was to invest the forces of conservatism with even more fear of change than they had previously held.

Polish Jewish life, which had for a time been typified by fairly coherent rabbinic lifestyles and learning, was fragmented and set on edge by these messianic movements. Some scholars suggest that these episodes traumatized rabbinic leadership, which thereafter became suspicious of innovative Jewish movements that emphasized spirituality and appealed to the masses. In addition, those German Jews who had settled in Poland had begun to shift their interests back toward their homelands in the German Empire, in which the first stirrings of the Jewish Enlightenment had begun. The quiescent Jewish religious lifestyles of early sixteenth-century Poland had proved to be not so much a situation of calm weather, but rather the eye of the hurricane, as the winds of early modernity began to blow, leading to changes that would transform Jewishness forever.

Hasidic and Mitnagdic Jewish Rivalry

Hasidic Judaism arose partially because of the "social convulsion" caused by Sabbateanism and Frankism. Hasidic leaders and their followers produced new answers and new challenges to rabbinic

Judaism. Beginning with the Baal Shem Tov (1698–1760), and followed by numerous other innovators, Hasidic leaders initially emphasized the potential of the common people to engage in joyous communication with God through song, meditation, harmony with nature, and attachment to the charismatic "rebbe" and his dynastic tradition. Hasidism was no mere variation on the familiar theme of rabbinic Judaism, Jacob Katz convincingly argues. Rather, "the values and characteristics of Hasidism" were "a displacement and substitution" for "traditional values."[35]

For the Jewish proletariat, Hasidism felt empowering, since a man's ability to serve God with passion was validated without his needing to belong to an intellectual elite. Hasidic men were encouraged to spend days, weeks, even months at a time in the courts of Hasidic rebbes. To listen to and learn the rebbe's new melodies, even to eat crumbs off the rebbe's plate, was to have access to holiness. Hasidism was, presumably, less validating for the women who remained at home, coping with children and the necessity to earn a living as best they could. Although a similar charge might be made about the rigors of rabbinical study (witness the many stories about Rabbi Akiva and his devoted wife), yeshiva study involved only a small elite, while Hasidic travel to the rebbe's court involved large numbers of non-elite men, many of whose families could least afford these absences from the household.

In these early years of Hasidism, a philosophy that appeared to deemphasize the prestige of sober Torah study—and the prestige and authority of rabbinic scholars—was intensely upsetting to rabbinic luminaries. These rabbis and their followers became known as Mitnagdim, literally "those who oppose." This pattern of action and reaction—in which an innovative approach to Jewishness causes long-established groups to create a name and an official ideology for themselves—would become very familiar with the passage of time. The more established group typically becomes more self-consciously doctrinaire and forceful as mentors push back against the newcomers. In the early eighteenth century, the conflict between the Hasidim and the Mitnagdim became so fierce that Mitnagdic luminaries such as the Vilna Gaon (1720–1797) repeatedly excommunicated Hasidic leaders. Yiddish writer I. L. Peretz characterized the common folk, looking back and forth between the Hasidic and Mitnagdic forms of Judaism, as caught in miserable confusion "Between Two Mountains."[36]

Excommunications did not squelch Hasidic approaches, however, and Hasidism became a mass movement. According to a new study by Glenn Dynner, *Men of Silk,* which "draws upon newly discovered Polish archival material and neglected Hebrew testimonies," this is partly because, in contrast with their image as simple spiritualists in tune with humanity and nature, charismatic Hasidic rebbes were "astute populists who proved remarkably adept at securing elite patronage, neutralizing powerful opponents, and methodically co-opting Jewish institutions." Early Polish Hasidic devotees comprised a broad socioeconomic and educational range, "from humble shtetl dwellers to influential Warsaw entrepreneurs." Hasidic rebbes taught that one could worship God in one's daily activities and that any common behavior could be invested with spirituality. This teaching gave Hasidic leaders a decided advantage: Having eliminated the need for a leader to isolate himself in an ivory tower of Torah learning, the Hasidic rebbes could present themselves as mystics while accessing worldly endeavors, including politics, business, and popular culture. Despite rabbinic opposition, "Hasidism's transformation into a mass movement created a revolutionary impact on Polish Jewish culture during the transition to modernity."[37]

It should be noted that today the Hasidic and Mitnagdic movements exert a powerful (and often unrecognized) influence on each other. Most forms of Hasidism, for example, have espoused rabbinic emphasis on study and conventional piety. Mitnagdic Judaism has also increasingly developed its own cult of charismatic personalities, especially in attitudes toward educational leaders and Jewish thinkers. Nevertheless, the Hasidic emphasis on the rebbe as a personal guide and advisor, rather than simply a halakhic decision maker, continues to provoke deep unease among those who discern the vague odor of the Hasidic rebbe as Christological figure, in that the rebbe serves as an intermediary between the individual Jew and God. Some in Orthodox and non-Orthodox Jewish communities decry statements affirming the living influence of the deceased Chabad/Lubavitcher rebbe. Upheavals and revolutions in ways of perceiving Jews and Jewishness increased and multiplied in the eighteenth century and beyond. Scholars have moved away from describing sharp demarcations of one historical period from another. Contemporary approaches focus on the gradual ways in which social groups, peoples, and countries develop and change. We have already seen how Hasidism challenged Mitnagdic rabbinic Judaism and yet remained attached to religious piety. In another foreshadowing of change, there is evidence that many individual Western European Jews had become relatively lax about their religious observances by the early 1700s. However, in both cases Jews had not changed their world views in any systematic way. Most still felt themselves tied to and part of the Jewish polity, and they evaluated their lives by Jewish standards. Scattered members of the commercial classes—some wealthy, cosmopolitan Jews, and a few intellectuals who interacted with non-Jews—had visions of a future in which Jews as a group would not be treated as a pariah people, and worked to effect those changes, but their efforts were limited to their own small geographical areas. These early foreshadowings would grow into a range of new paradigms when Western Jews launched their *Haskalah* (Enlightenment) move away from particularism toward universalism and the beginning of modern Judaism, which are the subjects of the next chapter.

3

Emancipating into Modern Jewishness

Piecemeal Emancipation and the "Brutal Bargain"

Despite differing forms of Jewishness in premodern Diaspora Jewish societies, for centuries Jews around the world shared the belief that God chose them for a special role in the world. The details of that role were vouchsafed to them in written guidelines for an appropriate way of life. Although communities differed in interpretations and individuals did not adhere to identical levels of observance, the conviction of chosenness and the hegemony of prescribed behaviors as a social ideal defined internal notions of Jewishness. Ironically, the hegemony of this particular Jewish societal model was probably at its most uniform in the two centuries preceding modernity's assault on it. Prior to Jewish emancipation, as Jacob Katz summarizes:

> Jews everywhere had had similar attitudes toward gentiles and parallel attitudes concerning all areas of human endeavor, from making a living to sexuality. Their basic institutions—the family, the house of study, the synagogue, the rabbinate—fulfilled similar functions everywhere. Heinrich Heine's witty remark that traditional Judaism was a

sort of "portable homeland" is not without a measure of truth. These fundamentals served the Jews over and over as a basis upon which to rebuild their society wherever they settled.[1]

Modernity brought sweeping individualism and secularization, and a spectrum of options that fragmented these unifying social ideals. This chapter looks at the Jewishness of the two Enlightenments, two versions of the Jewish *Haskalah*. First, the *Haskalah* across Western Europe transformed Jewish ways of looking at the world and at themselves, and precipitated the self-conscious study and reformation of Judaism as a religion. Later, East European Jews were transformed by the spread of secular social and political movements. East European *maskilim* (Jewish Enlightenment thinkers) invented Jewish versions of secular movements and created vibrant secular Jewish cultural expressions in Hebrew and in Yiddish. In both Western and Eastern Europe, new modern levels of Jewish diversity diverged not only in degree but also in kind from the more muted diversity that characterized Jewish societies from the medieval to the Enlightenment periods.

Comprehensive transformations in the life experiences of Jews depended on external changes. Put very simply, Europe's Jews were helped immensely by the universalistic, egalitarian philosophies of eighteenth-century Enlightenment thinkers, and often set back when Romantic Nationalism swept through Europe in the nineteenth century. Ideals of tolerance toward Jews began to be voiced sporadically by Reformation scholars, such as Erasmus and Grotius in sixteenth- and seventeenth-century Holland, and broadened by the German baron Samuel Pufendorf, who declared, "It follows as a law of nature, that every man should esteem and trust another as one who is naturally his equal." The idea that natural law supported egalitarian fellowship among people received its classic Enlightenment articulation by John Locke in 1688, as small Jewish communities reestablished themselves in England. Although Locke continued to reject Catholics and atheists, he declared that Jews ought not to be "excluded from the civil rights of the commonwealth" on the basis of religion.[2]

Looking back at the Jewishness of the late seventeenth, eighteenth, and nineteenth centuries, it is important to remember how controversial the idea of reducing Jewish otherness was, how piecemeal its implementation, and, above all, how utterly unlike the contemporary American ethos of pluralism the European mind-set was. British Parliament passed a law allowing Jews to become naturalized citizens in the British colonies in 1740, and in England itself in 1753. However, public outrage forced the repeal of the latter law in the same year. Tolerance of the Jews, rather than their acceptance as full equals, was the goal of some visionaries, and others promoted the moral improvement of the Jews leading ultimately to their conversion to Christianity. Joseph II of Austria encouraged the integration of Jews into Christian society in 1781–1782. Talk of the emancipation of the Jews was included in some utopian theories in Western Europe during the decades before the French Revolution (1789). America was the first country to actually emancipate the Jews, rejecting the idea of a "religious test" for "civil capacities" in the Federal Constitution of 1787 and severing the ties between church and state definitively in the First Amendment (1791).[3]

After the French Revolution, civil rights acquired a new emphasis, with lasting impact on modern Jews: Jewish emancipation would be based on Jewish deracination. French thinkers, influenced by Romantic Nationalism, worried that Jews would constitute a state within a state. Their goal was for each citizen to be a loyal Frenchman, without competing public loyalties, and for religion to be relegated entirely to the private domain, often referred to as a "personal confession," rather than being one dimension of Jewish peoplehood. Thus the "brutal bargain," as it came to be known, was this: "The Jews should be denied every-thing as a nation, but granted everything as individuals," as Comte de Clermont-Tonnère is famous for articulating.[4] When the French Constituent Assembly passed the first act of full emancipation of the Jews by a Christian state in 1791, Jews as individuals were offered opportunities, but not the communal ethnic pride that is familiar to contemporary American Jews. They were, instead, emancipated into individualism and secularized cultural homo-geneity. In entering what Katz called the "semi-neutral society,"[5] some Jews were ethnically neutralized.

The French model was critically important to transformations in the Jewish experience, because Napoleon tried to force those Continental European countries he conquered to emancipate their Jews. He set up a Central Consistory of French Jews (1808) with the task of accelerating French Jewry's acculturation. Most French Jews moved toward secularization and cultural, if not full, social integration, learning French, migrating to the cities, especially Paris, and becoming involved in education, modern professions, and politics.

Some countries found the idea of accepting Jews in their midst repulsive, and resisted. Many more repeatedly reneged on their promises. "The only way I see by which civil rights can be given to them [the Jews] is to cut off their heads in one night and to set new ones on their shoulders which should contain not a single Jewish idea," was German Johann Fichte's defiant response to the idea of Jewish emancipation. Faced with outraged resistance to Jewish emancipation, in some locations French troops literally burned down ghettos and led their Jewish inhabitants into the outside world.

By the time Napoleon's armies were defeated at Waterloo twenty-six years after the beginning of the French Revolution, in some countries Jews were emancipated in name, but were not socially or culturally accepted. In other countries, even nominal emancipation was an elusive goal. Moreover, by 1880 a backlash against emancipation or even tolerance had taken hold in many locations. With the swing of an ideological pendulum, the notion that it was a good and "natural" idea to treat Jews as equals was reversed. Rather than focusing on the qualities that unite all people, particularistic, Romantic Nationalism became the new ideological fashion—shifting the focus to one's own country and reserving one's affection and regard for one's own "folk" within that country. As nationalism became a more powerful ideology, so did hatred of the Jews. Once again, Jews were perceived as aliens. Ironically, the more they assimilated, the more Jews were subjected to suspicions of disloyalty.

Overall, Europe's Jews were certainly not emancipated with the same comprehensiveness and finality as utopian ideas had promised. Nevertheless, the *promise* of emancipation—and often the disappointment when that promise was betrayed—had changed Jewish life and expectations forever.[6] Although they had not been completely invited to join European societies, Jews had lost the idea that they belonged exclusively to the Jewish people and began to measure Jewishness by the lifestyles and ideas surrounding them.

Western Europe's *Haskalah:* Rationalism and the Jewish Enlightenment

For the Jews of Europe, modern changes seemed frustratingly slow in coming for some but too fast for others as they confronted transformations internal and external to the Jewish community. Jewish life was transformed in the cultural, religious, and political realms, although modernity's effect took different forms in different countries. In Germany, Holland, and to some extent in Hungary, much Jewish creativity went into reforming and modernizing Judaism as a "confessional" religion and religious culture. For

German-Jewish Reform thinkers, the ideal of the Golden Age of Spain served as a model for cultural symbiosis. Dignified and elegant Sephardi modes of worship, and cosmopolitan Sephardi ease of social interaction with non-Jewish neighbors each had a significant impact on many reformers.[7] In France, for substantial portions of the English and Austro-Hungarian Jewish populations, and for some Polish and Russian Jews, assimilation, individualism, secularization, and patriotic nationalism seemed like the path to acceptance. Occasionally, this meant baptism as Christians as well.

In response, a minority of newly self-conscious traditional Jews, especially in Germany and Hungary, pushed back at modernity by creating their own communal religious culture, and the various forms of Orthodoxy were born. One commonality of these diverse modern Jewish experiences, hard to recapture two centuries later, was the combination of intense yearning and explosive joy with which long-sequestered Jews viewed their emergence into the broader society. Relatively few paused to lament what they were leaving behind.

New forms of Jewishness often required Jews to divide up, compartmentalize, or differentiate aspects of their Jewish existence that had previously been united in an organic way of life. In pre-modern European Jewish societies, religious activities and cultural expressions had been interwoven with concepts of Jewish peoplehood. In Western Europe, the fracturing of religion from ethnicity was axiomatic: A revised and refined Jewish religion that fit into Protestant norms would be allowed, but public manifestations of Jewishness and Jewish ethnicity, in particular, were tantamount to political disloyalty. Western Jews embarked on a project to emphasize the most universalistic Jewish values, those that united Judaism and Christianity, and to eschew Jewish particularistic "Oriental" exoticism, which was branded as backward—at worst sinister and at best unattractive. As John Murray Cuddihy articulates this "ordeal of civility":

> Civility, as the very medium of Western social interaction, presupposes the differentiated structures of a modernizing "civil society." Civility is not merely regulative of social behavior; it is an order of appearance constitutive of that behavior. This medium is itself the message, and the message it beamed to the frontrunners of socially emancipating Jews came through loud and clear: "Be nice."[8]

The twentieth-century American insistence on being a "nice boy," therefore, derived not so much from historical Jewish culture as it did from the Westernizing Jewish attempt to be accepted by the Protestant middle class.

Change came from both the top down and the bottom up. Intellectual leaders were critically important in creating the modern Jewish mind-set. We can understand better how profoundly Jewishness changed by looking briefly at one pioneer of the Western Jewish Enlightenment, and arguably of all the modern forms of Judaism, Moses Mendelssohn (1729–1786). Mendelssohn changed the way Jews thought by introducing external philosophical ideas to measure, evaluate, and recast Jewish values and behaviors. This was a greater innovation than the mere dropping of some religious rituals, as some Western European Jews had already done. Mendelssohn remained ritually observant, but his frame of reference was Western and modern.

Mendelssohn encountered in Berlin a kind of nonsectarian society to which both Christians and Jews could belong. His interfaith social circle was "open and unfettered"—and thus "conspicuous" because in it "Jews and Gentiles mingled as though the barriers separating the two societies had already been torn down."[9] He was deeply influenced by eighteenth-century Enlightenment ideas as he championed a rationalist approach to Jewish history, theology, and culture. His love of philosophy led him first to Maimonides' emphasis on rationality, moderation, and intellectualism, and then to the "natural theology" of Gottfried Wilhelm Leibnitz and Christian von Wolff. To Mendelssohn, there was no inherent conflict between the rationalism of Jewish philosophy and that of the enlightened Christians with whom he interacted. He studied and wrote about German philosophy, Maimonides, and the Talmud. He married a Jewish woman, was a practicing and loyal Jew on good terms with most of the Jewish community, and interacted intellectually and socially with some of the greatest Christian minds of his day. Many Christian intellectuals regarded him as a personal and intellectual paragon.

However, as the years passed, Mendelssohn became aware that many of his admirers were astonished that he remained a Jew, and overtly wished to convert him to Christianity. By 1770, writing a critique of both Christianity and Judaism according to the tenets of pure reason, Mendelssohn articulated his own philosophy of rational Judaism, bringing together natural religion and divine revelation. For the remaining decade and a half of his life, much of Mendelssohn's focus was on Jews and Judaism, as he devoted himself to modernizing Jewish thinking and society so that they would be more consonant with Western Enlightenment ideals. His translation into German of the Five Books of Moses, which he wrote in High German but in Hebrew letters, and which included some sophisticated historical criticism, had the educational goal of teaching Jews correct German and opening them up to the idea of scientific, historical study of Jewish religious texts. Mendelssohn never lost either his belief in the importance of Jewish distinctiveness or his conviction that a truly neutral society of Jewish and Christian equals was possible.

For other Westernizing Jews who followed in Mendelssohn's wake, however, the opportunity to enter European socioeconomic spheres trumped the delicate balancing act implied by the neutral society. Mendelssohn's children were among that minority of well-educated, affluent, and ambitious Jews who enhanced their opportunities through baptism.[10] A small but significant group of Jewish cultural negotiators who sometimes converted to Christianity were the *salonières,* clever women who hosted "salons" in their homes. Some of these Jewish-born women initially presided in luxurious drawing rooms paid for by wealthy Jewish husbands. Their invitees were currently popular thinkers and other celebrities who conducted elegant conversations and repartee. The Jewish *salonières* parlayed their own charm, social skills, and intellectual wit into a vehicle for raising their social status and transcending what many of them felt was the great misfortune of having been born a Jew. Some *salonières* formed romantic relationships with their non-Jewish guests, and some of them divorced their Jewish husbands and married their Christian paramours.[11]

The vast majority of German Jews did not convert to Christianity, but moved, instead, into evolving approaches to Jewishness that were profoundly influenced by Western ideals and norms. Jewish intellectualism was transformed by the application of scientific principles to Judaic study, as a result of Jewish exposure to historical methods. The innumerable books published on Judaic subjects each year and the Jewish studies departments that we now take for granted in contemporary Western universities would have been unthinkable prior to nineteenth-century Germany, both from a Jewish standpoint, in which sacred texts had never before been subjected to systematic, historical-critical analysis, and from a non-Jewish standpoint, in which Jewish history and literature had seldom been considered outside the context of religious debates.

The new scientific analysis of Jewishness, which came to be known as *Wissenschaft des Judentums,* arose as an outgrowth of the University of Berlin early in the nineteenth century. Moving away from the cosmopolitan philosophical attempt to plumb universal truths, intellectual leaders at the university began to stress the study of individual nations, to look at the *Volksgeist*, the "unique qualities," the "common heritage and destiny" that defined each people.[12]

The idea of *Wissenschaft des Judentums* was shaped in part in the 1820s by Leopold Zunz (d. 1886), a brilliant young man who had earlier begun his education in a "dismal" Jewish school, where he acquired a deep talmudic knowledge and a bitter hatred of traditional Jewish life and attitudes. Under new administration by visionary and kindly proponents of the German *Haskalah* (Jewish Enlightenment), the school had reduced the hours of Talmud study and introduced German literature, French language and literature, history, and geography, emphasizing the potential of Jewishness to adapt to modernity, preparing him psychologically for the Reform Judaism he would later encounter. Zunz simultaneously considered becoming a rabbi and converting to Christianity. Along with his mentors and fellow students, Zunz regarded Judaism not as a peoplehood but simply as one of the several "confessions" (religions) found in Germany. Abandoning ideas of conversion, Zunz became a regular preacher at the liberal Beer Temple in Berlin, delivering messages with the goal of universalizing and secularizing Jewish culture. Nevertheless, Zunz was increasingly intrigued by the scientific study of folk cultures and philology, which he explored at the University of Berlin. The intellectual breakthrough articulated by Zunz and his scholarly circle of colleagues was the realization that the idea of *Wissenschaft* could be applied to materials like Talmud and Zohar. Analyzed linguistically and historically, taken out of sacred context, these Jewish cultural materials were appealing and worthy of study. Zunz wrote: "Only through science can we obtain for Judaism the status and appreciation which it deserves, and gradually arouse and unite all the better forces in Israel."[13]

Jewishness in nineteenth-century Germany was transformed sociologically as well as intellectually. Jewish families and societies changed because reformers and ordinary Jews alike evaluated Judaism and Jewish culture in comparison to surrounding middle- and upper-middle-class German culture. Social historian Marion Kaplan has demonstrated the extent to which Jewish women of the time were responsible for the project of shaping the Jewish family along the German middle-class model and for raising their children as the next generation of properly bourgeois adults. Jews took the concept of *Bildung*—the ceaseless self-cultivation of the indi- vidual—to heart, and assigned to Jewish mothers the task of negotiating between Jewishness and Germanness as they created "exemplary and refined families."[14] This German propriety came to typify German Jewish families all along the denominational spectrum. From Orthodox through Reform, a *yekke* (German Jew) was stereotyped as being careful, rational, refined, proper in utterance and carriage, and—unlike Jews from other locales— always on time.

The Reformer's Challenge

"Why should a man of European culture remain a Jew?" was the question that German Jews struggled with in the late decades of the eighteenth and the early decades of the nineteenth centuries, according to historian Michael Meyer. When Leopold Zunz crafted the idea of *Wissenschaft des Judentums,* he was enthralled with understanding the past, but he did not consider it as a way to pre- serve Jewish culture and make it interesting for Jews of the future. It was only with the development of the Reform movement's con- cept of "Mission" that such an idea was considered, along with the notion of Judaism "as a continuous development from the past and the study of Jewish tradition consciously utilized for the sake of the future."[15]

The Jewish reformers faced enormous cultural challenges. When philosopher Immanuel Kant considered Judaism's system of rabbinic codes, he found them redolent of a slave mentality, since traditional Jews seemed bound to an authority external to their own reason. Kant envisioned the Western moral man, by contrast, as "rational," developing an independent moral sense and following the dictates of his own conscience. This autonomous individual was a foundational concept of modern notions of citizenship, and to be accepted as appropriate citizens, Jews needed to demonstrate that they were capable of making moral decisions without external coercion. The German reformers set out to examine Jewish religious culture and to demonstrate that their faith, their philosophy, their synagogues, and their communal structures could meet the tests of rationality and morality.

In the first decades of European Reform Judaism, many changes took place because laymen wanted them to happen. Wealthy businessperson Israel Jacobson (1768–1832), for example, established a free school for Christians and Jews. By 1810 the school was full of children from both religious faiths. The first German Reform temple was built on the campus of this school, complete with robes, an organ, a choir, and a quiet and decorous prayer service. Many of the initial changes were aesthetic—and looked to the Protestant church as the touchstone of aesthetic excellence. Concerns revolved around synagogue decorum, the inclusion of choral and instrumental musical performances, and the redefinition of the rabbinic role as a theologian capable of giving elegant and effective sermons in the vernacular.

As rabbinic scholars gained control of the German Reform movement in the 1840s, the emphasis shifted to creating coherent policies and a cohesive movement. At rabbinic conferences in Wiesbaden, Brunswick, and Frankfurt, Reform thinkers stated guiding principles: Not everything in the Hebrew Bible and Jewish tradition had equal weight. Ethics and universalistic values were divinely revealed, but many of the details of Jewish law were tied to earlier societies and not binding on contemporary Jews. Judaism as an ethical system had evolved, and the study of Jewish history and texts would reveal the difference between the ephemeral and the eternal in Jewish cultures of the past. Judaism and Christianity shared principles of ethical monotheism. How these general principles played themselves out in practice was the subject of controversy among various thinkers, some of whom were rather conservative and some extremely radical in their suggestions. Most agreed that the *mission* of Judaism as a religious faith or "confession" was to convey universalistic ethics and good values, to be an *ohr lagoyim,* "a light to the world." Even secular organizations formed by Jews tended to use universalist, idealistic phrases.

Reform Judaism became the overriding form of Judaism in Germany by the end of the nineteenth century, accounting for 85 percent of affiliated German Jews. Unlike the Reform movement that reestablished itself in the United States, the German Reform movement received government support and had a fair amount of control over certain aspects of adherents' Jewish lives. Although Mendelssohn had imagined all of Jewish life as voluntary, German middle-class society expected decent, respectable people to belong to an officially approved congregation of like-minded coreligionists. Thus, the unified Jewish community, or *Einheitsgemeinde,* "was treated as the organizational framework of a religious community, like one of the Christian churches." Jews could be obligated to belong to the Jewish organizational network and support it financially in order to be perceived as upstanding citizens.[16] For Jews who rejected this vision of a remade Judaism, the Reform establishment was a mighty force to oppose.

Traditionalists Who Synthesized — or Rejected — Modernity

Reform Judaism appealed to the majority of modernizing Jews in Germany and central Europe. However, despite the official status and power the movement acquired, not all Jews wished to remake Judaism in so thoroughly a Western image. About 15 percent of German Jews tried to preserve traditional Jewish ways of life and rejected the ideas of the German reformers. Rabbi Samson Raphael Hirsch emphasized the idea that Orthodox Jews could and must combine rigorously observant "Torah" lifestyles with the *derekh eretz* (secular refinement and knowledge) of German culture. German Orthodox synagogues and homes synthesized Western and classical Jewish values. German Orthodox Jews, like their Reform brothers and sisters, took the idea of *Bildung* very seriously and lived thoroughly middle-class lives.

David Ellenson cites an episode that reveals the German Modern Orthodox mode of synthesis. When challenged by those who found the inclusion of references to animal sacrifices in the biblical temple inappropriate in a modern worship service, Rabbi Hirsch responded with a Maimonidean answer: One must understand animal sacrifices in a symbolic, rather than a literal way—but one must retain the references—rather than omitting them, as many Reform congregations had decided to do—so that the symbols stay alive.[17] The Positivist-Historical school, pioneered by Rabbi Zacharias Frankel and others, took the concept of a dynamic Judaism in modern times a step further: While retaining traditional Jewish rituals, they insisted that Judaism had evolved gradually, and that Jewish religious culture was continually developing and changing. Some scholars see the beginnings of contemporary Conservative Judaism in the Positivist-Historical combination of religious traditionalism and intellectual freedom.

In Hungary, about two-thirds of Jews identified with the reforming efforts of the Neologs (a group positioned approximately between Conservative and Reform ideas), and fewer than one-third of Hungary's Jews were Orthodox. Unlike in Germany, Hungary's Orthodox Jews were headed by fervently traditional rabbis who pushed back against the flow. Rabbi Moses Schreiber of Pressburg (d. 1839), best known by the name of his book, the *Hasam Sofer*, made an ideological decision to oppose the modernizing project per se, made famous by his dramatically reactionary statement, *"Hadash asur min ha-Torah"*—Anything new is forbidden by the Torah. In other words, regardless of the specifics, innovation itself is anti-Jewish. Historians caution us not to see this stance as a kind of "deer in the headlights" paralysis, but rather as a deliberate strategy to fend off the encroaching demands of modernity and, specifically, "to evade the danger of dissection" of Jewish values and lifestyles. Any "rationalistic appraisal" would surely lead to some diminution of devotion to Judaism, the Hasam Sofer thought, and thus, "Jewish tradition had to be preserved in its totality." In order for this to happen, his form of Orthodoxy sought to preserve the entire external as well as internal form of Orthodox life, including the use of Yiddish and Hebrew as much as possible. He was willing to pay the price of continuing "social and cultural isolation."[18]

Although they have both come to be viewed as "Orthodox," the German and Hungarian groups were actually very different from each other. The Modern Orthodox "accommodators" in Germany observed Jewish law but embraced Western ideas and lifestyles, while the Hungarian "resisters" self-consciously rejected Western mores for their own sake. Nevertheless, it should be understood that both of these Orthodox ideologies were deliberate responses to modernity. Once a religious group has had to confront modernity, it can never go back to being unself-consciously pre-modern.

Orthodox ideologies were influenced by the idea that religious groups consist of those people who share a religious outlook and values—that being a Jew is a matter of assent as well as descent. Indeed Neo-Orthodox, Positivist-Historical, and Reform Jews all downplayed Jewish ethnicity in response to German sociopolitical norms. Nevertheless, despite the shared Westernization of German Reform and Orthodox Judaism, Hirsch and Rabbi Esriel Hildescheimer, who supported him, convinced the German government that Orthodoxy was a different religion than Reform. By formally separating from the established Reform *Gemeinde* (governmentally supported Jewish communal umbrella organization), Hirsch was able to obtain government support for Frankfurt Neo-Orthodox Judaism. Ellenson argues that Modern Orthodox German Jews showed how much they had been secularized when they declared that they were a different kind of Jew than their modernizing neighbors. Significantly, both Hirsch and Hildescheimer had been educated at a German university and spoke perfect German, while their less Westernized Orthodox rabbinical opponents believed that the principle of a unified Jewish community superseded the threats posed by the Reform majority. Thus, the willingness to acknowledge Jewish sectarianism was a mark of secular modernity.[19]

In the previous century, for all their virulent conflict and rivalry, Mitnagdic and Hasidic Jews had both felt responsible to the same set of divinely ordained principles. Now, the Western European Jewish world was divided between those who felt obligated by the "yoke" of a rabbinic law, which they believed to have divine origins, and those who felt that only some aspects of traditional Jewish texts and beliefs were worthwhile, and others (including most of rabbinic law) could be discarded with impunity. The belief that there were different types of Jews was a difference of kind, not only of degree. The stage had been set for the evolution of diverse modern Judaisms in twentieth-century America. Western European Jewish Enlightenment thinkers had also created the academic field of Jewish studies (*Wissenschaft des Judentums*), Jewish philosophical inquiries that meshed Jewish and Western thinking, and a thoroughly Westernized middle-class Jewish lifestyle. These Western European creations became the model for American Jewish life, even though most American Jews trace their ancestry back to Eastern Europe.

East European *Haskalah*: Secular Modern Movements and a Jewish Enlightenment

Modern rationalism and intellectualism were the wellsprings of the Jewish enlightenment, the *Haskalah*, first in Western Europe, as we have seen, and later in Eastern Europe. Eastern Europe's Jews were never offered the "brutal bargain" that France proposed to Western Europe's Jews—nothing would make Judaism palatable in Poland and Russia! As a result, the road to modernization for Jews in Eastern Europe was quite different, and more diverse. Modernizing Jews in those countries did not reform their religion—although some attempted to modernize Jewish culture and societies—but instead streamed into secular modern movements of both general and Jewish varieties. Some modernizing East European Jews fled Jewishness entirely, becoming secular intellectuals and artists, cosmopolitan urban businesspeople, socialists, communists, Polish or Hungarian patriots. Others made Jewishness flower in new and unprecedented ways: Hebraists and Yiddishists creating new forms of Jewish literature and theater; champions of Jewish education for women; secular or religious Zionists.

Part of the impetus for change was economic. Serfdom was abolished in Russia under Alexander II, opening up capitalistic opportunities and causing a general migration from rural to urban areas. Jews, especially, began to resettle into large cities. Some Jews joined the urban working class, but others became part of growing bourgeois culture, attending Russian high schools and universities.[20] In addition, throughout late nineteenth- and early twentieth-century Europe, Romantic Nationalistic sensibilities had replaced the universalistic rationalism of the eighteenth- and early nineteenth-century Enlightenment. Nationalistic fervor made Jews in many locations want to be perceived as true patriots of the countries they lived in. In his masterpiece, *Three Cities*, Yiddish novelist Sholom Asch describes the assimilated Russian Jewish upper class ("St. Petersburg") and Polish Jewish intellectuals who fled from the shtetl and threw themselves wholeheartedly into Polish nationalism ("Warsaw"). This modernization did not result in Jewish renewal, as the children and grandchildren of Russia's Jewish elite tended to assimilate completely and convert to Christianity. In Poland and Hungary, Jewish patriots were increasingly perceived as outsiders and systematically denied the inclusion for which they had hoped. Finally, many of the best and brightest young Jews became socialists ("Moscow").

Socialism promised to make ethnoreligious identification irrelevant. The first socialist ideas were developed by German Jewish intellectuals Moses Hess, Karl Marx, and Ferdinand Lassalle. German Jews disproportionately participated in socialist and communist efforts, but the widespread grassroots Jewish embrace of the varieties of socialism involved Jews from Russia and Eastern Europe. Jewish names were prominent in the leadership of all sides of the competitive socialist and communist movements, both before and after the Russian revolutions in 1905 and 1917.[21] With achingly naïve utopian idealism, many young Jews believed that socialist movements would repair the world and do away with all kinds of inequalities, including antisemitism. However, just the opposite happened. Jews were vilified as "Judeo-Bolsheviks" for their participation in revolutionary activities and persecuted first by the czarist White Guard and later by anticommunists and fascists. At the same time, revolutionary troops often attacked Jews as innate capitalists, and later communist leaders, especially Stalin, persecuted Jews—including those who had devoted their lives to the movement—as enemies of the state.

In a different paradigm, many Jewish socialists embraced Jewish culture and ideals, although they vigorously rejected organized religion and ritual piety. They created Jewish versions of socialism, blending utopian ideals with elements of Jewish culture.

The Yiddish-speaking socialist *Bund* (association) focused its energies on the Jewish proletariat, the common folk and folk culture. Many members of the *Bund* were aggressively atheistic, blaming the rabbinate and religious individuals for promoting intellectualism and religious ritual instead of working to remedy the injustices of the world. To secular Jewish socialists, the rabbinic emphasis was not only anachronistic, but also destructive, in that it distracted Jews from becoming active agents in bettering their own destiny.

As Zionism gathered strength in European Jewish communities, alternative Zionist versions of Jewish socialism emerged, including the kibbutz (socialist agricultural communities) movement, which had both secular and religious groups, and secular Labor Zionism. The Bundists and the secular socialist Zionists both saw secular Jewish socialism as the salvation of the Jewish people—but they disagreed passionately with what the other movement represented. Both created competing educational systems for children to inculcate their own ideals—in their chosen languages.

Although many Jews, released at last from their enforced connections to the Jewish communities in which they were raised, fled from Jewish societies during the late nineteenth and early twentieth centuries, for others the period of the East European *Haskalah* was a time of intense, creative, and innovative Jewish expression. Jewish writing flourished—but here also two fiercely competitive secular camps emerged, one championing the reclamation of Hebrew as a language for modern literary expression, and one proclaiming Yiddish the language of the ordinary people. Authors in both movements had similarly grown up in pious Jewish homes and had attended Orthodox schools and *yeshivot* (seminaries teaching the Talmud and other rabbinic texts). They were deeply steeped in classic Judaism, and they used language, images, symbols, and themes that were drawn from those texts in their secular writing, even when their work criticized Jewish societies. Moreover, many of the *maskilim* (Jewish Enlightenment intellectuals) realized that the shtetl society that had so long typified East European life was quickly disappearing. As a result, some of their work aims to capture and elegize that disappearing world. The career of I. L. Peretz (d. 1915) crossed both Hebrew and Yiddishist movements and also incorporated both ironic critique and tender elegy; indeed, a whole industry of literary critics have charged each other with misunderstanding which of Peretz's writings are critical and which elegiac!

Many of the *maskilim* had suffered from traditional Jewish marriage patterns, having been married off as young adolescents to girls they hardly knew, and then having unhappy experiences living with their wives' parents. Not surprisingly, their fiction depicts these unhappy unions, as well as strong criticism of the treatment of women in traditional Jewish societies. Some stories depict harassed women staggering under the dual burden of raising children and raising money to feed them, while their inept, bullying husbands devote themselves to studying sacred texts or to visiting their Hasidic rebbe. Other literature of the *Haskalah* criticizes the Jewish community itself for ignoring the needs of its most impoverished and vulnerable populations, especially poor women. A powerful poem by the Hebrew writer Hayim Nahman Bialik (1873–1934), for example, portrays his widowed mother weeping into the dough she kneads by night, because she must work during the day to eke out a meager living to feed her children. Bialik uses language evocative of the Bible's "Woman of Valor" passage (Proverbs 31:10–31) with deep and bitter irony to spotlight what he sees as the failures of Jewish communities to live up to their purported social ideals.

The lives of Jewish women were profoundly changed in many ways during the period of the East European *Haskalah*. First, in terms of their secular intellectual development, Jewish women were the targeted reading audience of some late nineteenth- and early twentieth-century *Haskalah* writers, since traditional societies paid less attention to materials read by women. Jewish women often read not only the Yiddish pietistic texts, but also novels in Yiddish and, as they were increasingly attending secular schools, in other languages such as French and German. Often, the first contact that East European Jewish boys had with secular writing was borrowing the books read with impunity by their mothers and sisters. Thus, in sociological terms, literate Jewish women became brokers introducing secular concepts and attitudes into traditional Jewish homes.[22]

Because of women's increasing exposure to secular culture and values, both in their schools and in their home reading, attitudes toward providing Jewish education for women changed among pious Polish Jews. Sarah Schnirer, the daughter of a Belzer Hasid, was born in 1883 and received minimal Jewish education as a child, but pursued education on her own and later with Neo-Orthodox teachers in Vienna. She returned to Cracow determined to rescue Judaism for the next generation by providing intensive Jewish education for girls in an Orthodox setting. In 1917 she opened up the first Bais Yaakov school with twenty-five girls. The school expanded rapidly and new branches were established. Schnirer was able to succeed in her goal because she convinced leading Orthodox figures, such as the Hafetz Hayyim and the Belzer Rebbe, that women who received sophisticated secular education but inadequate Jewish education were likely to abandon Orthodox lifestyles. In 1937–1938 a total of 35,585 girls were enrolled in 248 Bais Yaakov schools in Poland alone.[23]

Artistic expression was an important element in the East European *Haskalah*. Many Westernizing Jewish writers and artists became part of polyglot bohemian artistic circles. Some of them formed lively, distinctly Jewish creative societies, organized around poetry and novels, theater, painting, music, and eventually film. Warsaw, especially, became the epicenter of developing Jewish culture and was teeming with Jewish creativity of all kinds, including works in both Hebrew and Yiddish.

Bourgeois and upper-class Jews in Austrian and Hungarian big cities also were drawn to sophisticated cultural secularism. The largely middle-class Jewish secular population yearned for the elegance of Vienna and Budapest—but meanwhile both cities were becoming more and more resentful of Jewish encroachments. One recent cinematic representation, *Sunshine,* usefully illustrates the example of the secularizing Jews of Hungary; in the film, actor Ralph Fiennes represents successive generations of Jews who threw their lot in with the non-Jewish, purportedly emancipated Hungarian society. The film depicts Hungarian Jews abandoning pious Jewish family life and becoming, in turn, pragmatic bourgeois; secular elites; patriots; intellectuals and artists; and soldiers, only to end up crushed, as individuals, because even after baptism they are still perceived as belonging to the pariah Jewish group.

Zionism and the "New Jew"

Modernity, as we have seen, seemed to make individuals sovereign in determining their own destiny. By the last decades of the nineteenth century, Jews in many countries no longer felt they needed to belong to a Jewish entity, unless they chose to do so. Because of the neutral societies that defined modern life first in Europe and later in the United States, a Jew could, in fact, live totally unconnected to any Jewish polity, without undergoing the psychological rupture of joining another religious group.

However, even in the full flush of modernity, history had a nasty way of reimposing Jewish group identity on the individual. For some Jews, the Alfred Dreyfus case, in which a totally assimilated French military officer was falsely convicted of treason—accompanied by sweeping and very vocal French anti-semitism—was a kind of wake-up call to the illusory nature of the European neutral society. Theodor Herzl, often called the father of Zionism, was an assimilated journalist. In conversation with freethinking philosopher and writer Max Nordau, the two men are said to have agreed, "Only antisemitism has made Jews of us." Political Zionism—the creation of a homeland for Jews where they would not be dependent on the good graces of others—was one answer to what now appeared to be the continuing challenge of antisemitism.

Zionist ideas predated Herzl's conversion to the cause, part of the strong trend of Romantic Nationalistic fervor sweeping the Western world. Secular Zionists looked to the creation of a Jewish political entity where Jewish life could become normalized, where Jews would be at home and could make their own history. From the First Zionist Congress in 1897 to the establishment of the State of Israel in 1948, the passion, commitment, and self-sacrifice of secular Zionists was a primary thrust in the realization of this ideal.

Nationalism and Jewishness were the major components of the modern secular Zionist movement, which adopted its own, Hebrew-speaking form of socialism in the emerging labor Zionist and kibbutz movement. Zionism precipitated important discussions about the definition of Jewishness in the modern era—discussions that are proceeding today with no less vehemence. One goal of the movement was to create a new kind of Jewishness, a "new Jew," by which they meant a person with none of the negative characteristics identified with Diaspora Jews. If, in the Diaspora, Jewish men were overly concentrated in intellectual and commercial pursuits, the new Jews would be spread evenly through all strata of society, from garbage collectors and bus drivers to farmers on up. Indeed, pioneering Zionists accorded special prestige to agricultural pursuits. The writer Micha Josef Berdichevski expressed this goal dramatically when he declared that modern Jews needed to choose: "To be or not to be! To be the last Jews or the first Hebrews."[24]

If Diaspora Jewish men were falsely accused of being cringing weaklings, incapable of self-defense, new Jews would be brave and forthright and totally responsible for their own military defense. If Diaspora Jewish men survived by their wits, always looking over their shoulders to see what the non-Jews thought of them, new Jews would speak their minds openly and would be accountable only to their own people and their own government, a government consisting primarily of Jews in a Jewish state. Israeli novelist Amos Oz, a fifth-generation Jerusalemite, remembers that in the decades before Israeli independence the "new Jew" seemed like a mysterious creature being created in Tel Aviv, where Jews were muscular and knew how to swim. "Swimming was unthinkable in Jerusalem," Oz reflects ironically, summing up Diaspora existence in one pungent phrase, and also making it clear that Jerusalem still shared aspects of Diaspora lifestyles and values. The "new Jew" was conceptualized almost exclusively in male terms, creating a still-extant situation in which Israeli women were theoretically equal with men, but had to struggle to achieve actual equity in many areas in a testosterone-filled environment. Among other results of this gender-biased conceptualization, the manifold contributions that women have made to the creation and history of the State of Israel are only beginning to be recognized and acknowledged.

Religious Zionists also played an important role in the creation of the Jewish state. For centuries, small clusters of religious Jews made their way to the Holy Land and lived, often in abject poverty, in Jerusalem or Safed. Although much of the Orthodox establishment opposed Zionism, religious Zionist groups such as Mizrachi expressed strongly pro-Zionist religious beliefs. During the era of the *Yishuv* ("settlement," 1880–1948), when Jews started to emigrate to Palestine in larger numbers working toward the goal of Jewish independence, religious Zionists were among those building urban and agricultural societies.[25]

Although some secular Zionist thinkers emphasized individual freedoms, the primary Zionist impulse focused on the Jewish polity, rather than the individual: Jews as a group had the power to create their own destiny. With the establishment of the Jewish state, Jewish religious groups expanded through immigration and procreation and have had considerable impact on and influence in Israeli society. Religious Jews place an emphasis on group values, norms, and behaviors superseding the independent interests of the individual. Although at the far ends of the spectrum ultra-Orthodox and secular Israelis have often been in conflict, they have shared, ironically, a conviction that the divergent groups they identify with need their loyalty. In Israel, unlike America, the group, rather than the individual, is the measure of all things.

The rise of Nazi power in the late 1930s did not end before it destroyed more than one-third of the world's Jews and annihilated rich European Jewish cultures. The actions of the Nazis, like the Dreyfus case almost fifty years earlier, made it clear that the elusive hope of integrating into a neutral society would not save individual Jews from Jewish history. Acculturated European Jews were often shocked that the Nazis considered them Jews, but, as Sander Gillman has shown, throughout the nineteenth and twentieth centuries racial antisemitism has often been exacerbated, rather than relieved, by Jewish secularization and assimilation.[26] For some Jews and non-Jews alike, the events leading up to and including World War II and its aftermath were powerful arguments for the establishment of the State of Israel.

Exodus to America—Another Kind of Zion

For millions of European Jews, the answers to violent persecution and constricted economic opportunities lay across the ocean, in America. As Philip Roth's protagonist, Nathan Zuckerman, summarizes it in *The Counterlife*:

[My grandparents were] ... simple Galician tradesmen who, at the end of the last century, had on their own reached the same prophetic conclusion as Theodor Herzl—that there was no future for them in Christian Europe, that they couldn't go on being themselves there without inciting to violence ominous forces against which they hadn't the slightest means of defense. But instead of struggling to save the Jewish people from destruction by founding a homeland in the remote corner of the Ottoman Empire that had once been biblical Palestine, they simply set out to save their own Jewish skins. Insomuch as Zionism meant taking upon oneself, rather than leaving to others, responsibility for one's survival as a Jew, this was their brand of Zionism. And it worked.... In the long run, I might be far more secure as a Jew in my homeland.[27]

America was not perfect, but it had the world's best record in terms of legal and social treatment of the Jews. In the eighteenth century, while European countries argued about the advisability of emancipating their Jews, New York (1777), Virginia (1785), the Northwest Ordinance (1787), and finally the Federal Constitution (1787) and the Bill of Rights (1791) passed resolutions and laws that resulted in Jews having complete religious freedom and putting them largely on an equal footing with their Christian neighbors. Unlike European settings, where the special case of the Jews was almost always singled out, it was Catholics, far more than Jews, who had to battle legal discrimination in America's early decades. George Washington's famous letter to the "Hebrew Congregation of Newport" (1790) specifically rejected the idea that Jews should have to earn tolerance and emancipation through their own "improvement."[28] In other words, Washington rejected the European idea that Jewish equality could only be achieved through deracination.

In addition to its unique religious freedoms, enshrined in law, America had a legendary reputation for economic opportunities—some impoverished immigrants expected to find gold in the streets. Wave after wave of Jewish immigrants found their way to America's seaports. In the middle decades of the nineteenth century, large numbers of German Jews who were disillusioned with emancipation efforts, German attitudes toward the Jews, and the economic ramifications of increased German antisemitism emigrated to the United States. America's Jews are believed to have numbered 3,000 in 1820, 15,000 in 1840, and 150,000 in 1860. The German Jews brought with them an entrepreneurial spirit and a willingness to travel. Many of them began as peddlers and worked their way up into legitimate businesses, establishing Jewish enclaves across the United States. Some also brought with them the values of Reform Judaism, and they eventually proceeded to build that movement. By the 1860s, conditions were worsening dramatically for East European Jews, and they too began to try their luck in America, swelling the U.S. Jewish population to 250,000 by 1877.[29]

Most of the first East European immigrants were neither well-educated nor pious—America had a reputation not only as a *goldene medinah* (a golden country), but also as a *treifeneh medinah* (a nonkosher country). However, each time the European situation reached a crisis pitch—a particularly merciless pogrom, a steep economic decline—more and more religiously committed Jews also found their way to America's shores, and the first Orthodox institutions began to be founded. Jews flocked to America in a sea of other immigrant groups, a polyglot migration, reaching its peak years between 1881 and 1924, that excited the fear and anxiety of long-established white Americans. The waves of immigration slowed to a mere trickle when a xenophobic, isolationist backlash against immigration prompted legislation closing the gates of immigration in 1924, by which time America had become home to 4.5 million Jews.

Those gates, unfortunately, stayed almost closed during the dramatic growth of worldwide antisemitism in the 1930s and during the Second World War. It was not until 1948, when American President Harry Truman pushed for special legislation to admit Holocaust survivors, that some 150,000 Jews joined their American coreligionists. Many more survivors emigrated to the newly established State of Israel. For decades, both in Israel and in the United States, Holocaust survivors often felt that their stories were not welcome. In the United States, refugees, often referred to as "new Americans," provoked uncomfortable feelings of difference among assimilating Jews now making their way out to suburbs that had previously been restricted to Jews.[30] In Israel, survivors' stories were often suppressed as one more example of the "old," victimized Diaspora Jew. It was not until the 1960s that, both in Israel and the United States, for different reasons, preserving the particular experiences of Holocaust survivors began to be considered an important communal goal. Israel's negativity toward Diaspora Jewish history began to diminish, and the Holocaust also became useful in explaining Israeli political policies. In America, as we explore further in chapter 4, ethnic difference and vulnerability became positives rather than negatives in the 1960s. The children of Holocaust survivors also began to speak out and tell their stories, making a case that the Holocaust experience had created uniquely identifiable forms of Jewishness.

For the majority of the world's Jews who did not choose to emigrate to Israel, the lessons of the vulnerability of individual Jews to Jewish history, whatever their form of modern Jewishness, precipitated ongoing struggle and discussion. During the years leading up to and after the Nazi era, some Jews both in Europe and the United States tried to escape their Jewishness through baptism to Christianity, name changes, and intermarriage. Some immersed themselves in increased dedication to religious and spiritual forms of Jewishness. Others, however, defiantly chose to continue identifying with the Jewish people despite their own individualistic and secular lifestyles, partly out of refusal to abandon a people thus singled out for persecution. Whatever their form of Jewishness, Jews live in history. Most Jews enter history by being born into the Jewish people. Others convert and become Jews by Choice. For all Jews, the contemporary period has been distinguished by its unprecedented varieties of Jewish expression. Our discussion turns now to the plethora of Jewish identifications forged by America's Jews.

4

Reforming American Judaism

A Large Movement with a Wide Tent

Reform Judaism can be said to have initiated the creation of the movements of contemporary American Judaism. The reformers' challenges in Germany and later in the United States precipitated the formation of self-conscious Jewish Orthodoxies and the development of the Conservative movement—both of which opposed Reform. As we shall see, the leaders of each form of Judaism saw their particular movement as *the* definitive version of Jewishness: Reform Judaism's Isaac Mayer Wise called his prayer book *Minhag America* (the American custom) because he hoped it would represent all of American Judaism. Conservative Judaism's Solomon Schechter spoke of "Catholic Israel" and hoped that his enlightened traditionalism would in fact speak to all Jews. And some Orthodox leaders of both the Modern and *haredi* (ultra-Orthodox) varieties have believed that they alone were transmitting authentic Judaism. Each of these Judaisms is, in its own way, a response to modernity, and Reform Judaism is arguably the first form of modern Judaism.

Since its creation, the Reform movement has enjoyed considerable power. About 85 percent of late nineteenth-century German Jews were Reform, and almost two-thirds of Hungarian Jews affiliated with a modified version of Reform. Although Conservative Judaism had the most adherents in mid-twentieth-century America, since the turn of the twenty-first century Reform congregations have had the most members of any wing of American Judaism. Today, the plurality of American Jews say they are "Reform," with or without formal affiliation.

The numerical growth of Reform Judaism might have been predicted. American Reform Judaism is in many ways the most mainstream form of Judaism. It is understood to be the most inclusive and welcoming of the major movements to all types of Jewish households, including interfaith, homosexual, and other households that differ from historical Jewish norms. After the movement's Central Conference of American Rabbis (CCAR) voted in 1983 to presume that children born of a Jewish father and a non-Jewish mother are Jewish (just as children born of a Jewish mother and a non-Jewish father are Jewish according to rabbinic law), increasing numbers of interfaith Jewish families found their way to Reform affiliation.

No less significant, the Reform movement today is more welcoming to traditional religious values and behaviors and has incorporated elements of Orthodox and Conservative worship, study, spirituality, and ceremony. As a result, Reform Judaism can arguably be described not only as the largest but also as the broadest of contemporary American Jewish religious movements.

Today many Reform temples seem to be going in two directions at once. On one hand, Reform Judaism incorporates greater numbers of traditional Jewish activities with every passing year. Recently ordained Reform rabbis, often with the help of their younger congregants, have introduced more and more Hebrew into worship services. A new Reform prayer book, called *Mishkan T'filah* (a tabernacle of prayer), has formalized the potential inclusion of paragraphs from traditional liturgy. Using the new prayer book, those individuals or congregations that wish to can worship primarily in Hebrew, utilizing many traditional prayers. Similarly, Reform temples frequently make use of liturgical melodies derived from Orthodox environments, including those of the Orthodox spiritualist Shlomo Carlebach and other Hasidic melodies, Orthodox cantorial compositions, and popular tunes from weddings and other lively yeshiva musical venues. Although the movement as a whole has not espoused the dietary laws, many deeply committed Reform Jews, along with their temples and other Reform venues, avoid biblically prohibited foods. The holiday of Sukkot (Tabernacles) has been "rediscovered," and many temples (and some individual families) build the temporary huts that are the hallmark observance of the holiday. In worship services, women and men often wear prayer shawls (*tallitot*) and head coverings, including contemporary Israeli knitted *kippot*. Eugene Borowitz, distinguished professor of Jewish Religious Thought at the movement's Hebrew Union College–Jewish Institute of Religion (HUC-JIR), calls this "the second phase of Reform Jewish piety."[1]

Some older congregants occasionally express dissatisfaction with the increasing amount of Hebrew and the lively melodies in the Reform worship services. "This isn't our tradition," some long-time Reform congregants feel about these very "Jewish" additions to their prayer services, but they are generally overruled.

Symbols of dramatically increased Reform warmth to historical Jewish activities are found in special events: The Union for Reform Judaism (URJ, formerly Union of American Hebrew Congregations, UAHC), Northeast Council, sponsored a conference for clergy, educators, and professional and lay leaders titled "Reclaiming Mikveh: Pouring Ancient Waters into a Contemporary Vessel," in June 2006. Reform Rabbi Elyse Goldstein opened a *kolel,* a Reform center for adult education, in Toronto in 1991. Both *mikveh* and *kolel* were concepts long associated with strictly Orthodox practitioners, but the Reform movement, in this as in other areas, has found ways to make these activities their own. In terms of education, the Reform community—dramatically reversing historical attitudes and trends—has created about a dozen Reform Jewish day schools and has participated in many transdenominational community schools. Israel and Zionism have become central to Reform Judaism as well, as rabbinical candidates have been required to study in Israel since 1970. After studying in Israel, many of them bring back an affection for certain traditional habits of worship and practice, which they then incorporate not only into their own lives but also into congregational settings.

On the other hand, Reform temples today are also characterized by infrequent member participation and increasing numbers of non-Jewish members. Relatively small numbers of congregants attend services on a typical Sabbath (an estimated 10–25 percent of members worship on a regular basis[2]), and the presence of children or teenagers is primarily limited to special occasions, such as the bar or bat mitzvah of friends. Despite the development of new forms of schooling, only a tiny segment of Reform children attend day school, in comparison with Conservative and especially Orthodox Jews, and Reform children and teens as a group have the lowest levels of Jewish education of any affiliated movement. Adult educational programs in many communities are flourishing, and segments of the Reform community are involved in adult education, learning much about Jewish history and culture, and acquiring impressive levels of knowledge about Jewish holidays and customs. However, these adult learners make up only a small—and primarily female—segment of the Reform community.

In the interfaith households that comprise a growing proportion of almost every Reform congregation, a mix of Jewish and Christian holiday observances is the norm. Again, one notes a "two-handed" situation: On one hand, the large number of interfaith families that join Reform temples are flocking to instead of fleeing from engagement with the Jewish community, which was at one time the prevalent situation. On the other hand, only one out of four children of interfaith marriages grows up to create his or her own Jewish home. Reform rabbis, educators, and lay leaders puzzle over the most appropriate approaches in serving the interfaith segment of the Reform community. Some are concerned that in focusing on families that include non-Jews they may be neglecting the in-married or conversionary families that form their Jewish "core," or they may be unwittingly changing or distorting Judaism so as not to alienate or disturb their non-Jewish congregants.

For the Reform movement, intermarriage has been a challenging issue that galvanizes leadership and laity alike and produces divisions within the movement itself. The official rabbinic recommendation of the CCAR is still to avoid officiating at marriage ceremonies between a Jew and a non-Jew. However, an increasing number of rabbis do officiate at selected intermarriages, usually when the couple promises to raise their children as Jews and to select Judaism as the exclusive religion practiced in their homes.

Custom-Making American "Classic" Reform Judaism

Despite these ongoing challenges, today's Reform Judaism incorporates many aspects of traditional Jewish environments that the movement emphatically rejected in its earlier American incarnation. Indeed, if a time traveler who was present at the 1885 Pittsburgh Platform meeting of American Reform rabbis and leaders attended many Reform congregations on a typical Friday night or Saturday morning today, the traveler would have trouble believing that he was truly in a Reform temple. "Classic," formal, and Westernized Reform traditions are being replaced in many locales by more particularly Jewish historical traditions. To understand how this happened, we briefly turn back to look at several telling highlights in the evolution of the movement.

In late nineteenth-century America, the modernizing reforms that were begun in Germany at the end of the eighteenth and the beginning of the nineteenth centuries were made even more sweeping in the American context. In chapter 3, we discussed the ways in which eighteenth- and nineteenth-century German Reform Judaism began by streamlining Jewish worship and ceremonial behaviors. Traditional Jewish worship habits were perceived as lacking in decorum and were changed accordingly.

We can better understand what disturbed the German reformers by looking at two examples of behaviors that were considered at odds with decorum: Latecomers to traditional ("Orthodox") Jewish services typically began the Hebrew service whenever they entered the sanctuary, and chanted through the prayers until they caught up to the rest of the congregation. Different worshipers might be standing up or sitting down and chanting to themselves, regardless of the prayer that the cantor was leading at that time. Reformers wanted all worshipers on the same prayer, all standing up or sitting down at the same time. Another example was the Torah-reading service, at which seven men were honored by being called to the service each Sabbath morning. In some synagogues, these honors were publicly auctioned off, with men calling out their financial contributions in the middle of the service. This was seen as undignified, and very unlike the austere, grand spirituality of the Protestant prayer services typical of the German middle and upper classes. German reformers wanted Jewish prayer services to be as quiet, dignified, and serene as those of their Protestant neighbors.

German reformers also removed what they saw as outmoded passages from the worship services, such as detailed descriptions of the sacrifices in the biblical Temple, prayers for their resumption, prayers for the return to the biblical land of Zion, and a number of complex, obscure liturgical poems (*piyyut*). Their goal was to clear away elements of the liturgy that they viewed as antithetical to the modern mind. Ideas that reformers viewed as non-Western were derided as "Oriental," and nonessential to Judaism. In addition, many felt that worship environments should be enhanced with edifying sermons in German and with instrumental and choral music, both of which seemed to them essential to modern worship. Their guiding principles were that Judaism evolves, that the moral precepts of Judaism are eternal, but that much of quotidian Judaism could and should be changed to conform to contemporary standards.

Reform Judaism changed when it reached America, although not instantaneously. The evolutions of Reform, Orthodox, and Conservative Judaism each illustrate how much casting about for definitions and boundaries these movements went through during their formative years. After German reformers emigrated to America during the nineteenth century, they established congregations Har Sinai in Baltimore (1842) and Emanu-El in New York (1843). These first congregations conformed to some conventions of traditional Jewish life: Men and women were seated separately and both covered their heads, and within the temple there was no violation of the dietary laws or Sabbath observance. These congregations were, however, modern and "reformed" in their care about decorum and other aesthetic principles: Temple Rodeph Sholom, in Philadelphia, imposed a fine on members whose behavior was disorderly in the 1840s.

Mixed seating was introduced in individual congregations in the 1850s and 1860s. Covered heads of male worshipers lingered somewhat longer. Rabbi Isaac Mayer Wise had, however, already publicly declared in 1850 that he believed neither in a "personal messiah" nor in "bodily resurrection," both considered fundamentals of Orthodox belief. Wise called himself an "Orthodox Reformer"—to distinguish himself from the "ultra-Orthodox" on the right and the "radical Reformers" on the left. However, Wise believed that he was proposing a form of Judaism that would unite all American Jews. As historian Jonathan Sarna notes:

> [Wise] had no intention of creating a separate movement or denomination within Judaism; his goal was to shape what he called *American* Judaism. He believed, in other words, that his moderate brand of Reform Judaism—the forms, formulas, customs, and observances that he modernized— would in time be recognized as the rite, or *minhag,* of *all* American Jews, displacing the many diverse European rites then practiced by different synagogues. To this end, he called the Reform prayer book that he published in 1857 *Minhag America....* Jewish unity, indeed, served as a leitmotif of his rabbinate.[3]

But Jewish life does not function in a vacuum; it is profoundly influenced by events in the communities in which Jews live. After the Civil War, new prosperity brought disruptions in many aspects of American life, and an atmosphere of optimism and experimentation pervaded social and religious contexts. Within the Reform movement, this atmosphere was a factor in the decision by Temple Emanu-El in New York (1864) and by Isaac Mayer Wise's congregation in Cincinnati (Beth Eichim, 1874) to ban men's wearing of head coverings in the temple. As this practice became the norm—just as the mass immigration of East European Jews to the United States was beginning in earnest in 1880, visitors to Reform temples were forbidden to cover their heads and asked to leave if they attempted to do so. The no-head-covering edict became a boundary marker for the Reform movement, which was at that time the largest established American Jewish religious movement, and effectively alienated East European Jews for decades. Similarly, the wearing of prayer shawls was banned, with the occasional exception of decorative rabbinic *tallitot* worn on top of rabbinical robes.[4]

The second American conference of Reform rabbis was convened in Pittsburgh in 1885 by Rabbi Kaufmann Kohler. By and large, the "Pittsburgh Platform" composed by the fifteen participating rabbis gave a coherent rationale for the changes that had already occurred in many congregations.[5] The document they created affirmed the "mission" of the Jewish people to serve as the "priest of the One God," while rejecting aspects of the Bible that were merely reflections of the "primitive ideas of its own age and times." In keeping with this distinction, the platform asserted that, "all such Mosaic and Rabbinical laws as regulate diet, priestly, purity and dress originated in ages and under the influence of ideas altogether foreign to our present mental and spiritual state." Insisting that Judaism is "a progressive religion, ever striving to be in accord with the postulates of reason," it was nonetheless vehemently not an atheistic document, insisting on a belief in the "Infinite One" and the immortality of the soul. It rejected, on the other hand, any expectation of a "return to Palestine" or a belief in "bodily resurrection and in *Gehenna* and *Eden* (Hell and Paradise)." Finally, it pinpointed working toward social "justice and righteousness" in order to deal with "the problems presented by the contrasts and evils of the present organization of society" as the "great task" of Judaism at that time. The Pittsburgh Platform's principles were affirmed at the founding of the Central Conference of American Rabbis (CCAR) in 1889 and remained an accepted articulation of American Reform Judaism until the Columbus Conference in 1937.[6]

Standardization of worship and practice was the goal of the American Reform rabbinical leadership. One of the primary tasks of this first CCAR meeting, convened by Isaac Mayer Wise, was to create a uniform Reform prayer book. Seven years later the two-volume *Union Prayer Book*, with most of its prayers in English, very few in Hebrew, and no German, was published. Within a decade it became the normative prayer book of the American Reform movement.[7] The Pittsburgh Platform, the CCAR, and the creation of the *Union Prayer Book* effectively standardized uniform behaviors for the movement's temples. American Reform

Judaism was distinguished from German Reform and from other developing movements of American Judaism. Within its own boundaries, it was largely homogeneous. This striving toward uniformity rather than diversity is one of the main hallmarks of pre-1960s American Reform Judaism.

Thus, ironically, the movement that cherished the idea that Judaism was founded upon "free will" discouraged Jewish expressions that departed from the Reform norm. From 1885 until the late 1960s and early 1970s, when the Havurah movement emerged, Reform worship was distinguished by its magnificent edifices and its tightly controlled institutions. Services were performed by robed, American-trained rabbis and musically accompanied choirs to a largely passive audience of worshipers. Participatory activities that had been part of traditional Jewish services—such as the calling up of individuals to read from the Torah during Sabbath and holiday services—were eliminated. The *haftarah*, a selection from the Prophets also chanted by a congregant in Hebrew during traditional services, was now read from the pulpit in English. Sermons were delivered with attention to formal rhetoric and elegance of expression, and rabbis whose rhetorical style captivated their audiences won the largest, most affluent and prestigious, and most coveted pulpits. The performance of prayers by outstanding voices, rather than by persons of any particular personal piety, were similarly selected by the "best" congregations. As Leon Jick, a Reform rabbi and scholar of American Judaism, remarked, "By this time the service as well as the general ambience of the Reform temple had been substantially Protestantized."[8]

East European Jews—and Influence—Enter American Reform

Classic Reform settings saw the influx of East European Jews during the 1930s, sometimes almost without established German

Jewish Americans noticing, and sometimes with their specific assistance and intervention. Although these Jews were not interested in retaining daily Orthodox Jewish practices, they often did bring with them distaste for the most austere, nonparticipatory versions of Reform worship styles. In addition, the dramatic rise of anti-semitism in Europe, most virulent in the very places in which Jews and Judaism were the most Westernized, intensified desire to express solidarity with Jews around the world.

These two forces contributed to the growth of interest in the use of Hebrew for worship and in Jewish holidays and rituals, and a lively connection with Zionism among many American Reform Jewish leaders, including Abba Hillel Silver and Stephen Wise and his rabbinical disciples. At first, Zionism had been vehemently rejected: The CCAR had passed a resolution that "we totally disapprove of any attempt for the establishment of a Jewish state" in 1897, the very year of the First Zionist Congress, and the Union of American Hebrew Congregations (UAHC) had declared in 1898, "We are unalterably opposed to political Zionism."[9] However, the issuing of the Balfour Declaration, indicating British support for a Jewish National Home in 1917, and the endorsement by the United States of that concept made it particularly tricky for the Reform movement to be against the establishment of a Jewish state altogether. Despite repeated official rejections of Zionism, some movement leaders were attracted to the idea that Jews should have their own state. The writer, public intellectual, and Zionist supporter Maurice Samuel commented in the late 1920s, "A gradual semi-furtive spiritual interest in the reconstruction of a Jewish Palestine has spread through the Reform world."[10]

The "peoplehood" aspects of Jewishness in general began to creep back into Reform Judaism, as the 1937 Columbus Platform, convened by an open Zionist, Rabbi Felix A. Levy, reversed several principles of the Pittsburgh Platform. For example, the Columbus Platform stated, "Judaism is the historical religious experience of the Jewish people." Judaism's universalism itself was seen as "growing out of Jewish life." While stating that the people of Israel live around the world and fully participate in the duties of citizenship where they live, the platform espouses "the rehabilitation of Palestine, the land hallowed by hopes and memories," and affirms "the obligation of all Jewry to aid in its upbuilding as a Jewish homeland, by endeavoring to make it not only a haven of refuge for the oppressed but also a center of Jewish culture and spiritual life." The document names as the foundations of Jewish life the "home," the "synagogue," "education," and "prayer," and specifies as cornerstones of the Jewish way of life "the preservation of the Sabbath, festivals and Holy Days," and the use of "Hebrew, together with the vernacular, in our worship and instruction."[11]

The resolutions of the Columbus Platform made few practical changes in the Reform Jewish experience, except in styles of worship and attitudes toward Israel. The new *Union Prayer Book,* published in 1940, has somewhat more Hebrew and, significantly, includes a few prayers that had previously been excised, including a prayer for the restoration of Zion. Zionism remained the subject of conflict among Reform leadership as World War II loomed, and that conflict became heated after the United States entered the war. At the CCAR convention in 1942, sixty-four attendees voted in favor of a Jewish army being established in Palestine, and thirty-eight voted against the idea. Some of the anti-Zionist rabbis, together with like-minded laypeople, formed an organization, the American Council for Judaism (ACJ), to articulate their opposition—since it was clear that the Reform movement itself would no longer serve that purpose.[12]

Although the American Reform movement was gradually being infiltrated by Jews of East European origin, with their taste for Jewish vitality over putatively Protestant austerity, a small influx of highly cultured German Jews who were fortunate enough to leave Europe in the 1930s brought with them a new infusion of the German Jewish world view. One of them was historian Manfred Jonas, who suggests that educated and assimilated German Jews both opened American Jewish minds toward worldwide Jewry and also accelerated American Jewish assimilation.[13]

Some intellectuals who came to America in the 1930s emphasized the impact of the German Jewish concept of *Bildung*—a religious culture emphasizing self-examination and continual character building—which German emigrees imported once again into the American Jewish scene.[14] *Bildung* demanded, among other things, the ability to make individual moral choices uncompelled by religious laws—the "free choice" beloved of Reform Judaism, diametrically opposed to the emphasis on obligation so central to Orthodox theologies. Orthodoxy continued to emphasize religious prescriptions, teaching: "He who is commanded and fulfills a commandment is greater [religiously] than he who fulfills a commandment without being obligated to"—a concept utterly at odds with the Reform Jewish moral compass. (It should be noted that even Orthodox German Jews were influenced by German ideas and perceived the necessity for ongoing *Bildung*.) Concepts like *Bildung* reinforced the Reform Jewish emphasis on free choice and were anathema to the concept of religious obligations, which would hold firm through later years of increasing ritual and ceremonial traditionalism.

Reform insistence on professionalism did not effectively extend to Jewish educational settings. In the 1920s many children in Reform-affiliated families received no Jewish education, and, for those who did, Reform Jewish education consisted primarily of Sunday school classes taught by congregants who themselves had minimal levels of Jewish education. Hebrew language, where it was taught, was often an "optional" subject. As an alternative venue for transmitting a sense of Jewish identity to children, some Reform leaders urged the formation of youth groups or "clubs," in response to Mordecai Kaplan's notion of the synagogue center. However, even this idea took time to be implemented with the establishment of the National Federation of Temple Youth (NFTY) in 1939.[15]

In the two decades following World War II, America was absorbed in an effort to establish peaceful normalcy. Family togetherness was greatly emphasized, and Americans married, had children earlier, and had larger families than they had in the Depression and war years. Middle-class morality was preached in magazines and newspapers, and individuals who appeared to be nonconformists were sometimes mistrusted and/or accused of lacking good morals or sound mental health. American Jews began to get married early, but not as early as their non-Jewish counterparts because Jewish attendance at institutions of higher education was far more common. Indeed, Jewish attendance at colleges rose sharply in the postwar years, partly because of educational benefits accorded to returning GIs, and partly because overt prejudice against Jewish students was much less acceptable after revelations of the Nazi genocide. Similarly, Jews had larger families than they had during the Depression and war years—but smaller families (2.8 children per Jewish woman) than non-Jews (3.5 children per non-Jewish woman), partly because of measurable Jewish commitment to family planning and birth control.

Americans in the 1950s viewed religion in an extremely positive light as a means of reinforcing family values and stability— "The family that prays together stays together" was one popular slogan. In this environment, Jewish religious and communal institutions flourished, and the number of Reform temples grew from 290 in 1938 to 520 in 1956. Many Reform religious schools incorporated midweek as well as Sunday school classes, along with the required teaching of Hebrew to religious school children. While many of the teachers were congregants, most large congregations hired professional educational supervisors for their schools. Most schools used the confirmation ceremony as a strategy to keep Reform youth in Jewish schools into their teen years. NFTY became more central as a movementwide priority and gained numerical strength. At Congregation B'nai Jehuda in Kansas City, "the *shofar* [ram's horn] replaced the trumpet in the Rosh Hashanah service after a sixty-year absence" in 1953, followed six years later by a resumption of "the chanting of Kiddush and the *Hakafot* (procession of the Torah scrolls on Simchat Torah)" and the hiring of a cantor.[16]

At the same time, Reform Jews, as the group most likely to move from cities to suburbs in these postwar years, were also the most likely to be self-conscious about not appearing to be "too Jewish" in their new, largely Christian neighborhoods. The work of sociologists Marshall Sklare and Joseph Greenblum suggests that suburban Reform Jews felt closest to those aspects of Jewish culture that overlapped with American values. Thus, they saw the most important aspects of Judaism as contributing to moral and ethical behaviors and a concern for society, but put little emphasis on studying Jewish history and traditions, or Hebrew and Jewish texts. Interestingly, Jewish suburbanites thought that working for the betterment of African Americans was more central to being a good Jew than observing Jewish rituals.

One of Sklare's most powerful pieces looked at "The Image of the Good Jew in Lakeville." Giving an actual suburb a fictitious name to protect its privacy, Sklare found that American Jews valued most highly those aspects of Jewish tradition that were consonant with American culture of a particular kind: well-educated, liberal, socially concerned, nonviolent. Sklare's subjects consisted of primarily Reform and some Conservative informants. These middle-American Jews felt very strongly that a Jew should be proud of being a Jew, partly because acknowledging one's origins and having feelings of pride and dignity about one's ancestry are deeply ingrained American characteristics. On the other hand, this pride did not extend to encouraging Jews to draw attention to themselves by dressing, eating, or speaking in any distinctive fashion.[17]

Philip Roth critically satirized the Jewish suburbanite's deep mistrust of more religiously observant Jews and their passion for conformity to the Protestant norm in his short story "Eli the Fanatic" (1959). In this story, the Jews of Woodenton, New York (a fictional community), are shocked and embarrassed when a group of Holocaust survivors try to establish a yeshiva in their community for school-age boys who have been orphaned in the death camps. They arrange for a lawyer, Eli Peck, to drive the yeshiva away from Woodenton, because they believe that the presence of these black-frocked Jews will endanger their standing in the Protestant community. Expressing distaste for the biblical narratives that his daughter learns in a Scarsdale Sunday school, one assimilated Jew declares that "science has disproved" everything in the Bible and that European Jews brought the Holocaust upon themselves by not adapting quickly enough to modern lifestyles and values.[18] As we saw in chapter 3, Marion Kaplan convincingly depicts the great struggle of Reform Jews in Imperial Germany (1871–1918) to make themselves into proper middle-class citizens.[19] However, Roth's story suggests that apathy, ignorance of historical Jewish culture, and the desire for physical comfort played more of a role than *Bildung* or Reform ideology in the sweeping transformation of Jews into middle- and upper-middle-class suburban Americans in the 1950s. In novels, plays, and films by Herman Wouk, Roth, and others, American Jews were portrayed as the ultimate incarnation of bourgeois complacency. Jews had become—perhaps even defined— the American middle class. But the evolution of the American Reform Jewish experience was far from over.

The 1960s Bring New—and Old—Styles of Worship and Practice

The comfortable accommodation with American middle-class morality and lifestyles was disrupted for Christians and Jews alike

in the social turmoil of the 1960s. These disruptions were culturewide, of course, but they affected American Jewish life in sharp
and important ways. Moreover, sociological changes laid the
groundwork for religious change as well, as an atmosphere that
privileged stability and conformity to larger societal norms gave
way to experimentation, individualism, and ethnic particularism.

The anti–Vietnam War protests in the late 1960s, for example,
disrupted middle-class life and values in an era of sweeping unrest
on college campuses, where dissident student groups erupted,
threw cherry bombs at Reserve Officer Training Corps (ROTC)
buildings, and occupied college administration buildings. Many of
the leaders of these dissident groups were Jewish college students,
as well as involved Jewish religious leaders. Conservative rabbi and
professor Abraham Joshua Heschel spearheaded the 1965 formation of the interfaith organization Clergy Concerned About
Vietnam, and a number of prominent Reform rabbis joined the
organization immediately. Rabbi Maurice Eisendrath spoke passionately against the war at the UAHC biennial, and the Reform
movement issued a statement supporting a cease-fire and a negoti-
ated settlement.[20]

When it came to Jewish life, young Jews used the dissident strategies they had learned in college to make demands of the organized
Jewish communal and religious worlds. Jewish students occupied
the Council of Jewish Federations General Assembly in Boston in
1969, demanding that the usually secular and philanthropy-
oriented Federation network pay more attention to what the students defined as authentic Jewish values and concerns. Although
some rabbinic leaders were declaring, "God is dead," and urging
their coreligionists to move forward to more sophisticated, existential understandings of Judaism in the post-Holocaust world,
their words provoked many Jews to confront painful questions,
rather than to abandon religion altogether. Together, activism and
spiritual searching helped to produce a readiness to experiment

with new forms of Jewish religious expression. The Havurah style of small worship and study groups, a replacement for large temple-oriented worship just beginning to emerge out of the Reconstructionist movement, had an impact on Reform congregants and temples as well, as even resistant rabbis and temple leaders began to understand that they would lose their market share of paying congregants if they did not provide venues for more individualistic styles of worship and other Jewish activities.

From this fertile soil grew three of the most powerful transformative social movements in the late 1960s and early 1970s—civil rights, feminism, and Zionism. American rabbis of every persuasion, especially large numbers of Reform rabbis, became visible leaders in the civil rights movement. They linked the struggle of African Americans to achieve meaningful freedom and equality with the most basic values of Jewish culture and with the historical experiences of the Jewish people. At the same time, the American celebration of African American "Roots," as one celebrated television series was called, sparked a parallel rediscovery of Jewish heritage among Jews from diverse backgrounds. As one social critic with a witty streak put it, "Jews discovered that if Black is beautiful Jewish is reasonably attractive." Ethnoreligious particularism, rather than the melting pot ideology, gave young Jews permission to explore aspects of life that made Jewishness distinctive. Within the Reform movement, renewed interest in Jewish texts and rituals, once considered outmoded, began to percolate.

This interest in things Jewish was nourished by Zionism and feminism, among other factors. Many American Jews experienced the perceived vulnerability of the State of Israel during the Six Day War in 1967 as a "wake-up call." Reform rabbis and laypeople began to spend more time in Israel and became attached to Hebrew, contemporary Israeli music, Jewish dance, and other aspects of Israeli culture, including the Israeli secular attachment to the holidays of the Jewish calendar year. Partly as a result, Reform prohibitions against head covering virtually disappeared, some clergy and congregants began wearing prayer shawls, and there was a greater tolerance of diverse styles as part of the diminishing of some distinctions between the Reform and Conservative movements. The formal choir began to give way to guitar-playing rabbis, in some settings, who played melodies they had heard first in Israel. Rabbis and other Reform visitors to Israel came home with diverse Israeli *kippot* (ritual head coverings), and some of them proceeded to wear their new acquisitions to temple.

At the same time, feminists pressed for genuine equality in Reform religious life, especially between men and women in religious and communal leadership. The Reform movement was the first American Jewish movement to ordain a female rabbi, Sally Preisand, in 1972. Reform Jewish women, many of whom had little or no Jewish education, became a powerful force in the revitalization of adult Jewish educational venues. Reform women were also "brokers" of a new interest in Jewish rituals and ceremonies. They wanted to learn and do because they felt they had been deprived of both. The bat mitzvah ceremony, just gaining widespread acceptance in the Conservative movement in the 1960s, spread to the Reform movement as well, as the movement reacquired the bar mitzvah as an accepted life-cycle event. Before long, the bat mitzvah ceremonies of adult women also became part of the Reform landscape. When Reform women put on head coverings and prayer shawls and learned to read from the Torah, their excitement about the skills that enabled them to participate in these activities sometimes ignited the interest of the men in their families. Women, long excluded by Orthodoxy from active participation in Jewish life, and then assigned a passive role along with the laymen in their Reform temples, helped to effect transformations for both men and women in Reform Jewish life.

Contemporary Developments: Choosing Covenantal Judaism — or Not

American Reform Judaism today offers its adherents the opportunity to incorporate aspects of Jewish religious culture drawn from many non-Reform Jewish environments. Rather than rejecting rituals, ceremonies, or languages as "Oriental" or non-Western, as it did a century ago, Reform Judaism today embraces a broad spectrum of Jewish activities. The newly edited Reform prayer book, *Mishkan T'filah,* is an exemplar of this adaptive approach. Each double-page spread provides worshipers with four options for the same section of the service, ranging from traditional to innovative, Hebrew or English.

The Reform strategy in adopting rituals, prayers, and other Jewish activities for the use of Reform Jews can best be described through several examples. In the current Reform prayer book, the *Shacharit* (morning) service begins with two prayers drawn from traditional preliminary, pre–morning service prayers. One prayer, *Asher yatzar* (God who has created), is recited by ritually observant Orthodox Jews after going to the bathroom, thanking God as the Creator of all the necessary bodily passages, without which human life could not exist. Many have noted that the prayer has a profound meaning far beyond its traditional usage. The Reform prayer book lifts *Asher yatzar* out of its toileting associations and places it in a sacred setting where its broader meanings are predominant.

A second strategy can be noted in the treatment of the *Elohai neshama she-natatah bi* (My God, the soul that you have given me) prayer. In Orthodox prayer books, this short prayer has two halves—one that asserts that the soul is eternally pure, and a second half that describes the death and resurrection of the soul. The authors of *Mishkan T'filah* have separated the two halves, making the first half one of the central prayers of the morning service, and eliminating the second half. Indeed, references to death and resurrection are generally replaced by other language in Reform prayers. Within the primary version of the *Tefillah* (sometimes called the *Amidah* or standing or silent devotion), for example, God is praised as the *m'khayeh hakol* (the One who makes all living things). An alternative version offers the words *m'khayeh maytim* (the One who resurrects the dead), as in traditional liturgy. What distinguishes the present Reform approach from that of the past is that traditional materials are selectively incorporated. If there is a piece or aspect of the older materials not consonant with Reform conceptions of Judaism, the strategy is adaptation rather than wholesale rejection.

Similarly, some Reform attitudes toward the concepts of God and of mitzvah (commandedness) have softened into an adaptation, rather than a rejection, of tradition. Reform Jews are invited to explore faith in a personal God and to enter into a theological "covenant" with that God. Additionally, a 1999 "Statement of Principles for Reform Judaism" declares: "Through Torah study we are called to *mitzvot* [sacred obligations], the means by which we make our lives holy."[20] Reform Judaism, unlike Orthodox or Conservative Judaism, insists that it offers adherents a choice: Reform Jews may choose to take on an attachment to Jewish rituals, ceremonies, or other activities, in which they feel obligated. However, it is always an individual choice whether or not they will enter into "covenantal theology" or "covenantal commandedness."

The volitional aspect of this approach is unique to Reform Judaism. However, the movement has in many ways drawn closer to more traditional wings of Judaism. Boundaries that once seemed clear between Reform and Conservative Judaism now appear to be fluid indeed. Differences between Reform and other wings of Judaism sometimes seem to be more sociological than theological, in that Reform congregants have much lower levels of Jewish education and much higher rates of mixed marriage than do Conservative- or Orthodox-affiliated practitioners. Nevertheless, the various wings of American Judaism have influenced each other. As the next chapters show, changes within the Reform movement exert sociological pressure for change within Conservative and Orthodox environments, celebration of traditionalism within Conservative and Orthodox communities has been incorporated into the American Reform movement, and aspects of Reconstructionism and Jewish Renewal color much of American Jewish life.

5

Shades of American Orthodoxy

Americans of diverse religious backgrounds flock to interviews with Hasidic rabbi Shmuley Boteach, a self-help guru whose book titles help to explain his enormous popularity on the American scene: *Kosher Sex, Why Can't I Fall in Love?, Dating Secrets of the Ten Commandments, Becoming a Hero in a Selfish Age.* Meanwhile, a reggae-influenced Hasidic musician calling himself Matisyahu (born Matthew Miller) is wildly successful as a touring musician and sells record numbers of discs, even though he describes his lifestyle as carefully Orthodox, punctilious about Sabbath observance and restrictions prohibiting physical contact between men and women.[1] In the Modern Orthodox world, an advertisement for the innovative Yeshivat Chovevei Torah (YCT) rabbinical program brags about its "ideal environment for training rabbis" by spotlighting as one of its prize rabbinical students a man who taught English to Tibetan refugees, is a human rights advocate, and practices kung fu and meditation.[2]

In all their diverse shades of existential being, contemporary American Orthodox Jews are profoundly influenced by their American context. Like other American Jews, their Judaism is flavored by American goals and values and assumptions about life and its purposes. The status of Orthodox Jewishness has changed since acculturated Jews in the first half of the twentieth century were concerned that Orthodox Jews would embarrass them by being devastatingly different. Joseph Lieberman, an Orthodox Jew, was the Democratic vice presidential candidate in the 2000 election, and while his politics provoked a great deal of controversy, his religious commitments didn't. Certain aspects of traditional Judaism seem to be regarded as exotic, rather than just esoteric: Madonna wears a kabbalistic red thread bracelet; some non-Jewish couples choose to marry under a *chuppah,* a traditional Jewish wedding canopy; and Yiddish words are so commonplace in American speech that Jewish teens and young adults sometimes have no idea that they come from their own culture.

The coalescence of American and Jewish culture has made life much easier for Modern Orthodox Jews who, like Senator Lieberman, want to live in two worlds at once, to be fully acculturated Americans and halakhically observant Jews. Conversely, for those fervently Orthodox—or *haredi*—Jews who wish to maintain clear boundaries between Jewish and non-Jewish values and behaviors, the task of being different becomes more demanding every year. Orthodox Jews who are determined to resist American culture are absorbed in an ongoing task of resealing porous boundaries. One favorite strategy is to declare more and more activities and foods off-limits. During the past few years, for example, broccoli, strawberries, and New York City water were all deemed off-limits unless they had certified Orthodox rabbinical supervision, since nonkosher microscopic bugs might lurk in those products.

Modern Orthodox and *haredi* Jews share a denominational name and hundreds of observances. Their model for Orthodox Jewish life is based on the premodern observances of communities that were guided by rabbinic law (as described in chapter 2). Most Orthodox Jews perceive Jewishness as a familial and communal enterprise growing out of a historical peoplehood, rather than a purely individualistic, spiritual attachment. The restrictions against traveling on the Sabbath reinforce that sense of community by creating physical proximity: Unlike non-Orthodox Jews, who often live great distances from other Jews, Orthodox Jews today tend to live within a two-mile radius of considerable numbers of other Orthodox Jews. Rather than embracing a philosophy of "free choice," such as defines Reform Judaism ideologically and other non-Orthodox Judaisms sociologically, Orthodox Jews usually refer religious questions to rabbinic authorities. Although many pick and choose among religious authorities and take considerable latitude in deciding which laws apply to them, Orthodox Jews of both the Modern and non-Modern varieties believe that following rabbinic law is their obligation.

Almost all Orthodox children attend day schools. The majority of Orthodox teens also attend Israeli educational programs for at least a year after high school. Unlike the situation at midcentury, when a large proportion of "nominally" Orthodox congregants were not Sabbath observers, and a minority of putatively "Orthodox" women used the *mikveh* (ritual bath) on a regular basis, today the majority of Americans who call themselves Orthodox comply with rabbinic laws—albeit some in their own fashion. Orthodox Jews have the highest and most regular attendance at worship services, and most participate on a regular basis in some kind of "learning," Jewish adult education, including *daf yomi* (daily study of one page of Talmud) classes in person, via telephone, or on the Internet. While Orthodox women have been very active in the adult education movement, Orthodoxy is the only stream of American Judaism in which men still outnumber women in worship services and as adult learners. This prodigious attachment to adult education has fueled an extraordinary renaissance in Jewish publishing: Record numbers of classical Jewish texts are purchased for home use. Nevertheless, despite the activities they share, Modern and fervently Orthodox Jews often feel as if they were living on different planets. An unknown observer has described them as "very

Orthodox" and "not very Orthodox." Their differences are not imaginary and can best be understood by looking at their relationship to modernity, as represented by American culture.

Dressing to Accommodate—or Resist—American Culture[3]

Today, Orthodox Jews go about their daily lives in America in clothing ranging from the specialized black garb of Hasidim and other *haredi* Jews, across the spectrum of Orthodox centrists who carefully balance societal propriety and religious devotion, to the most liberal American Orthodox who, in their blue denims, are virtually indistinguishable from non-Orthodox Jews and non-Jewish Americans. These diverging styles of dress reflect differences in religious practice and attitudes toward Jewish tradition and modernity, often in minute gradations that seem confusing to outsiders but significant and revealing to the practitioners themselves. This broad spectrum of Orthodox styles goes back to the second half of the nineteenth century when Sephardi, German Jewish, and diverse Middle and East European Orthodox Jews struggled over their particular approaches to defending the faith. As Yeshiva University historian Jeffrey Gurock reports, Orthodox "accommodators and resisters" mingled on America's shores more than a hundred years ago, and rabbinic hiring committees even then "worried about the various shades of Orthodoxy in America."[4]

This diversity is striking when one realizes that Orthodox Jews have always been a small minority and today comprise fewer than one in ten American Jews, when that population is broadly counted. However, Orthodox rates of affiliation are relatively high, and non-Orthodox rates of affiliation are relatively low. One out of five American Jews who belongs to a synagogue belongs to an Orthodox synagogue. In addition, Orthodox synagogues tend to be much smaller than Conservative and Reform congregations in terms of absolute membership for reasons discussed below, so there are a plethora of Orthodox places of worship: About fifteen hundred American synagogues describe themselves as "Orthodox."[5] These synagogues are closely related to differing Orthodox models—and thus very different Jewish experiences.

The largest Orthodox communities cluster in particular geographical areas, such as the greater New York metropolitan area (including contiguous sections of New Jersey and Connecticut, as well as Westchester and Rockland Counties in New York), Baltimore, Miami and West Palm Beach, Los Angeles, Chicago, and Cleveland. There is also an Orthodox presence in numerous medium-size American Jewish communities, such as Milwaukee, St. Louis, Columbus, Atlanta, Savannah, Dallas, Memphis, San Francisco, San Diego, and elsewhere. In most of these communities Orthodox Jews support the institutions they need for family life, such as Jewish day schools, kosher butchers and bakers, and ritual baths. In addition to these substantial Orthodox communities, Orthodox individuals can be found in many far-flung locales, especially those who are part of the Chabad/Lubavitch system of religious outreach to Jews across the world.

About two-thirds to three-quarters of American Orthodox Jews are classified by sociologists as *Modern Orthodox*; that is, they attend secular colleges and believe that university attendance is an "important part of life." The remaining third to a quarter are "fervently" Orthodox; that is, they discourage college attendance as likely to lead to estrangement from Orthodox lifestyles. More than one-third of Orthodox congregations do not belong to either of these categories, and of those independent congregations, about one hundred are non-Ashkenazi, catering to Jews from Syria, Iran, Iraq, other Middle Eastern countries, or other Muslim republics in areas such as the former Soviet Union.[6]

Internally, Orthodox communities can be roughly divided into three categories, since the sociological *Modern Orthodox* is composed of both those who call themselves *Centrists* and those who proudly embrace the adjective *Modern*. The *fervently Orthodox* category also incorporates many subgroups, but they are united by their "rejectionist" rather than "accommodationist" stance toward modernity.

Centrist Orthodoxy

Centrist Orthodox groups usually affiliate with the Union of Orthodox Jewish Congregations (marked by the logo of a U inside an O) and/or belong to the National Council of Young Israel. Centrists generally attend college, but have deep misgivings about many elements of contemporary American culture and try to keep their distance from anything that symbolizes them. (Some Centrist Orthodox secondary schools, for example, discourage students from wearing denim blue jeans or T-shirts with rock insignias.) Centrist Orthodoxy, which includes large numbers of religious studies faculty currently teaching at Yeshiva University, tend to be concerned not only about correct religious observances, but also about *balebatish* (proper) behavior, dress, and deportment, the definition of which is an amalgam of Orthodox and middle-class expectations.

Centrist Orthodox couples may meet at school or work, but more often through family, friends, or sometimes through a *shadchan,* a professional marriage broker. Nonmarital physical expressions of affection are frowned upon—the ideal is to be *shomer negiah,* to guard against illicit touching. According to some reports, the emphasis on nontouching among Centrist Orthodox singles has actually increased, rather than diminished over time, a testament to Centrist Orthodox rejection of general cultural norms.

After marriage, Centrist Orthodox Jews generally have higher fertility rates than the Modern Orthodox but lower than the fervently Orthodox, with an average of four to five children per family. They are often two-paycheck families, with mothers as well as fathers working outside the home, but they are less likely to think of themselves as "dual-career" families. Politically, Centrist Orthodox Jews, like fervently Orthodox Jews but unlike other segments of the Jewish community, are likely to be conservative in their voting patterns. Their children almost universally attend Orthodox day schools from kindergarten through twelfth grade and usually attend programs of religious study in Israel for at least one year (often two years) between high school and college. Centrist Orthodox Jews are more likely to attend colleges that are perceived as "safe" in terms of challenging their Orthodox beliefs, such as Yeshiva University, but a significant minority attend non-sectarian universities with large Orthodox populations.

Centrist Orthodox Jews generally do not consider themselves to be feminists (and may emphatically reject feminism as a concept) but have nevertheless cautiously adapted some feminist values into their communities. For example, baby-naming ceremonies for girls (beyond the father being called to the Torah on the Shabbat after the infant's birth to give her a name) are common, and bat mitzvah ceremonies are ubiquitous—although never involving girls or women having direct contact with the Torah scroll.

Centrist Jews usually have strong connections to Israel (although not all of them consider themselves Zionists), and some of their children eventually "make *aliyah*" (settle in Israel). Whether or not they identify as "Zionist," Centrist Orthodox Jews support Israel and tend to lean toward hawkish rather than dovish approaches to Israeli politics.

Modern Orthodoxy

Modern Orthodox lifestyles are similar in many particulars to those of Centrist Orthodox Jews (we have noted that, sociologically, they are usually grouped together), but their attitudes and values systems are quite different. They are an interesting community to study, because they blend observance of traditional Jewish prescriptions and rituals with an embrace of modernity as expressed by American culture. Like non-Orthodox segments of the Jewish community, they tend toward liberal rather than conservative voting patterns. In terms of Israeli politics, they encompass a larger number of peace activists and liberals than any other Orthodox group. Rather than focusing on appearing *balebatish* (proper), Modern Orthodox Jews often pursue a status of being au courant with intellectual trends and American culture and styles.

Men and women date and usually meet their spouses at school or work or through friends. Most of them are not averse to non-marital physical expressions of affection, and some of them are sexually active before marriage. Especially among older Modern Orthodox singles and divorcees, one hears reports of the *tefillin* date, in which men bring their phylacteries along for prayer services the morning after the night before. Their ideas about books, culture, fashion, and recreation are influenced by their colleagues and friends in the world outside of Orthodoxy.

Statistically, Modern Orthodox Jews as a group have extraordinarily high levels of secular education and occupational achievement. Both the 1990 and the 2000–2001 National Jewish Population Survey (NJPS) showed that they have the highest rates of spousal parity of all Jews; that is, Modern Orthodox husbands and wives tend to have virtually identical levels of secular education and occupational achievement. As a group they tend to travel broadly and to be involved in culture and the arts. Modern Orthodox Jews have a slightly higher intermarriage rate than Centrist or ultra-Orthodox Jews, but substantially lower than non-Orthodox Jews. Their families typically include two to four children. Their children usually attend day schools, but Modern Orthodox parents frequently make decisions in this regard based on what they see as the "best interests of the child," rather than automatically choosing an

Orthodox environment, as Centrist or ultra-Orthodox Jews generally do. Modern Orthodox parents may select community day schools or Conservative Solomon Schechter schools or public schools if they think a particular child will benefit from that non-Orthodox environment. When studying in Israel for a year between high school and college, Modern Orthodox teens tend to choose programs with a reputation for intellectual enlightenment as well as rigor.

Although most Modern Orthodox congregations are affiliated with the Orthodox Union within those congregations many individual members belonged for a time to a now-defunct organization called Edah, which had as its motto "The courage to be modern and Orthodox." Edah produced programs and materials exploring a broad range of Judaic subjects, asking hard questions about living fully within Jewish and Western culture. Its rise and fall have yet to be systematically analyzed, but both Edah and Yeshiva University's Orthodox Forum commissioned studies that self-consciously examined their own religious culture, an activity directly descended from the *Wissenschaft des Judentums*. This introspective analysis is one interesting demarcation of Modern Orthodoxy from Orthodoxies to its right.

JOFA, the Jewish Orthodox Feminist Alliance, an even more startling ideological organization, was founded in the mid-1990s. For people outside the Orthodox world, *Orthodox feminist* might seem to be an oxymoron, but JOFA biennial conferences have attracted two thousand attendees from around the world. Intellectually, Orthodox feminists have produced scholarly books and articles as well as advocacy initiatives that have transformed the status of women in many Modern Orthodox communities. Within segments of the Modern Orthodox community, women serve as synagogue board members, committee heads, and presidents, participate in and teach classes to coed groups, and give sermons and lectures. It is a Modern Orthodox cultural ideal for girls to be given the intellectual tools to study the Talmud and other complex historical texts, preferably in coed environments or in classes that parallel those of boys.

Orthodox feminists often participate in Women's Tefillah (prayer) Groups (WTGs), in which women and girls worship and read the Torah together. The WTG Internet Listserv is one vehicle facilitating communication between Orthodox feminists internationally. In Israel, and in large American Jewish communities, such as New York, Washington, D.C., Chicago, Boston, and elsewhere, new independent "Partnership" congregations have sprung up in which men and women sit separately, divided by a *mekhitzah* (curtain or screen used for separation), but share the prayer service leadership and participation to the full extent not prohibited by rabbinic law. In many locations, these Partnership congregations, interestingly, have become "scenes"—magnets for singles from other wings of Judaism as well.

Ultra-Orthodoxy

Haredi (also variously described as ultra-Orthodox, Right-Wing Orthodox, fervently Orthodox or fundamentalist Orthodox) Jews are the most countercultural of all Orthodox Jews. This diverse group can be divided into Mitnagdic (non-Hasidic) ultra-Orthodox Jews who belong to Agudath Israel of America or are involved in one of the right-wing *yeshivot* (rabbinical seminaries), and a variety of Hasidic sects—each with their own particularistic garb and attitudes toward people outside their group. They reject the automatic espousal of Western norms, examining behaviors closely to determine the extent to which they may enhance or detract from Jewish values. For example, many *haredi* young families do not own television sets, or own only monitors so that they may play videos or DVDs of their own choosing. On a positive note, their children do not spend hours each week parked in front of television sets like the typical American child.

All these groups discourage college attendance, except for purely vocational reasons. Ideologically, the intrinsic value of Western culture is rejected—although Jewish fundamentalists, unlike non-Jewish fundamentalists, enthusiastically embrace technological and medical advances. Adherents revere rabbinic authority, and individual preferences are often subsumed to communal standards. Ultra-Orthodox societies emphasize gender role definitions, although—again, in contradistinction to Christian and Islamic fundamentalist communities—many young mothers work outside the home, an activity which, rather than being stigmatized, often brings additional status to the husband of a woman with prestigious paid employment.

Most *haredi* Jews dress according to very specific preferences that not only comply with their interpretation of Jewish law but also make them instantly recognizable to each other. Particular styles of dresses, stockings, and suit jackets, as well as head coverings, signal religious affiliations to the initiated. Closest to Western dress among the ultra-Orthodox is the clothing of the non-Hasidic *yeshivish* (connected with rabbinical seminaries) communities, where men wear black suits, wide-brimmed black felt hats, and large black velvet *kippot* (skullcaps), and married women cover their hair with expensive, beautifully styled wigs, and their arms (to the elbow) and legs (to the knee) with fashionable apparel. Bare legs and silky stockings are frowned upon, and visible stockings of some kind are the norm for women. Although it is readily identifiable, non-Hasidic *yeshivish* clothing is a version of modern Western garb, rather than an allusion to eighteenth-century Polish nobles, as many of the Hasidic outfits are.

Yeshivish haredi Orthodoxy is primarily distinguished by its societywide ideal for singles and young married men to devote years to the full-time study of Talmud, and thereafter to continue Talmud studies on a regular basis after working hours. In premodern European settings, only a small, intellectually gifted segment of the population aspired to spending substantial amounts of time studying. However, in *haredi* American Jewish communities today, large numbers of young men hope to spend at least the first few years of their married lives unencumbered by the necessity of earning a living. This idealistic communitywide expectation has emerged partly in response to democratic notions of equality (at least among males) and parallel societywide American social trends. (Non-Orthodox and non-Jewish middle-class and upper-middle-class Americans, for example, have for the past twenty years had a tendency to postpone beginning their life's work until well after the completion of college.) In the *haredi* world, this trend of postponement has another purpose: to keep young men out of mainstream secular culture until they are well established in their married adult lives, and thus, presumably, less vulnerable to the blandishments of a profane world.

In the *haredi* community most marriages are arranged through professional marriage brokers and parental negotiations. This has led to the current practice of the families of bridegrooms demanding several years of financial support from the families of the brides: A "good" boy currently "goes for" many thousands of dollars of financial commitments. The many gradations of this pricing have their own nicknames, instantly understood by insiders, such as "His family demanded that he get standard Lakewood" (a *haredi* learning-oriented community in Lakewood, New Jersey). Thus, in addition to traditional preferences for sons over daughters, having female children has become in *haredi* circles a substantial financial burden.

The Hasidic Ultra-Orthodox

Hasidic groups range from those who are very insular to those who are energetically engaged in outreach to other Jews. At the insular end of the spectrum, groups such as the Satmar Hasidim do not feel particularly close to other Orthodox Jews and have almost nothing to do with non-Orthodox Jews and non-Jews. They live in urban enclaves in Brooklyn and elsewhere and in contemporary rural *shtetlach* (urban villages) such as Kiryas Joel in upstate New York, in which they can reinforce their isolation from what they see as polluting influences. Readings in Satmar high schools are carefully supervised, and classes go only through the eleventh grade to ensure that their teens will be ill-equipped to attend college. In Satmar neighborhoods, non-Hasidim and women of all kinds are discouraged from walking near especially holy or important buildings. Purity is an extremely powerful concept in these isolationist communities, and separation is seen as the most effective way of guaranteeing that purity. In response to criticism, Satmar Hasidim would note that they have an excellent record of success in transmitting Jewish culture from one generation to the next and in producing numerous Jewish children and grandchildren.

At the other end of the Hasidic spectrum, Lubavitch Hasidim, also known as Chabad, have outposts all over the world in which Hasidim conduct famously successful outreach programs to non-practicing Jews. The central Lubavitch office in Brooklyn has hundreds of international "listings" that Chabad *shluchim,* emissary-teachers and outreach workers, can sign up for. They are sent to their assigned posts—in China, Paris, La Jolla, Minsk, Hawaii—typically with a small amount of seed money to get things set up, and then it is up to them to create a viable outreach program. It is their mission, quite literally, to "make Jewish souls." In seducing underengaged Jews into a relationship with their own Jewishness, Chabad typically uses warmth, hospitality, and the delights of traditional Shabbat observances as effective strategies. Anecdotally, the most common praise for Chabad outreach efforts offered by previously secular Jews who have come under their aura is, "They didn't ask anything of me, and the food was great!"

Troupes of Chabad outreach workers—some of them quite young—are often seen in "Mitzvah Mobiles"—vans with paraphernalia for Jewish prayers such as prayer shawls and prayer books inside. They urge Jewish men to enter and pray. This kind of missionary activity is deeply unsettling to many American Jews, because it seems to go against the grain of both American and Jewish sensibilities. However, although they are sometimes described by skeptical outsiders as indulging in "brainwashing," the assertion is not accurate, first, because it is not Chabad policy to isolate individuals by encouraging them to reject their nonreligious families, and, second, because they do not expect the vast majority of their protégées to become fully observant. Instead, Chabad hopes to influence them to experience Jewishness on a more regular basis.

Another aspect of Chabad behavior, however, that has received harsh criticism from Orthodox as well as non-Orthodox Jews, is Chabad's increasingly messianic fervor in recent years. Ideologically, Chabad today is divided into those who believe that the deceased Lubavitcher rebbe, Menachem Schneerson, is actually the messiah, and those who do not share this belief. For many non-Lubavitch Jews, the declaration that a deceased person is the messiah, no matter how exceptional that individual may have been, is perilously close to early Christian belief or to Mormon preachings. Some Mitnagdic rabbinic scholars have argued that Chabad/Lubavitch should be declared outside the sphere of the Judaic belief system.[7]

The Evolution of American Modern and Antimodern Orthodox Models

To understand the current situation of America's Orthodox Jews, it is helpful to look back very briefly at the experiences of Orthodox immigrants during the great wave of East European immigration (1880–1924), at the concomitant formation of Orthodox institutions during the late nineteenth and early twentieth centuries, and at Orthodoxy's unpredicted rise to self-confidence and even triumphalism toward the end of the twentieth century.

As previously noted, many Jewish immigrants to the United States had already abandoned regular religious practice before they left Europe. Others were said to have thrown their *tefillin* (phylacteries) overboard as they sailed to America. However, substantial numbers of Jewish immigrants hoped to keep their religious traditions alive, especially those who fled Europe and Russia after the turn of the twentieth century. For these Jews, as individuals and as families, maintaining religious observance was a genuine struggle, often involving financial and other hardships. Nevertheless, many persisted. First-person interviews and memoirs capture the fortitude of immigrants who remained religiously observant, men and women who turned down six-day-a-week jobs, passionately uttering in Yiddish, "I'll eat bread and water but I won't work on Saturday." Much of the published history of Orthodox Jewry in the United States focuses on Orthodox rabbis and other leadership figures, but in our examination of the varieties of Jewishness it is important not to forget the contributions made by ordinary Orthodox working people who remained remarkably true to their traditions despite the dislocations of immigration and the staggering socioeconomic challenges.

Synagogues were the primary external symbol of the diversity of Jewish experience in nineteenth-century America. By 1850, sizable Jewish communities typically had several synagogues—some long-established ones reflecting Sephardi heritage, and newer, or breakaway synagogues, reflecting Western or Central European countries of origin. An ongoing influx of German Jews, some of them well-educated, had already brought pressure to bear on Reform congregations, putting an end to the Sephardi "Orthodox" near-monopoly of earlier periods. The new German Jewish prominence also precipitated the creation of consciously Orthodox responses to the challenges of modernity, evident in the growing American Reform movement.

At midcentury, the numbers of East European Jewish immigrants began to multiply, and with them came yet more diverse liturgical customs, and houses of prayer to articulate them. A massive wave of East European Jews commenced in 1881, and American Jewish institutional life began to reflect this traditionalist Jewish influx. Each group of Jewish immigrants sought to replicate the liturgies and idiosyncratic prayer customs of their hometowns, animating the creation of multiple small and large unself-consciously Orthodox synagogues, known as *landsmanschaften* (Old World–style synagogues composed of people from the same hometown). Different types of Orthodox rabbis were imported and sprang homegrown from the American scene with these newly numerous and diverse Orthodox populations.

Rabbi Jacob Joseph was brought to the United States from Vilna in 1888 by the emerging Association of American Orthodox Hebrew Congregations, an organization that arose in response to the Reform Pittsburgh Platform of 1885. Rabbi Joseph was accomplished in Judaic studies and skilled in both Hebrew and Yiddish written and oral expression, having proceeded from a traditional Lithuanian *cheder* and yeshiva schooling to the great Mitnagdic (non-Hasidic) Volozhin Yeshiva. However, unlike two earlier Sephardi Orthodox rabbinical imports, Italian-born Sabato Morais of Philadelphia and London-born Abraham Pereira Mendes of Newport, who had studied at the University of Pisa and University College in London, respectively, Jacob Joseph had little in the way of secular education. These three are revealingly symbolic of the diversity of Orthodox rabbis upon whom fell the task of opposing the forces of Reform Judaism during the second half of the nineteenth century. Although they were all identified as *Orthodox,* their educations, life experiences, and attitudes toward non-Orthodox Jews differed dramatically. While Morais and Mendes, for example, fell within the group of Orthodox rabbis who believed it was necessary and desirable to cooperate with the Reform rabbinate in combating external threats, such as the vigorous Christian missionary movement, Rabbi Joseph could understand only one kind of Orthodoxy—his own—and kept his distance from non-Orthodox Jews.[8]

By the beginning of the twentieth century, established Orthodox organizations epitomized these two very different approaches. Prototypical American modernizing Orthodox congregations acquired an organizational name when they created the Association of American Orthodox Hebrew Congregations in 1887. When the Orthodox Jewish Congregational Union of America, encompassing forty-seven congregations in eleven states, was formed in 1898, its platform included a detailed argument against specifics spelled out in the 1885 Reform Pittsburgh Platform. The boundaries were carefully drawn between modernizing Orthodox and American Reform, with the yet-to-become Conservative middle ground not yet clearly delineated. Indeed, American Judaism at the beginning of the twentieth century appeared to be split into two, not three, groups.[9]

The Americanized, "accommodating" Orthodox rabbinical organization emerged first. The Orthodox Union had a stated mission to protect "Orthodox Judaism whenever occasions arise in civic and social matters ... and to protest against declarations of Reform rabbis not in accord with the teachings of our Torah." As Gurock notes, the Orthodox Union was actively engaged with realities on the ground, fighting "against blue laws," protecting "the rights of Sabbath observers," advocating on behalf of "the modernization of Jewish educational techniques." Additionally, American-born rabbis, such as Bernard Drachman and other Orthodox Union leaders, strove to make traditional Judaism more appealing to Americanized Jews. They fought this battle on two fronts—the synagogue and the classroom—with a goal of bringing order and excellence to both institutions.[10]

By contrast, the Orthodox "resisters," with their isolationist tendencies, joined the Agudath ha-Rabbanim, a group officially formed by sixty immigrant rabbis from Russia, Poland, and Austro-Hungary who were currently living in Canada, New York, Boston, Philadelphia, and the Midwest. Their goal was to replicate the Eastern European environments they had left behind, rather than to grapple with the American milieu and come up with creative new solutions. The Agudath ha-Rabbanim battled against sermons in English, which they saw as a grave threat to traditional Judaism, insisting on Yiddish instead. They wanted to control the lucrative kosher meat industry, and saw the Americanized rabbis as a threat to their authority.[11] In this difference of emphasis, the Orthodox Union and the Agudath ha-Rabbanim foreshadowed a difference in approach that is evident to this very day.

The great majority of the new immigrants remained along the Eastern Seaboard, although some were deliberately brought to other areas of the country and others joined relatives and friends in midwestern communities or followed the German Jews who had preceded them to cities all over the country. For Jews who settled in the South, the Southwest, or the Midwest, experiences were notably different from those living in Boston, New York, Philadelphia, and the Baltimore/Washington area. Nevertheless, Orthodox life and leadership around the country was at first primarily shaped and affected by developments in New York and, to a lesser extent, Chicago. Yeshivat Etz Chaim, which was later incorporated into Yeshiva University's Rabbi Isaac Elchanan Theological Seminary (RIETS), was founded in 1886, and the Jewish Theological Seminary (JTS)—an "accommodating" Orthodox institution in the pre–Solomon Schechter years—opened in 1887. Later, the Hebrew Theological College of Chicago (often called the "Chicago Yeshiva") opened in 1922, two years before large-scale immigration to America was brought to a halt by legislation. The early JTS and the Chicago Yeshiva were in many ways

Modern Orthodox, expecting (or at least not opposing) their students' acquisition of secular as well as yeshiva education. RIETS struggled with its relationship to modernity, but took a Modern Orthodox stance for extended periods of its existence.

Overtly antimodernist American Orthodox rabbinical institutions were created later, as some European rabbis of the "resister" persuasion finally recognized the European threat to Jewish safety and emigrated. Fervently Orthodox institutions were established in Brooklyn, including the Talmud study arm of Mesivta Torah Vodaath in 1926; in Baltimore, Ner Israel in 1933; and in Cleveland, the Telshe Yeshiva in 1941. The Chaim Berlin advanced yeshiva moved from Brooklyn (1939) to Lakewood, New Jersey, in 1943.[12] By giving an American voice to modernity-rejecting Orthodoxy, and by rejecting not only Reform Judaism but also the modernizing Orthodox, the Agudath ha-Rabbanim helped to create American ultra-Orthodoxy and also to define it by rejecting the liberal traditionalist stance that would soon become Conservative Judaism.

Orthodox East Europeans, who followed the Orthodox German Jews' preference for beautiful, orderly, impressive edifices and services, created palatial synagogues with imported prominent cantors who were robed and behatted in the most elegant fashion. Their imitation of Reform magnificence was sometimes openly articulated. However, it was precisely what they rejected of Reform worship and what they retained of Orthodox punctiliousness that defined the boundaries between themselves and Reform congregations: Orthodox congregations had no organs; they prayed in Hebrew; the worshipers covered their heads and wore prayer shawls; they maintained the traditional, lengthy services. Thus, although they were light-years away from the noisy, disorderly, and sometimes none-too-clean East European worship environments that German reformers had vehemently rejected, these elegant new Orthodox congregations were both modern and Orthodox—and not Reform.

While both the modernizing and the antimodernizing Orthodox congregations declared their fidelity to Jewish law, their punctiliousness did not extend to the private lives of many congregants. Immigrant men often frequented the comfort of Orthodox synagogues to begin Sabbath celebrations after work hours on Friday night, but economic necessities pushed them out the door to their workplaces on Saturday morning. Many an immigrant woman rushed home from the counters of the store she managed to light Shabbat candles—and then returned to work. Immigrant memoirs testify that those who absented themselves from work for all the Jewish holidays were likely to lose their jobs. Thus, while the two types of Orthodoxy were drawing the boundaries between themselves and the Reform congregations and institutions that challenged them, the ordinary people within those congregations were already making their own accommodations with the reality of American life. What sociologists would later come to call "nominal" Orthodoxy was born in these immigrant struggles—Jews who thought of themselves as Orthodox and most comfortably prayed in Orthodox synagogues, but were not reliably Orthoprax (fully practicing) in their own behaviors. In later generations the same economic necessities were often no longer in place, but the nominal Orthodox behavior persisted for decades.

Synthesizing America into Orthodox Lives

Middle- and upper-middle-class Modern Orthodox Jewish professionals and laity in major metropolitan areas across the United States during the interwar years took pride in what they saw as their successful combination of Americanization and Jewish traditionalism. Motivated not by the economic necessities that created nominally Orthodox behaviors among struggling immigrants and their children, upwardly mobile Modern Orthodox Jewish attitudes were shaped by the desire for cultural integration—a determination to be physically indistinguishable from other middle-class white Americans.

Modern Orthodox educational institutions saw as their mandate the deliberate synthesis of Jewish and Western culture. Yeshiva University proudly declared that it was the home of *Torah U'Mada,* sacred learning and scientific knowledge. In the flagship Modern Orthodox day school, Ramaz, on New York's fashionable Upper East Side (and also in the heart of German-populated Yorkville) Orthodox boys were taught by the senior rabbi, Joseph Lookstein, that the yarmulke (head covering, now often called a *kippah*) was an "indoor garment," as Modern Orthodox males did not wear identifiably Jewish head coverings outside Jewish environments. Very few private individuals built a *sukkah,* the ritual hut where observant Jews are supposed to eat, study, and even, if possible, sleep during the week of the fall harvest festival of Sukkot. Rather than disturb their neighbors by building these flimsy and decidedly non-middle-class structures, most Modern Orthodox Jews in the interwar years honored their Sukkot obligations by blessing the food they ate after services in the synagogue's unobtrusive *sukkah.* As historian Jenna Weissman Joselit reports:

[Modern] Orthodox Jews were very much like everyone else: they enjoyed social dancing and mixed swimming, fancied sleeveless attire during the summer season, and traveled widely ... eating out in a non-kosher restaurant while observing the ritual amenities did not confound them at all; if anything it served as a measure of their own success in linking the two cultures.[13]

Seen through their own eyes—and not the critical and disapproving prism of the more self-consciously ritualistic American Modern Orthodoxy that developed during the second half of the twentieth century—these interwar Modern Orthodox Jews felt that they were enabling historical Judaism to survive. To the extent that they interacted with Conservative or Reform Jews, Modern Orthodox Jews felt they had good reason to consider themselves pillars of authentic traditionalism. They transmitted a form of Orthodoxy embedded in American middle-class comfort and fashion. Their boundaries were primarily observance of the Sabbath and the dietary laws, which tended to be strict enough within their homes that more rigorously Orthodox grandparents could eat there, and the avoidance of nonkosher meat, poultry, and seafood when eating outside the home.

The concept of worrying about the *kashrut* of items such as candy bars or ice cream was far beyond most ordinary Orthodox Jews at midcentury. Instead, these items seemed like symbols of benign American pleasures, and benign pleasures were treasured as part of their birthright as free Americans. They attached great importance to making their lives and cultural and religious expressions consistent with American middle-class norms. Thus, Orthodox wedding music often consisted of classical and romantic contemporary tunes; the vibrant European klezmer-style music that acquired such great cachet late in the twentieth century would have seemed quite alien and retrograde to many prepluralism Modern Orthodox American Jews.

In a period now nostalgically remembered as a kind of edenic innocence by some in the more rigorously observant Modern Orthodox world, pre–World War II Modern Orthodox American communities did not feel constrained to articulate an official doctrine or philosophy that would give coherence and institutional roots to their distinctive hybrid lifestyle. While Modern Orthodox rabbinic leaders like Lookstein or Leo Jung occasionally made references to the German neo-Orthodox milieu and teachings, America's Modern Orthodox leaders remained largely ignorant of the powerful model that had preceded them. Mordecai Kaplan noted in his diaries that Modern Orthodox practitioners were largely self-satisfied with the social and religious norms they had created, felt little need for external approbation, and, for the most part, were little educated in the intricacies of biblical and rabbinic texts, Jewish history, or Jewish cultural output such as modern Yiddish and Hebrew literature, music, or philosophy. As one of Kaplan's commentators put it, they were "not troubled too much by abstract problems of Judaism."[14] Nor were they much troubled by the dwindling *haredi* societies they encountered, which they misjudged as not likely to survive in America.

Day Schools and the Text-Based Revolution

The complexion of Orthodox life in America began to change in the middle of the twentieth century. As we have seen, a small number of *haredi* rabbis had begun to emigrate in the pre–World War II years. After the war, with the influx of 150,000 Holocaust survivors, including a disproportionate number of *haredi* Jews, however, Modern Orthodoxy's relationship with existential religious issues—and with their *haredi* brothers and sisters—was disrupted and in many ways transformed. Conservative Judaism, discussed in the next chapter, had already made significant inroads into nominal Orthodox vitality—indeed the Conservative movement at mid-twentieth century was populated primarily by defectors from Orthodoxy. The more intensive Orthodoxy of many new immigrants was thus positioned to have even more of an impact than it might have had if the numbers of Orthodox Jews had been higher.

The Orthodox Jews who had come to America during the mass immigration period of 1881–1924 had arrived with millions of other immigrants, with little idea of how to navigate in the modern milieu of their new country and no socioeconomic safety net. By contrast, many of the *haredi* Jews who arrived in the 1940s and 1950s had been effectively resisting modernity in Hungary since the edict of the Hasam Sofer: "Anything new is forbidden by the

Torah." As Jack Wertheimer points out, "these Orthodox Jews had already experienced sustained exposure to the corrosive forces of modernity, and had developed a set of strategies to deal with them."[15] Once in America, they applied their religious and social organizational energies to creating more intensive Jewish schools than had ever existed here before, multiplying the number of day schools many times over. Additionally, their tendency was toward Orthodox resistance rather than accommodation, and they were little interested in working together with the other wings of Judaism or even with more liberal types of Orthodox Jews. Finally, American Orthodox Judaism had moved away from a relaxed, mimetic transmission of religious culture to a more rigid, text-based, earnest Orthodoxy. In a famously influential article, historian Haim Soloveitchik discussed the ways in which younger Orthodox Jews looked to their rigid rabbinical teachers rather than their accommodating families as religious authorities, and, as a result, American Orthodoxy had itself become more self-conscious and rigid.[16] The incremental move rightward of American Orthodoxy had begun.

Most day schools were not truly *haredi*. Some were ideologically and proudly Modern Orthodox, including such flagship schools as the Flatbush Yeshiva (1927); Boston's Maimonides, under the leadership of Rabbi Joseph B. Soloveitchik, a towering figure in the Modern Orthodox world; and New York's Ramaz, under the leadership of two generations of Rabbis Lookstein, also men deeply committed to the legitimacy of the modern approach (both established in 1937). Much later, clusters of innovative new schools devoted to intellectual excellence arose, schools that self-consciously synthesized Jewish and Western educational values.

The vast majority of day schools then and now would probably be classified as Centrist Orthodox, affiliated with the *Torah Umesorah* (Torah and tradition) umbrella organization created in 1944. The Conservative movement's Solomon Schechter schools,

Reform day schools, and especially nondenominational Jewish community schools have recently acquired greater market shares. According to a recent study, in 2004 there were over 200,000 students in approximately 760 day schools, of which about 80 percent of the students were enrolled in Orthodox schools.[17] However, regardless of the educational philosophy of the day school, finding day school teachers who genuinely believe in a non-*haredi* approach is far more difficult today than it was decades ago. Day school teaching (like education in America in general) is neither a very high status or a very well compensated profession. Today, given the ease with which Jewish professionals can find work in many fields outside the *haredi* world, American-style success is often a more compelling value than devoting one's life to the education of young people. As a result, except for the most prestigious (and best-paying) Modern Orthodox day schools, many children and teens are enrolled in schools in which the beliefs of the teachers are decidedly less liberal than the beliefs of the parents and community.[18]

Triumphalism — and Tension

Orthodox Judaism is stronger in the United States today than it has ever been before, and one might argue that it is stronger than it has been in any Westernized country since the emancipation of the Jews. High levels of Jewish education are ubiquitous due in large part to the growth of the day school movement. Orthodoxy today is doing a better job of retaining its young people than in any previous American decade. The Orthodox retention rate is under half, at 42 percent, but on the other hand, Orthodox children represent 40 percent of children in synagogue-affiliated families, compared to 27 percent in Conservative- and 33 percent in Reform-affiliated households. Cultural transmission appears manifestly healthy among Orthodox Jews, and rates of intermarriage for Orthodox youth who graduate from day schools are well under 10 percent. JTS Provost Jack Wertheimer has suggested that this is the "Orthodox moment"[19] and elsewhere has praised Orthodox family styles, noting that the Orthodox are the only American Jews having enough children to replace themselves.

Many Orthodox Jews, however, ask the question, "If things are so good—why do they feel so bad?" Like Orthodox historical scholars, many ordinary Orthodox Jews are not so sure that Orthodoxy is as strong as it seems. Of particular concern to many is the impact of *haredi* attitudes on Orthodox life. Steven Bayme, national director of communal affairs at the American Jewish Committee, for example, says, "Real modern Orthodoxy must stand up," noting that increasingly "the voices of ultra-Orthodoxy have prevailed even within centrist Orthodox institutions."[20] Jonathan Sarna calls the mood "a sense of triumph mixed with trepidation" and speaks of a leadership vacuum, a "brain drain" of talented young Orthodox Jews moving to Israel, and profound confusion about the old Orthodox question of "how to confront modernity," including the modern question of women's roles within Judaism.[21] Looming ominously, the increasing tendency of Israeli rabbinical leadership to isolate and delegitimatize all but *haredi* Orthodox rabbis threatens to further split the movement along ideological lines. American Orthodox Judaism, no less than Conservative and Reform, is currently experiencing a struggle for the definition of the very core of its being.

6

Conservative Judaism at the Crossroads

Conservative Judaism has been at a crossroads since it emerged as a centrist movement in the early decades of the twentieth century. By the 1920s, a growing number of Conservative congregations were positioning themselves squarely between Orthodox and Reform modes of worship. These congregations appealed to the offspring of East European immigrants who had streamed into America between 1880 and 1924. To Americanizing and yet traditional Jews, the appeal of Conservative Judaism, with its familiar and largely traditional liturgy, was in its perceived balance. Most of the Hebrew prayers were retained unchanged, but they were mixed with English readings in a quiet and decorous environment. Families sat together in mixed pews, American style. Knowledgeable rabbis, many of whom had attended Orthodox rabbinical seminaries before they received ordination from the Jewish Theological Seminary (JTS) of America, gave modern sermons in unaccented English, and displayed a seemingly more relaxed attitude toward congregants' ritual observances than Orthodox clergy.

As a result, Conservative congregations grew into the largest movement of American Judaism during the period of post–World War II suburbanization in the 1950s, and attracted the largest membership of American Jews throughout the middle decades of the twentieth century. In this growth period, Conservative Judaism pioneered a characteristic American Jewish focus on youth, creating a strong supplementary Jewish education program and a summer camping system, which, in turn, helped to sustain its position as a defining Jewish experience. Through its Hebrew-speaking Ramah camps and its youth groups, United Synagogue Youth (USY) and the Leadership Training Fellowship (LTF), the Conservative movement created a strongly committed lay cadre, as well as a larger lay group with less intensive Jewish connections.

The crossroads centrality of American Conservative Judaism served it well for almost one hundred years. Today, however, although Conservative Judaism maintains its middleman position in American Jewish life, it has lost part of its "market share," both to the Reform movement on the left and to Orthodoxy on the right. Thus, Conservative Judaism today is at a crossroads in a different way, as it considers its options concerning changing trends in American Jewish life.

Before analyzing the present situation in light of past evolutions of Conservative forms of Jewishness, we pause to define an important characteristic of the movement—Conservative Judaism is in some ways not one, but two movements with the same name: a smaller, Jewishly knowledgeable, ideologically Conservative "elite" movement; and a much larger, mostly less educated, and Jewishly less active Conservative "folk," without particular knowledge of or concern about Conservative ideology.

Conservative "Folk" and "Elites"

To understand the varieties of Jewishness, sociologist Charles Liebman insists, one must pay equal attention not only to "elitist ideologies" but also to "folk religion," or "popular religious culture." Liebman distinguishes between two populations who characterize "elite" and "folk" approaches:

> The elite religion is the ritual, belief, and doctrine which the acknowledged religious leaders teach to be the religion. Thus, the elite religion includes rituals and ceremonials (the cult), doctrines and beliefs (ideology), and a religious organization headed by the religious leaders.... Folk religion is not self-conscious; it does not articulate its own rituals and beliefs, or demand recognition for its informal leaders. Therefore, in the eyes of the elite religion folk religion is not a movement but an error, or a set of errors, shared by many people. Folk religion is expressed primarily through ritual and symbol.... It is relatively indifferent to the belief structure.[1]

While many religious groups consist of folk and elite segments, Liebman argued that this division was particularly characteristic of the American Conservative Jewish movement. "The fact that the folk identified with Conservative Judaism did not mean they were Conservative Jews as the Conservative elite, JTS leaders and alumni, understood Conservatism."[2]

Today, that division still stands. Rabbis, cantors, educators, and deeply committed Conservative lay "elites" continue to incorporate many aspects of traditional Jewish lifestyles into their daily, weekly, and cyclical yearly routine. Their homes include Sabbath and holiday observances, they attend synagogues on a regular basis, and their food intake is guided by the principles of *kashrut*. They are among the most active populations in charities on behalf of worldwide Jewry. With the growth of the Conservative Solomon Schechter Day School system, Conservative elites today are more likely to send their children to day schools than to supplementary religious schools. These Conservative youth elites attend Jewish camps, make trips to Israel (often as part of their day school curriculum), and sometimes spend a year studying in Israeli *yeshivot* between high school and college.

These most committed Conservative Jewish elites incorporate many aspects of modernity into their lives and their concepts of Judaism. They embrace the research of biblical historians and sociologists of religion, and they see Judaism as a religious culture that has evolved in complicated ways over the millennia, contributing much to world culture and borrowing much from it as well. Indeed, the Conservative movement today and over the past century has produced some of the greatest scholars scientifically examining Jewish history, culture, and life, and has incorporated scholarship emanating from other streams of Judaism as well.

Almost from the beginning, however, the Conservative movement has been characterized not only by its elite, but also by a far larger group of "folk" practitioners. The behaviors and values of these Conservative "folk" differ strikingly from those of its elites, and these differences have become more pronounced with passing decades. For example, in terms of ritual observance, Conservative folk support the idea that their synagogues and rabbis should observe Sabbath and the dietary laws, but most are not necessarily convinced that these laws should apply to them or to their homes.[3] Among Jews who pay dues to Conservative synagogues, about one out of four report that they have two sets of dishes and buy only kosher meat. Four out of ten say they light Sabbath candles every Friday night, and about half attend synagogue services at least once a month. In terms of these rituals that make demands on a regular basis, the majority of American Conservative Jews are content to "make the rabbi their vicarious Sabbath," in the words of the late novelist, Arthur A. Cohen.[4] Observance of yearly ceremonies, on the other hand, is almost universal among members of Conservative synagogues: Four out of five Conservative members fast on Yom Kippur, light Hanukkah candles, and attend Passover seders.[5]

Attitudes toward Jewish education also reflect differences—and in some cases opposite directions—between folk and elite Conservative populations. Prior to the proliferation of day schools in the Jewish community, Conservative elites often enrolled their children in four-day supplementary school religious programs, but now they often opt for the more comprehensive Solomon Schechter day schools. By contrast, Conservative folk pressure their synagogue administrators to reduce the number of days of their religious school programs. As elites have moved into the day school system and folk utilize supplementary school systems with half the previous hours, an even greater cultural literacy gap between day school and supplementary school populations has emerged. Thus, when an American Jew identifies himself as a "Conservative Jew," that declaration may reflect one of two very different communal norms—the elite level or the folk level—with very different Jewish experiences and assumptions.

The movement's official policy has adapted in some ways over the decades to the broader communal norms of its folk. In one telling example, the movement's Commission on Laws and Standards ruled in 1950 that Jews were permitted to use electricity on the Sabbath and that they could ride to and from the synagogue on the Sabbath—but not to any other location.[6] For many years this ruling had little impact on the behavior of most rabbis, who continued to eschew automobile travel on Sabbaths and holidays. Truth be told, it had little impact on the behavior of most folk Conservative Jews as well, in that the vast majority continued to use their cars for whatever type of travel suited them on Saturdays.

Sociologically, what the ruling did was to make travel to and from the synagogue "kosher," in the eyes of Conservative rabbinic law, free from the stigma of being a transgression of the Sabbath. Conservative rabbis—who would not themselves travel on the

Sabbath—could still feel that their congregants were not transgressing the Sabbath in order to attend their synagogues, and they could thus urge them to attend regularly.

In the ruling on driving to the synagogue, the concept of the authority of rabbinic law was maintained for rabbis and other Conservative elites, side by side with the flexibility of the law and responsiveness of the rabbis to changing times. These changes made for a greater feeling of comfort in both segments of the Conservative population.

The ruling made Shabbat travel normative for laypeople within the movement, on an ideological as well as a behavioral basis. Within several decades, many (but by no means all) younger Conservative rabbis would follow suit and personally adopt the policy of traveling to and from the synagogue by automobile. The question that emerged then, and now faces the movement over different issues, is the extent to which the traditions of the past or the trends of the present would most influence not only the practice of the folk but also the ideology of the elite.

American Conservative Judaisms Evolve

To understand contemporary Conservative Judaism and the challenges it faces, we now look back at certain highlights of its origins and development. Scholars argue over the genesis of the movement: Some insist that Conservative ideology has always been an important foundational factor and trace that ideology back to nineteenth-century Germany and the moderate traditionalists who espoused Positivist-Historical Judaism.[7] Historian Moshe Davis, for example, points out that attitudes very similar to what would become Conservative ideology were already apparent in the European Historical School, which viewed Judaism as "evolving" organically over the centuries. American religious thinkers found these ideas appealing and incorporated them into American contexts, preparing the ground, as it were, for the growth and development of a well-defined and specifically American movement that emerged in the early decades of the twentieth century.[8]

Others see Conservative Judaism primarily as an American phenomenon, with pragmatism as the shaping force, emphasizing the impact of congregations seeking an American compromise. Marshall Sklare, a pioneer in the field of sociology of the Jews, stressed the movement's dual nature and very American character in his landmark study *Conservative Judaism* (1955). Sklare noted that American Jews tended to form Conservative places of worship when they moved into gentrified urban areas or, increasingly, the suburbs.[9]

While Sklare's sociological understanding of Conservative Judaism focuses primarily on the folk—the laypeople identifying with the movement—historian Mordecai Waxman poses a compromise approach to Conservative ideology. The movement has been characterized not by "a doctrine but a technique." This technique is in itself a kind of ideological crossroads, emphasizing notions of Catholic Israel—the unity of Jewish peoplehood; Positivist-Historical Judaism—respect for the Jewish past; and Vertical Democracy—not the rule of the present majority alone, but decision making that takes into account the traditions of the past and the needs of the future as well. Waxman distinguishes these three guiding principles of Conservative technique from Orthodox and Reform approaches. He suggests that when Reform Judaism rejected much of biblical and rabbinic law and insisted on the idea of Judaism as a religion (or "confession") alone, and not as a principle of peoplehood, it was rejecting the notions of Catholic Israel and Vertical Democracy, the Jewish people in their historical, religious development. Orthodox Jews also rejected these principles when they insisted on the supremacy of religious law over the needs of the ordinary people.[10]

The tension between Jewishness of the past and the present was built into American Conservative Judaism as it evolved. The crossroads nature of the Conservative movement, and its ability to morph in differing directions, is exemplified by two key figures: Rabbis Solomon Schechter (1847–1915) and Mordecai Kaplan (1881–1983). Holographlike, their evolving positions reflect and symbolize the movement's conflicts between tradition and modernity. Schechter moved from a position almost indistinguishable from Orthodoxy to help create Conservative Judaism as a separate movement, and Kaplan, who received both Conservative and Orthodox ordination, became a major figure in the Conservative movement and then created a new movement, Reconstructionist Judaism, which championed folk religion.

As we discuss in the next chapter, Kaplan's "Reconstructionist" views of Judaism have had a profound effect on all of American Judaism. Even within our consideration of Conservative Judaism, it is significant to recognize Kaplan, like Schechter, as an icon of shifting allegiances and boundaries.

Schechter, whose name is memorialized in the branding of the Conservative day school system, was born in Romania, the son of a Hasidic *shochet* (ritual slaughterer). Nevertheless, as a very young man Schechter embraced the rationalist approach to Jewish history and Judaism, studying at the Berlin *Hochshule fuer die Wissenschaft des Judentums* (1879) and at the University of Berlin. Schechter moved to London in 1882 and became a prominent rabbinic scholar. He revolutionized Judaic scholarship with his discovery and retrieval in the 1890s of a rich mother lode of archival materials, some of them nearly a thousand years old (and most of them referring to Sephardi Jewish communities), from the Cairo Genizah. Despite his embrace of historical scholarship and the idea of the organic evolution of Judaism, Schechter was known as a spokesperson for traditionalism. However, Schechter also coined the phrase *Catholic Israel*,[11] which argues that the mainstream Jewish experience is defined by empirical and communitarian criteria, or is the way the majority of Jewish societies live.

Schechter never followed the idea of Catholic Israel to its logical conclusion—but decades later Mordecai Kaplan did, as he created Reconstructionist Judaism and clearly articulated the idea that "Judaism is what Jews do."

Schechter moved to the United States to become the president of the Jewish Theological Seminary in 1902. However, because Conservative Judaism was not yet clearly defined and differentiated from Orthodoxy, some Orthodox leaders initially saw Schechter as their standard bearer. Thus, the president of the Orthodox Union, H. Pereira Mendes, enthusiastically called Schechter a "bulwark against Reform Judaism." As paradoxical testimony to JTS's early lack of clearly defined boundaries, Reform leaders also saw Schechter as an ally. Temple Emanu-El lay leaders Jacob Schiff and Louis Marshall supported "Schechter's seminary," which they hoped would serve to Americanize and appropriately Judaize the children of immigrants.[12]

Ironically, neither Schechter nor his colleagues at the time intended to begin a separate stream of Judaism. They thought of themselves as traditionalists. At the core of Schechter's concept of Catholic Israel was his belief that his new seminary, combining modern thought and rigorous ritual observance, would be a Judaism for all those who cared about *halakhah*.[13] Far from embracing pluralism, Schechter, with his Catholic Israel—like his Reform and Orthodox counterparts—saw himself as the standard-bearer for a single Judaism that would take American Jewishness from the past to the future.

A Conservative Jewish Empire at Midcentury

At its height, Conservative Judaism was the most quintessentially American religious movement, according to Marshall Sklare, who documented the ways in which Jewish immigrants and their children attempted to maintain Jewish traditions while looking, sounding, and behaving like bona fide Americans. He asked questions about behaviors, attitudes, and beliefs when he spoke to the Jews who had moved to more upscale urban apartment houses or out to suburban American environments in the decades after World War II.[14] Already in the 1950s and 1960s, the gap between the professors at JTS, the rabbis and cantors, and the Conservative laity was striking. Conservative laypeople, unlike the scholars and professional practitioners, defined what it meant to be a Conservative Jew not by ideology but by what they perceived as Conservative practice.

One of the most recognizable signposts of the Conservative religious experience at midcentury was loyalty to a relaxed version of kosher eating. In 1955 the majority of Conservative Jewish homes observed *kashrut*, often partially to enhance the ease with which older, more Orthodox relatives could share Sabbath and holiday meals. Conservative housewives often fiercely guarded the *kashrut* of their kitchens, even if the family was more lax in meals outside the home. Far fewer numbers of Conservative Jews strictly observed *kashrut* in restaurants or social situations, although many avoided biblically prohibited foods, such as pork products, shellfish, and milk and meat mixtures. Unlike the Reform Jews to their left, who had abandoned *kashrut* as an essential aspect of Judaism, and unlike practicing Orthodox Jews to their right, who observed *kashrut* so strictly that it impeded their social contacts with others, Conservative Jews retained the concept of *kashrut* but observed it loosely enough to socialize with diverse friendship circles. As Sklare articulated this compromise: "(1) the isolating function of the dietary laws no longer operates as far as most of Conservative Jewry is concerned; (2) nevertheless, the role of *kashrut* as an aspect of Jewishness is still manifest."[15]

The ritual male head covering, yarmulke or *kippah*, was virtually never worn on the street by Conservative boys or men, and was seen only in Conservative synagogues, schools, and on special occasions in the home. Both Conservative and Reform Jews placed much less emphasis on extensive Judaic knowledge or strictly observed ritual behaviors than on being an exemplar of moral, ethical, and socially concerned behavior. Thus, Conservative Jewishness had something in common with the Reform Jews of Lakeville, who similarly felt that every good Jew should work for social justice, including helping African Americans achieve justice, and that good Jews should be honest in business dealings. Conservative Jews, however, demarcated their approach by the traditionalism that differentiated them from Reform Judaism and the flexibility that divided them from Orthodoxy.[16]

Jews who announced "We're Conservative" in 1955 positioned themselves firmly—and proudly—in the center of the American Jewish denominational spectrum, neither as strict as the Orthodox Jews to the right ("We're not fanatics!"), nor as ritually streamlined as the Reform Jews to the left ("That place doesn't even look like a synagogue—they made us take our yarmulkes off!"). Conservative Jews thought of themselves as Americans on the street and Jews in the home and heart—the essence of moderation. The typical Conservative household in the 1950s had some semblance of Sabbath and holiday observances and attended synagogue at least several times a year. Even among those who attended services regularly on the mornings of Sabbaths and holidays, many went to work or ran errands, including shopping, in the afternoon. In terms of the Jewish education of children, a typical pattern was to send boys to afternoon supplementary Hebrew schools for several years, culminating in a festive bar mitzvah ceremony at age thirteen. Far fewer girls than boys from Conservative homes attended Hebrew school, because bat mitzvah ceremonies were not yet common in American synagogues. Although women sat side by side with men, they had no public ritual roles in Conservative synagogues. Rabbis sometimes called women up to lead English responsive readings.

Conservative Jews generally had warm feelings for Zionism and Israel—although few had actually visited the Jewish state—and felt Israel was an important haven for unfortunate, persecuted Jews around the world. The typical Conservative household had a blue Jewish National Fund (JNF) charity box on the kitchen counter and sent money to plant trees in Israel through the JNF for birthdays and other special occasions. Conservative Jews had largely Jewish friendship circles—although they believed friendships should be dictated by common interests, rather than religion or ethnicity—and a sense of solidarity with Jews around the world.

Except for the elite cadre, they were not especially well educated in terms of Jewish history and culture, but most Conservative men were familiar enough with liturgical Hebrew to follow the traditional services that were common in their synagogues. Conservative women worked for the synagogue and diverse Jewish causes through congregational Sisterhood women's organizations. The Sisterhood venue gave many women a chance to express their devotion to synagogues that gave them, as females, few other opportunities for social bonding or public Jewish roles. Many Conservative Jewish women attended college, but few worked outside the home, in keeping with American middle-class post–World War II social norms. Many Jewish women poured their energies into synagogue Sisterhoods and national Jewish organizations, like Hadassah, the Women's Zionist Organization of America.

Men, too, had their Brotherhood or Men's Club organizations, which sponsored events throughout the year. A common Conservative Brotherhood or Men's Club activity was the Sunday morning brunch after religious services, occasionally punctuated by some type of educational program. Indeed, until the Jewish feminist movement emerged out of second wave feminism in the late 1960s and early 1970s, weekday religious services themselves were their own kind of "men's club." In each synagogue, a small number of elite laypeople (many of whom had grown up in Orthodox homes and retained traditional attitudes) were distinguished by their Judaic knowledge and religious observance. These people were often the core of the morning prayer service (*minyan*) attendees, and from among that group the rabbi often drew his confidants.

Challenge and Change: Civil Rights

Important social movements in the 1960s and 1970s challenged this comfortable world and changed many aspects of the Conservative Jewish experience. The civil rights movement, emerging second wave feminism, the spread of antiauthoritarianism in various student movements and in the "hippie" and drug cultures, and the trauma of the 1967 Six Day War each changed attitudes and shifted priorities. For Jews across the denominational spectrum, working for civil rights became a passionate activity. Rabbis from the Conservative and Reform spheres both took highly visible roles. Among others, Abraham Joshua Heschel, a beloved rabbinic leader and scholar at The Jewish Theological Seminary, marched in Selma with the Reverend Martin Luther King Jr., and wrote: "Racism is Satanism, unmitigated evil." Heschel urged Jews to respond actively:

> Let us cease to be apologetic, cautious, timid. Racial tension and strife is both sin and punishment. *The Negro's plight,* the blighted areas in the large cities, are they not the fruit of our sins? ... This world, this society can be redeemed. God has a stake in our moral predicament. I cannot believe that God will be defeated.... The only remedy is *personal sacrifice.*[17]

As a group, Jews identified strongly with the traumatic experiences, suffering, and struggles of African Americans. Inspired by leaders like Heschel, many saw voluntarism and philanthropy for such causes as not just an American patriotic but also a Jewish activity. American Jews were also affected by the civil rights ethos in a more directly Jewish way. Some who had been reticent about flaunting their Jewishness began to seek out more information about Jewish history and culture and to show more intensive Jewish identification. The ethnoreligious pluralism that emerged out of the civil rights struggle was one of the factors contributing to a resurgence of interest in Jewish history, culture, and folkways.

Gender Egalitarianism and Conservative Judaism

Another utopian social trend that transformed American Judaism and had profound implications for the Conservative movement was second wave feminism. By the early 1970s, Jewish women in all wings of American Judaism had been influenced by feminism. Although the Reform and Reconstructionist Judaism movements would more quickly advance the idea that women could be rabbis, ordaining the first Reform female rabbi in 1972 and the first Reconstructionist female rabbi in 1974, the impact of feminism on the Conservative movement was far more traumatic and thus, arguably, more profound. Feminism galvanized the Conservative movement, splitting the movement's leadership and eventually providing a defining boundary on the right: By the end of the 1980s, Conservative Jews differed from Orthodox Jews because they believed that both *halakhah* and egalitarianism were sacred principles.

Within the Conservative movement the impetus toward feminism arose not only from American concerns about equal rights but also from the circumstances of an elite Conservative education. Conservative-raised girls who had been part of the LTF intensive supplementary school education, or had attended Jewish day schools, and had learned both prayer liturgy and conversational

Hebrew through many summers at Camp Ramah, grew up into women who were uncomfortable with and angry about their position as second-class citizens in their Conservative synagogues. They formed an advocacy, worship, and study group called Ezrat Nashim, a play on the Hebrew term for the women's section in a synagogue, with the literal meaning "women's help." Ezrat Nashim's campaign to change Conservative women's roles in public Judaism was aided by rabbis who felt that the exclusion of women from roles in public Judaism was immoral, an outmoded remnant of earlier sociological understandings of gender roles. The Conservative Rabbinical Assembly (RA) had already voted in the 1950s to permit women to be called to the Torah for *aliyot,* but halakhically it was a much bigger step to count them for a *minyan* (prayer quorum), which was approved in 1974. As the 1970s proceeded, with the dramatic example of female rabbis being ordained by Reform and Reconstructionist Judaism, pressure increased on Conservative leaders to follow suit.

Seminary Chancellor Dr. Gerson D. Cohen and Rabbi Wolfe Kelman, executive vice president of the RA, became determined that Conservative Judaism would not be left behind in this important modernizing move. At the annual RA convention in May 1977, the majority of the rabbis voted to ask for the formation of an interdisciplinary commission to study the role of women as spiritual leaders, to be presented to the RA in the two following years. The commission's report recommending ordination for women appeared in 1979, followed soon after by a strongly worded opposition paper, crafted by Saul Shapiro and sociologist Charles Liebman, warning that ordaining women would alienate the most committed core of Conservative laity. Opposition to the ordination of women was articulated by some of JTS's most illustrious Talmud scholars. Nevertheless, in 1980 the RA voted 156 to 115 in support of women's ordination, and in 1984 the seminary faculty voted to admit women to the rabbinical program. Amy Eilberg, the first woman to receive Conservative ordination, graduated in 1985, and by 1992 JTS had ordained thirty-two women rabbis. Today, the vast majority of Conservative synagogues in the United States are completely egalitarian, although a minority have retained differences in the treatment of men and women; in Canada, however, Conservative egalitarianism is far less common, in keeping with Canada's generally more conservative Jewish stance.

Shortly after the ordination decision was announced, a small number of pulpit rabbis and congregations split off from the Conservative movement to form the Union for Traditional Conservative Judaism, under the spiritual leadership of scholar Rabbi David Weiss-Halivni, who hoped that it would become the organizational hub of committed, traditional Conservative Jews and more liberal Modern Orthodox Jews. In order to enhance this hoped-for amalgam, the movement changed its name to the Union for Traditional Judaism—the UTJ, omitting the "Conservative" name brand. The new movement formed a rabbinical seminary, or *Metiftah*. Spirits were high for a short time when the Fellowship of Traditional Orthodox Rabbis officially joined forces with the UTJ. However, the UTJ never attracted the volume of congregations, pulpit rabbinical support, and lay leaders it had hoped to, in part because UTJ's male leadership avoided tackling the issue of women's roles directly. This was a key issue for Modern Orthodox liberals, who found a far more compelling home in JOFA, the Jewish Orthodox Feminist Alliance. When Edah, the liberal Modern Orthodox organization, closed its doors in 2006, UTJ leaders took out ads in Jewish newspapers urging Edah supporters to support UTJ, to little effect.

The UTJ continues to come out with learned *responsa* on halakhic issues and bulletins on the latest in *kashrut*. Thus, eclipsed by Conservative egalitarianism on the left and egalitarian passions among Modern Orthodox on their right, the UTJ has yet to carve out its own institutional niche.

From Comfort to Discomfort in the Center

In contrast to earlier rulings that only affected individual or personal behavior, the Conservative movement from the 1970s onward faced demanding policy decisions that profoundly affected the entire movement on an ideological as well as a pragmatic level and changed the lives of individuals and families within the movement. The ideological issue that galvanized the Conservative movement in the 1970s and 1980s was gender egalitarianism—decisions about women's roles in public Judaism, including leadership roles. Today, Conservative leaders wrestle with issues such as the appropriateness of admitting openly homosexual candidates to their rabbinical program, with some younger leaders strongly advocating the "moral" choice of doing so and traditionalists resisting it under the mantel of "authentic" Jewish law. Some urge the Conservative movement to follow the lead of the Reform movement in considering the children of Jewish fathers, as well as of Jewish mothers, to be Jews, while others cite centuries of tradition. Some declare that the Conservative movement, while guided in many ways by rabbinical law, is not a "halakhic movement" in the way that term is often understood,[18] while others insist that the organic evolution of rabbinic law means that one can be fully, halakhically observant even while working carefully toward change.

In struggling with these issues, Conservative Jewish leaders are torn between traditional Jewish values, articulated by centuries of rabbinic discourse, and Western values embodied in contemporary American culture. This tension is arguably the defining characteristic of contemporary Judaisms. As they consider future policies of the Conservative movement, rabbinic and lay leaders try, wherever possible, to find legal precedents to lend legitimacy to their decisions. Even in the absence of traditional precedents, however, they may decide that such contemporary sacred values as eradicating homophobia and creating more inclusive Jewish communities for diverse Jewish households override prior rabbinic rulings.

Conservation or Transformation in the Twenty-First Century?

Conservative Judaism today runs a broad gamut. At the most liberal end are near-Reconstructionist or near-Reform congregations that push the Conservative envelope toward liberalism. As historian and JTS Provost Jack Wertheimer has noted, Conservative congregations, especially on the West Coast, have been far less concerned with halakhic restraints:

> Like their counterparts in the other movements, Conservative rabbis have, both literally and figuratively ... "come down off the *bimah.*" Many younger rabbis sit or stand among the congregants rather than on a pulpit above them.... A number of Conservative synagogues have also followed the example of Reform and Reconstructionism in the use of musical instruments in the service, a practice contrary to rabbinic law and therefore generally avoided in earlier generations.[19]

By contrast, at the most halakhic end are traditionalist egalitarian congregations like Hadar in New York City, an independent, postdenominational congregation in which Conservative and Orthodox men and women share leadership in an essentially Orthodox liturgy and worship style. As sociologist Steven M. Cohen notes, the "slew of independent congregations" that bring together Conservative and Orthodox young adults—including large numbers of singles—are both a testament to the success of Conservative educational and camping institutions and a warning about the inability of the youngest members of the Conservative elite to find a home within the movement itself:

> Conservative Jews fell in number from 915,000 in 1990 to 660,000 in 2000. Of Jews affiliated with the three major denominational movements, Conservatism fell from 46 percent (and first place) in 1990 to just 36 percent (and second place, behind Reform) in 2000.... It has declined most precipitously in the younger age cohorts.... Rather than providing these committed and educated young adults with ongoing opportunities for movement involvement (retreats or reunions of fellow alumni of the movement's great educational system), and thereby grounding them in an alternate source of Jewish social networking, the movement has chosen to let escape many of its "best and brightest" youngsters.[20]

Cohen and many Conservative Jewish leaders are anxious about the movement's future because the proportion of Jews identifying as Conservative has decreased dramatically.

The movement has been whittled away from two directions by defections into other wings of Judaism to the left and to the right, which have undergone their own evolutions. Cohen reports that the number of Jews shifting from Conservative to Orthodox affiliation doubled from 5 to 10 percent in the decade from 1990 to 2000. While Conservative Judaism initially grew because many American Jews thought Orthodoxy was too "medieval" and Reform was too "un-Jewish," rejecting concepts of Zionism, Jewish peoplehood, and Hebrew as a useful Jewish language,[21] today Modern Orthodoxy has lost its medieval veneer and Reform its Protestant ethos, as we discussed in the two previous chapters. The socioeconomic Americanization of Modern Orthodoxy and the increased traditionalism of the Reform movement have made it more difficult for Conservative leaders to define their niche in the marketplace of Jewish religious expressions.

One of the primary immediate challenges facing the movement is how to deal with the growing number of intermarried families. Unlike the feminist transformation of Conservative Judaism, which was championed primarily by elite women and some men, contemporary pressure to relax attitudes toward intermarriage derives from the Conservative folk. Traditionalists in the movement argue that more inclusiveness toward interfaith families will inevitably lead to less intensive connections with traditional Judaism.

Professor Arnold Eisen, succeeding Ismar Schorsch as chancellor of the Jewish Theological Seminary, is known for his writings on contemporary transformations in Jewish religious belief and practice, and on the profound effect of individualistic values on today's American Jewishness. Eisen suggests, "Normalcy and covenant both require adaptation to new circumstances. Only the tension between them is a constant."[22] Under his leadership, the elite and folk of the Conservative movement will wrestle with the current pressure to adapt in order to ride the wave of the future.

Eisen and other Conservative leaders are not considering these issues in a vacuum. The strongly articulated opinions and experiences of Conservative folk have an important influence on Conservative leaders. The decisions that Conservative Jews make at this twenty-first-century crossroads may be the most momentous since the movement emerged as a distinct entity one hundred years ago and will deeply affect the future experiences of Jews who find their home in the movement. Only time will tell whether Conservative Jewishness will be able to use the "tension" that has been a "constant" to maintain its position as a centrist movement.

7

An American Kaleidoscope
Reconstructionist, Renewal, and Secular Forms of American Jewishness

The diversity of Jewishness in America is expressed not only through the three oldest organized "rivers" of Reform, Orthodox, and Conservative American Judaism, which themselves include internal diversity, but in the smaller "streams" of Reconstructionist Judaism and the Jewish Renewal movement. Nondenominational or postdenominational institutions attract increasing numbers of supporters and are producing their own leaders in schools such as the Academy of Jewish Religion and the Boston Hebrew College Rabbinical Program. The proliferation of transdenominational community day schools has also supported postdenominational attitudes. In addition, a large and growing segment of American Jewry connects to Jewishness not religiously but through some form of secular identification. Frequently, these streams flow out of the larger ones, and sometimes reconnect with them over the course of time. Reconstructionist, Renewal, and secular forms of Jewishness interact with other forms of Jewishness, often have a great impact on them, and sometimes change each other's direction and flow. In addition, individuals as well as movements interact with each other: Many (perhaps most) American Jews have looked to more than one form of religious and/or secular or cultural Jewishness as they negotiate their Jewish identity.

Reconstructing American Jewish Life

Reconstructionist Judaism can be said to be the only form of purely American Judaism, created in the United States without any European antecedents. Reconstructionist Judaism began as a movement grounded in the social scientific rationalism and pragmatism of twentieth-century America. Without overt pressure to adapt to Protestant norms, twentieth-century American Reconstructionist Judaism focused on the "folk," the ordinary Jewish people, and the way they understood and lived their own religious culture. The epigram most closely associated with the movement is its founder's pithy "The past has a vote, not a veto," and the operational Reconstructionist slogan could be (greatly) simplified as "Judaism is what Jews do." These sayings clearly reflect what many American Jews believe. Even though the percentage of American Jews identifying as Reconstructionists hovers around 3 percent, the movement has influence and significance far beyond its numbers.

The founder of Reconstructionist Judaism, Mordecai Kaplan, received his training within more traditional European and American wings of Judaism. Kaplan was born in Eastern Europe (Lithuania) in 1881 but moved to the United States as a child. Like Schechter, he grew up in the world of Orthodoxy—his father was a *mashgiach* (ritual supervisor) of kosher slaughterers—but his intellectual development and religious experiences were entirely American. Kaplan earned two rabbinical ordinations: one Conservative, at JTS (1902), and one Orthodox (1908), from the European Rabbi Isaac Jacob Reines, the founder of modern religious Zionism. Kaplan's first rabbinic position was at the Orthodox Congregation Kehilath Jeshurun, where he helped to found the Orthodox Young Israel movement, which was initially a liberal, lively, participatory environment. In 1909 Kaplan moved to the Jewish Theological Seminary to head the Conservative Teachers Institute.

By the time Kaplan proposed his "Program for the Reconstruction of Judaism" in 1920, he had come to believe that "Orthodoxy is the bane of Judaism." He was one of the chief architects of the Jewish center concept of the synagogue—the synagogue as a "second home" that offered social and athletic as well as religious aspects of life—and founded the Jewish Center on New York's Upper West Side. He left these more traditional affiliations and resigned from the Jewish Center in 1922 to found a new congregation called the Society for the Advancement of Judaism (SAJ), continuing to teach at the Jewish Theological Seminary until his retirement in 1963.[1]

Kaplan, who urged Jews to deconstruct, thoughtfully consider, and "reconstruct" a Judaism that could be meaningful to the modern mind, is regarded as one of the great thinkers of twentieth-century American Judaism. In his seminal work, *Judaism as a Civilization,* he described an inclusive construct that incorporated diverse elements, such as Israel as a country with Jewish culture, the Hebrew language, Jewish literatures, the Jewish legal system, artistic expressions, and Jewish customs and folkways. Kaplan rejected *supernaturalism* in favor of *naturalism.* Rejecting the traditional understanding of a transcendent God who created the world, revealed divine guidelines in the Torah, and guides history from afar, Kaplan's notion of Divinity resembles the immanent deity of the Romantic movement: God is the process of working toward social responsibility, morality, and world peace, as apprehended by human beings, both Jews and non-Jews alike. Many Jewish folkways had wisdom and meaning in the modern world, but others did not, Kaplan posited, and should be rationally considered and discarded.[2]

As historian Jonathan Sarna points out, many Conservative rabbis and thinkers privately agreed with Kaplan's rational revision of an organically conceived Judaism, finding its air of comfort with modern concepts and ways of approaching the past "extraordinarily liberating." However, few of them actually followed Kaplan into the new movement he created.[3] Not surprisingly, sociologist Charles Liebman argued that Reconstructionist Judaism's tenets, built on American attitudes of a religion "of the people and by the people," reflects the way most American Jews think of Judaism, regardless of their official affiliation.[4]

In the twenty years between Kaplan's retirement and his death in 1983, Reconstructionist Judaism underwent shifts in emphasis that launched major new trends throughout the American Jewish community, including egalitarianism in the 1960s and early 1970s, embrace of homosexual participation in Jewish leadership in the 1970s and 1980s, and increasing interest in spirituality and mystical experience in the 1980s and beyond. Kaplan's attention to the experience of God in nature contributed to trends in both mystical and spiritual explorations and also to the concept of *ecokashrut*, the idea that working on behalf of ecological causes is a profoundly Jewish idea with bases in the Bible and other Jewish religious sources. Each of these directions, which were nurtured in the Reconstructionist environment, changed Jewish life across denominational lines.

The Reconstructionist Rabbinical College (RRC) in Philadelphia spearheaded egalitarian directions in American Judaism. The RRC included women as soon as its doors opened in 1968 and also immediately accepted as fully Jewish the children of a Jewish father and a non-Jewish mother, anticipating by almost two decades the "patrilineal decision" of the Reform movement in 1983. Although the RRC ordained its first woman rabbi, Sandy Eisenberg Sasso, in 1974, two years after the Reform movement, it accepted women into its rabbinical program earlier. The college has been the home of much important Jewish feminist scholarship, including explorations of women in the Bible, liturgy and rituals, and gender and power. Because the RRC's ordination of women predated the Conservative movement by a decade, some women who considered themselves basically Conservative by conviction studied for ordination at RRC and obtained their first positions at Reconstructionist congregations. The school's Jewish Women's Study program continues to attract female rabbinical candidates who are especially interested in exploring feminist issues as part of their rabbinical training. New egalitarian programs have focused on the religious lives of Jewish girls and women, in the "Rosh Hodesh Project" and other initiatives.

The RRC has also led the way toward the inclusion of gay and lesbian rabbinical and lay leaders. That change first took place quietly, on the ground, and then was officially ratified. Observers noted that gay and especially lesbian rabbinical candidates pursued their Jewish educational training at the RRC before the faculty voted on the issue in 1984. Rebecca Alpert and Jacob Staub comment on this groundbreaking initiative:

> The RRC took a courageous step in admitting gay and lesbian students. The decision opened up the discussion of the role of gay and lesbian Jews for the whole Reconstructionist movement. In 1992, a joint Reconstructionist Commission on Homosexuality, which included rabbinic and congregational representatives, published a lengthy document in support of gay men and lesbians in Jewish life. The report emphasized the ways in which gay men and lesbians are like others in the Jewish community who are involved in loving, long-term relationships. The statement welcomed gay men and lesbians into the community as leaders and teachers.[5]

The Reform movement eventually followed suit, and it seems likely that, under the leadership of Professor Arnold Eisen, the

Jewish Theological Seminary will be next. Thus, more than two decades after the RRC made what was at the time a controversial decision, that decision continues to have repercussions in American Jewish religious life.

According to a study of recent issues and trends in the American synagogue, about 100 congregations nationwide affiliate with the Federation of Reconstructionist Congregations and Havurot. Another 120 affiliate with the National Havurah Committee, and an additional 35 affiliate with Aleph: Alliance for Jewish Renewal, which, as discussed below, sometimes have links with the Reconstructionist movement. As Wertheimer summarizes the current state of congregational life:

> Many of the congregations meet in their own buildings, and approximately two-thirds have rabbis. In the more established congregations, the Sabbath morning service is the focal event of the week, whereas in the smaller *havurot* twice monthly Friday evening services are central. Reconstructionism proudly embraces an especially large percentage of intermarried families.... 44 percent of self-identified Reconstructionist adults were intermarried.[6]

Reconstructionist congregations today tend to be smaller than the typical Conservative or Reform congregation. In some ways, they are more avant garde, in that they are willing to try spontaneous new approaches to prayer and congregational activities. Some Reconstructionist congregations are composed of members with excellent Jewish educations, who promote a fairly intense schedule of study and worship. Others are more casual and less intense. In many congregations the rabbi-figure does not play a traditional rabbinical role. In keeping with the movement's stress on egalitarianism of status, as well as of gender, some congregations regard the rabbi as a facilitator rather than a leader. Some congregations, in fact, have para-rabbinic or lay rabbinic leaders, rather than leaders with classical rabbinical training. Reconstructionist Judaism may be small, but, like other American Jewish movements, it is diverse.

Renewing Jewish Spirituality

Perhaps the most sweeping changes in American Jewish congregational life were both shaped and symbolized by the independent Havurah movement, which borrowed a name (and some personalities) from a similar, slightly earlier initiative in Reconstructionist Judaism. The Havurah movement was born in the 1960s, a time of civil unrest and social change that focused on, among other things, young people's disillusionment with the churches and synagogues of their parents, which they faulted for being overly concerned with buildings and congregational finances (humorously termed the *edifice complex*) and too little concerned with social justice and/or spiritual explorations and expressions.

Some American Jews took on the American Jewish organizational establishment, both through protests and by creating Jewish groups in their own image. Havurat Shalom was established in Somerville, Massachusetts, in 1968, under the leadership of Arthur Green, who would later head the RRC and, still later, a new, postdenominational rabbinical seminary at Boston's Hebrew College. Havurat Shalom, like other countercultural efforts of the time, declared its antipathy for "self-satisfied, rich suburbanites" and "smug institutions," and saw as its mission "a new model of serious Jewish study." Adopting a commune ethos, the group prayed by candlelight, sat on the floor, and explored new models for spiritual expression. Many of them had been raised within the Conservative movement, which they condemned for its "bleak" lack of depth.[7]

Versions of Havurah-style worship and study groups began spreading within all three wings of Judaism in cities across the

United States. Typically, the group would break off from an established synagogue and find a place to meet on a regular basis, either in members' homes or in a church classroom or social hall. The Havurah groups placed a great deal of emphasis on participatory behavior. In the beginning, most of the groups were run by men, since men had more liturgical skills. However, with the simultaneous growth of the Jewish women's movement, as more and more women acquired liturgical skills—and demanded equal leadership opportunities—Havurot (plural for Havurah) became characterized by gender egalitarianism. Indeed, some in the Havurah movement took a militant stance on the issue. Although for years the annual Havurah convention was quite eclectic and tolerated many different styles of worship, eventually the leadership voted not to support any Orthodox groups in their ranks who wanted to pray with a *mekhitzah* separation between men and women.

Countercultural, hands-on Judaism was greatly enhanced by the publication of *The Jewish Catalogue* in 1973, a kind of how-to book modeled on *The Whole Earth Catalogue*. The book provided instructions on how to create one's own Jewish experiences without depending on synagogues and other Jewish organizations. It placed a premium on do-it-yourself Judaism—baking your own matzah, making your own Hanukkah candles—and very little emphasis on more traditional activities, such as Torah study or ritual observances. Indeed, in a sardonic essay titled "The Greening of Jewish America," Conservative sociologist Marshall Sklare satirized the catalogue's slant by writing that the authors of the catalogue seemed sad that there were so few opportunities for working with wax in the Jewish calendar year.[8] Regardless of Sklare's scorn, *The Jewish Catalogue* was repeatedly reissued and continued to serve as a widespread sourcebook even as newer, more radical texts were published and circulated. Writer Bill Novak, who created a periodical called *Response* as a vehicle for Jewish countercultural writings, characterized the movement as an intentional "bypass" of organized American Judaism:

> The counter culture I have spoken of is a new and growing organism. It is very small in actual numbers, but involved in it are some of the brightest and most creative young people in Jewish life today. The overall movement is intentionally vague, ad-hoc, and decentralized, for its members have learned to fear structures more than anything else.[9]

That "new and growing organism" eventually went in two directions. For many, there was a kind of regression toward more bourgeois lifestyles. After bitterly fighting the Havurah phenomenon, a number of congregations began instead to co-opt their local Havurah, inviting participants to meet in the synagogue instead of in off-site locations. Indeed, many Havurah members were ready to be co-opted, because they had gotten older, married, and had children who now needed Jewish educations and were approaching bar and bat mitzvah age. The Havurah located in the synagogue enabled them to continue to feel countercultural even as their lives conformed more and more to middle-class norms and concerns. Delighted with the success of this tactic, some synagogues created their own small Havurah worship-and-study group in the chapel or classroom, a preemptive strategy for congregants displeased with large congregational worship formats.

Others in the Havurah movement, by contrast, became more radical and experimental, influenced by Eastern religions and growing American spiritualist trends, in a movement frequently now called *Jewish Renewal*. Renewal congregations tend to be small, to meet infrequently, and to explore unconventional and experiential modes of spiritual expression, rejecting typical Reconstructionist services as excessively cerebral. Jewish Renewal has expanded in an environment that celebrates mysticism and spirituality. Madonna and other celebrities famously espouse Kabbalah, and, in what one reporter calls "a grass-roots religious movement," young Americans seeking dates on Internet websites, including Jews, often identify themselves as SBNR—"Spiritual But Not Religious"—to indicate that they don't like "how negative atheism sounds."[10] Jewish Renewal is nourished not only by this fascination, but also by specifically Jewish musical, emotional, and spiritualist elements. Rabbi Zalman Schachter-Shalomi, one of the most influential figures in the movement, has urged Jews to recapture "intimacy and ecstasy" in their relationships with God, drawing on tales of Hasidic masters as examples of people "wrapped in a holy flame."[11]

Jewish mysticism is sometimes combined with other religious traditions in services, leading to combinations such as "JuBus" (Jewish Buddhists), "Jufis" (Jewish Sufis), and "Hinjews" (Hindu Jews). Tai chi and yoga meditation exercises are routinely used in some Renewal services. The Renewal movement has its own prayer book, *Ohr Chadash: New Paths for Shabbat Morning,* and runs a summer retreat, *Elat Chayyim.* Historian Jack Wertheimer suggests that "Renewal has become somewhat less touchy-feely under the recent leadership of Rabbi Daniel Siegel, but it nevertheless remains highly experimental."[12] Given the loose organization and the principles of nonconformity that characterize the Renewal movement, it seems destined to continue providing a home for wide-ranging varieties of Jewishness.

Secular and Cultural Jews

From its beginnings, *Jewishness* had a connotation of peoplehood, with a distinctive set of social values and cultural expressions, as well as religion. During the biblical and Second Temple periods, geography also helped define Judaism. Early Jews were people who lived in or who had come from Judaea. In the contemporary period, these interwoven threads are often disentangled. For secular Jews, the religious threads of the picture are removed, and land, social values, culture, and/or peoplehood become most prominent as the primary sources of identification.

The concept of secular Jews—people who identify as Jews, who do not remove themselves from the Jewish people, but reject the concept of God—arguably began with the brilliant Jewish philosopher Baruch Spinoza (d. 1677). Spinoza was eventually excommunicated by the Jewish community of Amsterdam, but he himself never rejected his Jewish identity and never converted to Christianity. In a famous essay, Isaac Deutscher called Spinoza and other Jewishly identifying atheists "non-Jewish Jews" and traced their lineage all the way back to a talmudic figure called Akher, literally "the Other." Akher rejected the basics of Jewish belief but remained a close friend of his rabbinical colleagues. Such Jewish heretics, Deutscher asserts, "belong to Jewish tradition."[13]

The viewpoint that diverse voices have long characterized Jewish cultures is shared by Israeli writer and thinker Amos Oz, who sees the development of Secular Jewish Humanism as the logical evolution of the diversity of Jewish experience: "The culture of Israel has a kind of anarchistic core," he claims. "We don't want discipline." He too takes Jewish diversity back to the basics: "The people of Israel always quarreled with its prophets, and the prophets always quarreled with God. The kings fought with the people and with the prophets." In Oz's summary of the history of Judaisms, the mainstream is "a polyphony, a chorus of voices," characterized by "a culture of argumentation." According to this view, Jews who look to authoritative voices inspired by God are "enclaves of blind submission," fundamentally different than historical Jewish communities, "a deviation from mainstream Judaism, even as they claim to be its truest expression."[14]

The concept is diametrically opposed to that of Jewishness as purely a personal religious commitment, or, in the language of nineteenth-century German Jews, strictly "a confession." As Herb

Silverman, president of the Secular Coalition for America, notes, "Many gentiles are confused by the term 'Jewish atheist' because 'Christian atheist' really is an oxymoron. To be a Christian, one must believe in Jesus."[15]

Some secular Jews in Israel today insist that geography once again is the primary identifying characteristic of the Jew. Israeli novelist A. B. Yehoshua, for example, insists that all Jewish identification is transitory except that which consists of living in and identifying with the Land of Israel and speaking Hebrew, the language of the land and the people. Yehoshua has expressed these views in many contexts, rejecting any value of Diaspora Judaisms—and any hope for their survival—and depicting those who believe in and practice any form of religious Judaism as no different than the most right-wing Israeli Orthodox sects. Not surprisingly, Yehoshua describes these undifferentiated religious Jews in the most unflattering terms, as people believing in and conducting their lives according to outmoded superstitions, while neglecting their true responsibilities to the people and the Land of Israel (the ultra-Orthodox do not serve in the Israeli Defense Forces). Claiming that Israel has no connection to historical Judaisms, Yehoshua believes that the only significant and enduring identity is Israeli, the way a Frenchman's identity is French, a national identification with a national language and culture.[16]

A conviction that contemporary Jews are free to select and emphasize aspects of Jewish culture and to deemphasize or reject others is, of course, not limited to secular Jews. Many modern liberal theistic Jews (Jews who believe in God), especially Reform and Reconstructionist Jews, also subscribe to a Judaic approach that privileges free will. Moreover, the state of belief—or disbelief—is often fluid, and individuals may subscribe to differing feelings in response to events or life-cycle changes. This fluidity itself would not be possible without the secularization of Jewish life within the cosmopolitan social and intellectual environments into which Jews were thrust with the advent of modernity. Spinoza seems to many the prototype of modern secularism because he transcended narrow religious boundaries and prescriptions. Deutscher argues that Spinoza made a greater contribution to the history of philosophy than Christian philosophers René Descartes and Gottfried Wilhelm Leibnitz, who could not free themselves from "the shackles of medieval scholastic tradition." Influenced by Spain, Holland, Germany, England, and Renaissance Italy, Spinoza rejected the Jewish notions of chosenness and a God of Jewish history, and instead forged an independent understanding of a universalistic God and ethical system.

Jewish Secular Socialism

The intellectual inheritors of Spinoza's broad vision were public intellectuals such as Karl Marx, Leon Trotsky, and Sigmund Freud. They drew from their ancient culture, but they were not limited by it, and were, in Deutscher's words, "non-Jewish Jews."[17]

Deutscher meant this terminology as a compliment, but it is doubtful that it would be understood as such by secular American Jews today. Contemporary secular Jews are as diverse as any other group of Jews, and we may say that secular Jewishness itself today is "polyphonic."

Some secular Jews are the intellectual descendents of East European secular socialists. Abraham Cahan, for example, arrived in New York in the 1880s as an anarchist. Within a few years, he had substantially adapted his brand of socialism to the labor movement to fit his new environment and went on to help found the International Ladies Garment Workers' Union and the social Yiddish daily newspaper *Forverts* (*The Forward*). Within a few years of his arrival, Cahan was writing novels in English, including Yekl (on which the 1974 film *Hester Street* was based) and the critically acclaimed *Rise of David Levinsky,* which brilliantly critiques the aridness and lack of courage and humanity in the capitalist enterprise.

Many working Jews were secular socialists, even as some simultaneously pursued their capitalistic dreams. Alfred Kazin wrote movingly about his cousins—single, working women who adored cultural expressions—speaking with passion and insight about dancers Anna Pavlova and Vaslav Nijinsky, film, and socialist doctrine. In 1910, for example, two-thirds of the women employed in the garment industry were Jewish! Jewish women, unlike the daughters of some other ethnic groups, were allowed to travel to and from work without chaperones, to keep most of their earnings, to attend high school and college after work, and to participate in labor unions if they wished. As a result, secular young immigrant women were a major force in the emerging labor movement.[18] Reading back to that important and often forgotten period, Barbra Streisand created a popular image of one of these idealistic, secular, but very ethnically Jewish young women in her retrospective film *The Way We Were* (1973).

Socialism is no longer an engaging concept for most American Jews. Gone are the places that nurtured the intense Jewishness of socialist immigrants, usually living in areas of dense Jewish population, such as the Bronx, New York, or Montreal, Canada. Their children—most of them now middle-aged or older—often remember going to secular Yiddish schools, hearing Yiddish spoken on the street, and receiving from their parents a hearty disdain of religious piety. For most people who grew up in socialist, Yiddish-speaking, antireligious Jewish environments, only the disdain for religiosity remains of that world. Secular socialist Jewishness was largely a one-generation phenomenon.

Secular Social Activism

Replacing socialism as a central organizing principle of Jewishness are ideas like working to make the world a better place, often referred to as *tikkun olam*. For much of the twentieth century, generations of Jews worked within the general and Jewish organizational worlds to express what they saw as a Jewishly inspired commitment to social justice. Some had primarily universalistic approaches and joined the Peace Corps or other nonsectarian organizations.

A significant segment of American Jews felt responsible for Jewish communities around the world and worked for secular Jewish organizations such as the Joint Distribution Committee, Jewish federations, and a host of others. Jonathan Woocher, observing the deep belief such Jews had in "sacred survival" of the Jewish polity, dubbed their commitments "Jewish Civil Religion." Although Woocher insists that this "is *not* simply a species of Jewish secularism,"[19] the majority of its proponents for most of the twentieth century did in fact define themselves as "secular Jews," as opposed to "synagogue Jews." Today, most American Jews who choose to work for Jewish organizations are also synagogue members. Secular Jews today are much more likely to devote their world-improving energies to nonsectarian organizations or, when they focus on Jewish causes, to new, specifically secular organizations, such as the Jewish Fund for Social Justice or Ruth Messinger's American Jewish World Service.

American Secular Jewishness

When most American Jews say, "I'm really kind of a secular Jew," what they mean is, "I'm not very religiously observant." Their words do not necessarily imply agnosticism or atheism, as much as their understanding of themselves as disinterested or lax in Jewish practice and engagement. The fact of their Jewishness may or may not be significant relative to their core psychological identification, but it does not occupy any central place in their regular activities. Because America today is basically a friendly place for Jews, even weakly identified young American Jews seldom bother to deny their Jewish descent.

The current comfort with the Jewish label marks a change from the first half of the twentieth century, when this particular type of secular Jew loudly declared American identity while proclaiming the irrelevance of Jewish descent. In the 1930s, '40s, and '50s, many among the relatively small number of interfaith marriages involved this variety of secular Jews, who were anxious to leave behind what they saw as the restricted, constraining world of Jewish identification. Memoirs of Jews in the arts and entertainment industries pungently reveal the voices of those who thought their Jewishness more or less irrelevant. Ben Hecht, writing in 1954, related the following anecdote about his frustrating attempt in 1942 to get Hollywood's powerful Jews to intercede on behalf of "stateless and Palestinian Jews":

> I called on David [Selznick] the next day and was happy to find there was no cringing stowaway in my friend. Nevertheless, he was full of arguments. They were not the arguments of a Jew but a non-Jew.
>
> "I don't want anything to do with your cause," said David, "for the simple reason that it's a Jewish political cause. And I am not interest in Jewish political problems. I'm an American and not a Jew. I'm interested in this war as an American. It would be silly of me to pretend suddenly that I'm a Jew, with some sort of full-blown Jewish psychology."
>
> "If I can prove you are a Jew, David," I said, "will you sign the telegram as co-sponsor with me?"

The two men agreed that Selznick would name three non-Jews and Hecht would call each of them, with Selznick "eavesdropping on an extension," and ask them if Selznick were Jewish. Selznick's

list included Martin Quigley, publisher of the *Motion Picture Exhibitor's Herald;* Nunnally Johnson; and Leland Hayward. Each had the same affirmative answer. Hayward, the most vociferous, simply exploded: "For God's sake, what's the matter with David? He's a Jew and he knows it." Hecht recalls, "David honorably admitted defeat. Apparently in everybody's eyes but his own he was a Jew. His name went on the telegram."[20]

By contrast, for a deeply committed group of principled atheists who are attached to Jewish values and culture, secular Judaism is not a default mode but an important expression of Jewish identity. Secular Jewish Humanists believe that Jewish culture has very important teachings for Jews and for the world. They believe that these gifts are unconnected to belief in God or any type of supernaturalism. They are convinced that the growing number of secular Jews around the world are being deprived of their own cultural birthright because they mistakenly imagine that they can only participate in Jewish culture if they are "believers." Emphasizing the universalism and the basic secularism of Jewish ethical and moral messages, Secular Jewish Humanists are deeply engaged by their vision of Jewishness and have established organizations, programs, and schools to help spread their message.

The Society for Humanistic Judaism (SHJ), established in 1969, was long under the leadership of Rabbi Sherman T. Wine. It lists as its goals:

- Enables Humanistic Jews throughout the world to communicate with one another.
- Creates celebrational, inspirational, and educational materials.
- Helps to organize Humanistic Jewish chapters and Havurot.
- Serves the needs of individual Humanistic Jews who cannot find communities that espouse their beliefs.

- Promotes the training of rabbis, leaders, and teachers for Humanistic Jewish communities.
- Belongs to an international community of Secular Humanistic Jews.

As this mission statement list makes clear, for Jews affiliating with the Secular Humanistic Jewish movement, principled atheism—"independent of supernatural authority"—and attachment to Jewish values, ideas, and the Jewish community go hand in hand.[21]

According to SHJ Executive Director Bonnie Cousens, "Humanistic Judaism began as an idea in a single congregation. It grew and flourished in the hearts and minds of the congregants. And it spread. First to two congregations, and then ... to others. Now there are 32 congregations and communities across North America."[22] The International Federation of Secular and Humanistic Jews (IFSHJ) has annual conferences, complete with scholarly lectures on topics in Judaica and Sabbath services, at which participants sing nontheistic versions of traditional melodies, such as "I lift mine eyes up unto the hills, from whence comes my help? My help comes from myself." Humanistic congregations have Sunday schools, and children in the congregations have bar and bat mitzvah ceremonies at age thirteen. The goal of the SHJ clearly is not to ignore Jewish history and traditions, but to express Jewishness in a secular, cultural, nonsupernaturalistic way.

One of the chief proponents of the IFSHJ is British philanthropist Felix Posen. The Posen Foundation has given generous grants to twenty-five schools in Israel and across the United States to implement an academic program that teaches courses on secular Jewish culture. These courses are particularly targeted at nonobservant students, who frequently have little exposure to Jewish history and ideas. Titled the Posen Project, the program requires grantees to teach a prescribed sequence of courses with curricula designed by Myrna Baron, executive director of the New

York–based Center for Cultural Judaism. The goal of the program is to make Jewish intellectual, cultural, and ethical texts and ideas available to students who would not ordinarily take Jewish studies courses.[23]

Very different is the attitude in many European, South American, and Israeli settings, where a fiercely antireligious secularism is not uncommon. For these secular Jews, Jewishness is simply an ethnicity, with neither religious nor peoplehood aspects. Born Jewish (and often with many Jewish friends) these secular Jews proudly declare themselves to be primarily French or Argentinean or Israeli, with no connections to the Jewish religion or to the Jewish people. Clearly, the category of secular and cultural Jews is as diverse as other forms of contemporary Jewishness.

8

Jews by Choice

Converts in the Jewish Community

Most Americans who consider themselves Jews were "born into" Jewishness through ethnic descent. Some, however, become Jewish through assent, converting to Judaism in a process that usually involves study, immersion in a *mikveh* (ritual bath), and, for men, an actual or symbolic circumcision. For some, the decision to convert to Judaism is linked to dating, living with, or marrying a Jew. For others, the journey into Judaism is unconnected to romantic involvements. After the conversion ceremony is completed, these Jews by Choice, as they are often called, are considered by Jewish law to be full members of the Jewish faith and the Jewish community.

Conversion is a topic of intense interest today because more than one-third of American Jews are married to non-Jews, and close to half of recent "Jewish" marriages are mixed marriages between individuals of Jewish and non-Jewish descent.[1] Furthermore, four out of five cohabiting Jews are involved in interfaith relationships. However, although the number of Jews marrying non-Jews has climbed from decade to decade, the proportion of spouses deciding to convert to Judaism has not risen commensurately.[2] Both the 1990 and the 2000–2001 National Jewish Population Surveys indicate that the number of people converting to and from Judaism during recent decades has been about equal.[3]

Converts to Judaism help to create households with distinctively more Jewish demographic and ethnoreligious profiles than families with one Jewish and one non-Jewish spouse. Conversionary households almost universally aim to raise their children as Jews, according to their own description.[4]

By contrast, the proportion of intermarried couples hoping to raise children within Judaism and no other religion has remained at about one-third, according to National Jewish Population Surveys conducted by the United Jewish Communities (UJC) in 1990 and 2000–2001.[5]

Mixed-marriage families that choose to raise completely Jewish children are sometimes very successful and have received both popular and scholarly attention. In her article, "Can a Gentile Wife Raise Jewish Kids?" for example, Gabriele Glaser paints a glowing picture of non-Jewish mothers who are "*enjuivée,* infused with Judaism," who read "Jewish magazines" and prepare Rosh Hashanah brisket and "sumptuous and spiritual Passover seders."[6] A most notable example of the Christian parent committed to raising a Jewish child is Professor Harvey Cox, a Sabbath-and-Jewish-holiday-observing Harvard Divinity School Christian theologian married to a Jewish woman. Cox has written and spoken articulately and in detail about his attachment to the Jewish cycle of holidays and life-cycle events. In perhaps his most passionate mission statement, he challenges Christian parents of Jewish children, "to reassure Jews by words and actions that we are also committed to a future for the Jewish people" by ensuring that there will be a new generation of Jews.[7]

Statistically, however, such households are unusual, and for the 1.5 million Americans who grew up in mixed-marriage households, having more than one religious tradition often seems both normative and normal.[8] The 2000–2001 National Jewish

Population Survey (NJPS) revealed that, among American Jews ages twenty-five to forty-nine, those with two Jewish parents had a 28 percent mixed-marriage rate, whereas those with only one Jewish parent had a 77 percent mixed-marriage rate.[9] Thus, rising rates of intermarriage are greatly increased by the second- or third-generation intermarriage of children who grew up in interfaith families. Conversion to Judaism, by contrast, offers the potential for more Jewishly engaged households.

Three Types of Converts

Converts are not a monolithic group, and their levels of Judaic connections can vary dramatically. Jews by Choice can be divided into roughly three different profiles: Activist, Accommodating, or Ambivalent converts to Judaism. Activist converts have very high levels of Jewish connections, sometimes exceed the Jewishness of their spouses, and statistically raise the Jewish index of the whole cohort of converts. Accommodating converts try to establish the level of Jewishness that their partners seem to wish. Ambivalent converts, on the other hand, have mixed feelings about their choices to convert and are the group of converts most likely to incorporate Christian observances into their familial holiday calendar.

About 30 percent of Jews by Choice can be described as Activist converts. This group tends to report stories of powerful spiritual journeys into Judaism and say they feel part of the Jewish people and Jewish destiny. Many Activists start on the road to conversion before they meet the Jew to whom they will become engaged or married.[10] Others do not investigate formal conversion until they meet a Jew they wish to marry, but are interested in Jews and Judaism from an early age, and once on the road to Judaism they tend to give up other religious observances and to be fully committed to living Jewishly. Converts who join Orthodox or Conservative congregations are disproportionately Activist converts, but Activists are prominent in Reform lay and professional leadership as well.

One segment among the Activist convert population becomes extraordinarily, intensely involved in Jewish life, including taking Jewish leadership roles. These star-level Activist converts are characterized by three factors: (1) They moved toward Jewish identity even before they met their current partner or spouse; (2) they are involved with or married to a deeply committed Jew, often someone with extensive Jewish education and vital Jewish commitments and interests; and (3) they have found Jewishly committed social networks who support and reinforce their commitments to Judaism.

Very attracted by Jewish holiday celebrations, Activist converts are often particularly fond of Shabbat and go to great lengths to ensure that Shabbat is marked on a regular basis. Not infrequently, it is the Activist convert—not the Jewish spouse—who initiates these activities. Sometimes the extended families of the Jewish spouse are dismayed by the religious intensity of the Activist convert. Contradicting data indicating that converts relate primarily to Judaism as a religion, rather than to the Jews as a people, Activist converts often relate intensely to Jewish peoplehood. Characteristically, the Activist convert is intensely supportive of Israel and frequently volunteers to take leadership roles in the wider Jewish community.

The majority—but not all—of Activist converts are women. Both jokes and anecdotal stories about such converts often conclude with the astonished born-Jewish husband watching his intensely Jewish-by-Choice wife scurrying around her kosher kitchen, and wailing, "Oh my God, I married my mother!" Activist converts include men and especially women who become prominent rabbis and spiritually moving cantors, dynamic synagogue presidents, brilliant Jewish scholars, and devoted communal professionals. While men are certainly among the Activist converts, they are more likely to be women, because the total number of female converts far outweighs male Jews by Choice and because women in general greatly outnumber men in Jewish adult educational contexts.

Accommodating converts make up the largest segment of Jews by Choice—almost 40 percent. They often remember having warm feelings toward Jews and Judaism during their childhood and adolescence. Although the Accommodating convert typically does not think about conversion until asked to consider it by the romantic partner, spouse, family, or rabbi, this convert overcomes any initial reluctance and acquiesces with some eagerness to the process of classes and conversion. Unlike the Activist converts who often take the initiative in upgrading the family's Judaic observances, accommodating converts usually let the born-Jewish spouse take the lead in terms of household religious rituals and ceremonies, diligently and sometimes enthusiastically enabling a variety of Jewish connections and practices. Not infrequently, the Accommodating convert joins Jewish organizations, but grounds most of her Jewish life in the home, extended family, and friendship circles. Accommodating converts are, not surprisingly, very influenced by the strength of Jewish commitment—or lack of it—of the Jewish spouse, family, and friends.

Ambivalent converts, making up about 30 percent of those who undergo a formal conversion process, have second thoughts about agreeing to become Jews.[11] A number of Ambivalent converts simply don't care for organized religion and don't think of themselves as "religious" individuals. Sometimes they agree to convert because it seems important to their partner or in-law parents, and sometimes "for the sake of the children." Like other converts, many Ambivalent Jews by Choice have some feelings of warmth toward Jewish social and intellectual styles, but, unlike the enthusiastic Activist or Accommodating converts, they are wary that the household not become "too Jewish" in terms of ritual practice. When asked, Ambivalent converts may identify themselves as Jews, but also express anxiety about losing connection to their original faith. Many Ambivalent converts dislike the notion of a Jewish "chosenness" or special mission. A few think they have mistakenly given up their prior religion. Some worry about endangering their souls.

Moderately Ambivalent converts sometimes initially leave behind aspects of family or personal background willingly. As time passes, however, second thoughts often surface, sometimes triggered by life-cycle events, such as a birth or death in the family. Ambivalent converts sometimes find themselves feeling guilty about neglecting their original cultural heritage. There are also often residual feelings of resentment about having given up Christian beliefs or, more often, holidays. Depending on the personalities involved, some may exert subtle—or not so subtle—pressure on born-Jewish spouses to retain or resume the celebration of non-Jewish festivities within their households. Most often, moderately Ambivalent converts feel passively Jewish, but this Jewishness does not affect their lives or thoughts deeply.

Historical Jewish Approaches to Conversion

Looking back at the biblical period, no formal procedure for a non-Israelite joining the Israelite people is described in the Hebrew Bible, although a text in Exodus 12:48–49 lays out the conditions under which non-Israelites can change their status and participate in sacrifices and other communal activities:

> If a stranger who dwells with you would offer the passover [offering] to the Lord, all his males must be circumcised; then he shall be admitted to offer it; he shall then be as a citizen of the country. But no uncircumcised person may eat of it. There shall be one law for the citizen and for the stranger who dwells among you. (Translation: *Etz Hayim: Torah and Commentary*)[12]

It appears that Israelite behaviors and modes of worship, with their accompanying regulations, including circumcision, could be taken on by male non-Israelites who lived within the geopolitical boundaries of Israelite society. Non-Israelite women, on the other hand, were sometimes taken in marriage by Israelite men (such as the non-Israelite wives of Joseph, Moses, and other prominent biblical figures).[13]

"It never occurred to anyone to demand that the foreign woman undergo some ritual to indicate her acceptance of the religion of Israel," historian Shaye Cohen explains. "The woman was joined to the house of Israel by being joined to her Israelite husband; the act of marriage was functionally equivalent to the later idea of 'conversion.'" However, after the destruction of the First Temple in 586 B.C.E. and the subsequent Babylonian exile, Jews faced a completely new set of circumstances. No longer living primarily in their own country, they were far more vulnerable to other cultures and had a new need to establish clear boundaries defining a non–geographically determined identity. As Cohen puts it, "Attitudes changed when conditions changed":

> Judaea lost any semblance of political independence, the tribal structure of society was shattered, and the Israelites were scattered among the nations. In these new circumstances marriage with outsiders came to be seen as a threat to Judaean [Jewish] identity and was widely condemned. The Judaeans sensed that their survival depended upon their ideological (or religious) and social separation from the outside world.[14]

No longer able to depend on culture and geography, rabbinic Judaism put procedures in place to make conversion official. Historian Lawrence Schiffman notes, "During the exile, Judaism had been transformed from a nationality which depended on a connection to the land and culture to a religious and ethnic community which depended on descent."[15]

During the subsequent Second Temple period (520 B.C.E.–70 C.E.), the Judaean nation-state was quite powerful during certain periods. At the peak of its power under the Hasmonean kings, attitudes about conversion underwent a significant shift. During this period there was an upsurge in interest in Jewish proselytizing activity, some of it quite vigorous. The writings of the Jerusalemite historian Josephus Flavius (38–100 C.E.), for example, suggest that during the Hasmonean period in the reign of King Hyrcanus (about 128 B.C.E.) there was a mass conquest and conversion of peoples from the states neighboring Judaea. The Idumaeans and others were given a choice between being expelled from their country or "submitting to circumcision and having their manner of life in all other respects made the same as that of the Judaeans. And from that time on they have continued to be Judaeans."[16] While scholars argue about aspects of Josephus's reportage, two matters are salient to our discussion: (1) At least at the time of Josephus's writing a process for becoming Jewish and joining the Jewish people included circumcision and taking on the religious and other laws of the Judaeans; and (2) the Hasmonean kings seemed unambivalent about implementing wholesale conversions.

The actively proselytizing phase of early Judaism was diminished with the destruction of the Second Temple by the Romans in 70 C.E., and further limited after the brutal crushing of the Bar Kochba revolt in 135 C.E., followed by the eclipse of the Judaean nation-state and the dispersal of the Jews throughout the Mediterranean basin and the Near East. The transformation of Jewish identity and the ascendancy of rabbinic Judaism that followed the post–Second Temple period set the stage for the now-familiar formal process and ceremony through which a non-Jew becomes a Jew. This process was established by first- and second-century-C.E. Rabbis, partially in response to the dramatically changed conditions, and is depicted twice in ancient rabbinic literature, in the Babylonian Talmud, *Yevamot* 47a–b, and in the post-talmudic tractate *Gerim* 1.1.[17]

Cohen asserts that "the primary purpose of the ceremony was to introduce a measure of order and verifiability in a situation where previously chaos had reigned." In its talmudic descriptions, the conversion ceremony consisted of three sequential actions:

1. Acceptance of Jewish religious law as a conceptual obligation. Importantly, merely practicing some of the commandments would not satisfy the acceptance aspect of the process.
2. Ritual circumcision for males. While there is considerable initial talmudic discussion about the necessity for circumcision, it becomes a required step in the conversion process.
3. Immersion in a *mikveh* or ritual bath is an absolute requirement, according to rabbinic law, for both men and women.

All three of these actions were to be performed publicly—the witnesses became, in effect, a kind of certificate of authenticity if the actual conversion were ever called into question.[18]

According to talmudic narratives, the conversion process was only entered into after rabbinical authorities were completely convinced of the sincerity of the would-be convert. The Talmud expresses considerable skepticism about persons who wish to convert to Judaism in order to gain something, especially a financial advantage. Lengthy discussion is devoted to the possible advantages that would-be converts might be seeking through conversion to Judaism, and a conversion for the purpose of material gain (or for any purpose except wishing to serve the Jewish God and join the Jewish people) is considered inappropriate. Talmudic writings express differences of opinion as to whether an insincere conversion can be considered valid after the fact.[19]

With the rise of Christianity and its establishment as the accepted religion of the Roman empire, conversions to Judaism became rare—partly, no doubt, because a series of Roman-Christian laws decreed death both for converts and the Jews who converted them. Circumcision of Christians was banned, which made conversion to Judaism close to impossible. At this point, Jewish emphasis on the turning away of proselytes became more pronounced than it had previously been. Thus, proselytes were to be told of the suffering implicit in the practice of Judaism, of the potential persecutions, of the great difficulties of the Judaic lifestyle. If, however, the proselyte persisted, and continued to wish to convert to Judaism, at that point Jewish authorities allowed the conversion to proceed, with the assumption that becoming a Jew was a privilege that the proselyte had earned through determination and devotion.

For the nearly two thousand years of rabbinic Judaism before the dramatic changes wrought by the emancipation of the Jews, the Enlightenment, and the many transformations of modernity, converts were part of many Jewish societies. Indeed, over the centuries some converts have attained extraordinary status as Jewish rabbinic leaders and thinkers. Rabbinic code books and responsa literature over the centuries have dealt repeatedly with conversion—its policies, practices, challenges, and concerns. While attitudes toward converts to Judaism have varied and continue to vary, most rabbinic writings have followed the lead of Maimonides (1135–1204 C.E.) who insisted that once a sincere, halakhic, formal conversion has taken place Jewish law requires that converts be treated with respect and consideration. A reminder perhaps most familiar to Jews from many backgrounds is found in a passage from the Haggadah, read yearly at the festive Passover seder meal, that even the patriarch Abraham had an idol-worshiping father, and thus every Jew symbolically descends from idol-worshipers who converted to Judaism:

Mitkhilah ovdei avodah zarah hayu avoteinu ...

From the beginning, our forefathers were idolaters. But now, God has drawn us close to worship him. As it is written: And Joshua said to all the people, this is what the God of Israel says: Your forefathers lived across the river [Euphrates], and Terakh, the father of Abraham and Nahor, worshiped pagan gods. Then I took your father Abraham from across the river, and I brought him through the land of Canaan. (Author's translation)

Contemporary Communal Conversations about Conversion

Conversion has become a controversial topic because it touches so closely on the existential question of what Jewish identity means in a globalizing, multicultural world. In Diaspora countries, including the United States, Jews compose a tiny minority of the population, despite extraordinary Jewish educational, occupational, and socioeconomic successes, sociocultural acceptance, and cultural and political influence. Numbers are part of the motivation for heated discussions about conversion. Although some social scientists argue that the absolute numbers of Jews in America have increased, most agree that the percentage of people identifying as Jews in America has drifted downward to about 2.5 percent of the overall population; in comparison, Christians compose approximately 80 percent.[20]

Some see a vigorous communal emphasis on conversion as a way of recouping losses. Those who argue that non-Jewish spouses should be treated and counted as Jews without formal conversion are also often concerned about numbers; they assert that insistence on conversion can be off-putting to many non-Jewish spouses and that interfaith families need to be drawn into Judaism without stressing conversion.

Approaches to conversion in the American community today run a very broad gamut. Pronounced differences exist between the various wings of Judaism, with most Orthodox rabbis articulating stricter, more circumscribed attitudes and Reform rabbis adopting the most liberal approaches; Conservative rabbis often position themselves in the middle, but closer to Orthodox standards than to Reform. The vast majority of intermarried and converting Jews who affiliate join the Reform movement; a considerably smaller group affiliate with the Conservative movement; and a dramatically smaller segment affiliates with the Orthodox movement. Equally important, the children of Reform Jews are statistically far more likely to marry non-Jews—and thus to be put into a situation where they might think about conversion—than the children of Conservative or Orthodox Jews.[21]

Thus, Reform temples include the largest group of potential converts, although the movement as a whole has moved away from overt emphasis on conversion and toward an atmosphere of inclusiveness that makes Judaism and Jewish environments feel welcoming to all types of families. In addition, many Reform rabbis have very large congregations with many responsibilities, and report that they have limited time to devote to bringing congregants through the process of conversion. As a result, the potential for conversion in Reform temples is often not actualized to its fullest extent.

Orthodox rabbis are the group of American Jewish clergy who are called upon least often to deal with intermarriage and conversion. Nevertheless, they do confront requests for conversion on a regular basis, and Orthodox rabbinic responses to these requests fall along a continuum. Proponents of high boundaries believe that conversions should only be performed according to the strictest Orthodox standards and that prospective converts must commit to leading completely ritually observant Jewish lives.[22]

Many contemporary American Orthodox rabbinic courts have brought this same strictness to their policies with regard to adopted children. Thus, non-Orthodox couples who adopt children and want an Orthodox conversion so that the children they raise will be fully accepted by Jews around the world often experience difficulty in finding an Orthodox *beit din* (rabbinical court) that is willing to convert their adopted children to Judaism. However, more liberal Orthodox Jews encourage sincere conversion and believe in lowering the boundaries to doing so. They base their approach on the many classical rabbinic sources that simply require potential converts to be told about some of the most difficult laws and some of the easiest laws, without requiring promises of completely Orthodox behavior before a conversion. One offering from *Yevamot* 47a–b is influential among liberal segments of the contemporary Orthodox community:

> Our masters taught: If, at the present time, a man comes to you seeking to be a proselyte, he should be asked: What makes you wish to be received as a proselyte?.... If he says, "I am fully aware [of the suffering of the Jews] but I am scarcely worthy of [the privilege of becoming a Jew]," he is to be received at once and instructed in a few minor and a few major precepts. He should be told of the sin of not giving gleanings, forgotten sheaves, corner crop, and poor man's tithe.... [A list of further examples follows.] One should take care not to impose on him too many commandments nor go into fine details about him.[23]

The Conservative movement includes rabbis with divergent opinions on conversion, ranging from strict rabbis and lay leaders who advocate endogamy and stringent halakhic conversion guidelines, to more liberal thinkers who believe that the movement should emphasize *keruv* (a Hebrew word for drawing a person closer to Judaism) and put less stress on boundary maintenance. Rabbis in both wings of Judaism base their decisions on legal precedents within the corpus of rabbinic legal writings from medieval through modern times.

The extent to which American cultural standards and expectations have changed is most vividly illustrated by looking at Reform Judaism. Thus, as Reform scholar Daniel Schiff points out, in the early decades of the twentieth century the Reform movement displayed near-unanimity in its advocacy of endogamy, urging conversion in cases of marriage across religious cultural lines. American Reform leader Kaufmann Kohler's 1919 statement against officiating at mixed marriages clearly articulates the expectation that a Jewish home must have only one religion, because "if man and wife belong to two different religions, it will be a house divided against itself. Without harmony of views in a matter so vital to the future, there is no real unity."[24]

By the 1980s, however, intermarriage had become so common in most Western countries that the more liberal elements in each wing of Judaism struggled to forge revised standards that could be applied to changing Jewish families. In 1983, the Central Conference of American Rabbis passed a resolution declaring that "the child of one Jewish parent is under the presumption of Jewish descent. This presumption of the Jewish status of the offspring of any mixed marriage is to be established through appropriate and timely public and formal acts of identification with the Jewish faith and people." Later Reform responsa dealt with situations where that identification becomes murky, emphasizing that "patrilineal descent must testify to the child's positive and exclusive Jewish identity." Many rabbis interpret this to mean that children of one Jewish parent must demonstrate their Jewishness by being raised in the Jewish faith and by affirming their Jewishness at an appropriate age.[25]

The emotionalism evoked by intermarriage and conversion issues in general and by the patrilineal descent decision in particular was exacerbated by the "Who is a Jew?" controversy in Israel.

On several successive occasions (1972, 1974, 1977–1978, 1983–1985), Israeli religious parties attempted to establish consistent, halakhically-based principles for conversions performed in the Diaspora and to incorporate them into the Israeli Law of Return, which guarantees all Jews citizenship in the Jewish state. Their goal was to only accept as Jews people who had been converted by an Orthodox *beit din*. American Conservative, Reform, and Reconstructionist rabbis and laypersons alike felt that these stringent new rulings would effectively disenfranchise them. American leaders energetically and ultimately successfully lobbied the Israeli government not to put these standards into law.[26]

In the interim, the Israeli government and communities have recently faced their own "Who is a Jew?" crisis, as thousands of Russian Jews and their non-Jewish family members (and significant others) emigrated to Israel, further complicating attempts to draw clear lines between Jew and non-Jew within Israeli society. At least 300,000 nonhalakhic Jews are estimated to have entered Israel under the Law of Return, and many Jewish Israelis—including Israeli women—living or traveling abroad marry non-Jews and give birth to halakhically non-Jewish children. Most recently, Israel's government has made strides in dealing with increased demands for conversion by creating the Joint Institute for Jewish Studies (informally called by a more accurate name: the Joint Institute for Conversion), which brings together rabbis and leaders from the three wings of Israeli Judaism to work together to instruct prospective converts. Partially as a result of this and other efforts, the number of Israelis receiving conversion certificates has escalated to 3,599 in 2004, and even greater numbers are projected in future years.

Conversion and Jewish Identification

Conversion to Judaism is almost always a process in the contemporary context. For some, the attraction of Judaism is primarily religious and spiritual. Others are first attracted by Jews, rather than Judaism: They grew up in Jewish neighborhoods or had mostly Jewish friends. Converts often remember perceiving Jewish families as being warm, close, responsible, and concerned. Many were attracted to Jewish humor and said that Jewish families were relaxed, witty, and had fun together. Converts also often say they are attracted to Jewish interpersonal styles—verbal, egalitarian, flexible—or to Jewish political styles—feminist, liberal, concerned about social justice. Consciously or unconsciously they sought out primarily Jewish friendship circles in high school. For some, this was a deliberate decision. For others, "It just happened." During college as well they made mostly Jewish friends and often dated primarily Jewish men or women. Others don't consider the possibility of converting until they begin seriously dating a Jew or until their first child is born. However, regardless of when they first started thinking about choosing Judaism and the Jewish people, becoming a Jew was an idea they worked with over a period of time, frequently going back and forth about it in their own minds. According to their recollections, it took months at the very least, and sometimes years, until some were ready to make a decision to convert to Judaism.

Non-Jewish spouses of Jews who don't convert before marriage often "live a Jewish life" for several years before they decide to formally convert. Moreover, the notion of a conversion that is not part of an organic process is offensive, even for many who eventually choose to convert into Judaism. Conversionary households often end up negotiating holiday and other religious issues with their Christian extended families. Although Christian families are much less likely to try to introduce Christian practices into a family that has chosen to be Jewish than they are in an interfaith family, testing behavior often continues for decades. Although conversion thus does not erase all tension over holidays between the conversionary household and the non-Jewish extended family, systematic research conducted on intermarried and conversionary households over the past three decades demonstrates that conversion makes a profound difference in individual and family identification, behaviors, and attitudes.

Beyond the conscious decisions people make, conversion opens the way for a pro-Jewish drift. Part of the reason for a pro-Jewish trajectory is related to the impact of the norms of social networks: Once they have converted, Jews by Choice are more likely to make more Jewish friends and to take a more active role in Jewish organizations. For many, conversion also lessens feelings of conflict about accommodating two religious traditions. After conversion, families typically take on more Jewish religious rituals and holiday celebrations, and the majority decide to confine Christian celebrations to visits to the extended family and friends. Many converts are encouraged by the goal of becoming Jews just like their spouse and their children. "It meant that now we were all one of a kind, rather than Daddy being one thing and Mommy and the kids being another," as one converted father put it. Many new converts express the belief that they have helped their families have religious integrity.

Despite diverse narratives of Jewish exploration, research shows that conversionary households are, by and large, interested in maintaining and increasing their Jewish connections. Some comment that the Jewish community does not give sufficient thought to the special challenges they sometimes face. In addition to advocacy for endogamy and conversion, synagogues and Jewish communal institutions have been called upon to provide more services and strategies for conversionary families. Jews by Choice must deal with psychosocial and familial complexities not faced by born Jews, and many converts urge the Jewish community to create a mentoring community for converts and conversionary households. They hope rabbis, families, and community members will support the Jewish identity of Jews by Choice, who bring new dimensions of energy and commitment to contemporary Jewish societies.

Conclusion: Diversity and the Future of the Jewish Renaissance

Jewishness has always been diverse, as we have seen, but nothing compared to the varieties of the Jewishness that emerged as modernity transformed Western societies. Concepts of an organically evolving Jewish religious culture, the opportunity to examine that culture rationally and scientifically, and secular ideas and movements produced an unprecedented range of variations in how Jews defined their own Jewishness. Today, in an environment celebrating cultural pluralism, the phrase "That's a very Jewish thing to do" can refer to a spectrum of activities, from international social justice efforts, to work on behalf of Jews worldwide, to religious rituals and ceremonies recalling biblical narratives. "A Jewish attitude" might be describing universalistic moral and ethical precepts, or Jewish political or social "styles," or concern about regular Torah study.

Contemporary Jewish communities, as we have seen, are the inheritors of modern religious transformations. The vast majority of American Jews are descended from immigrants who came from Eastern Europe and Russia, where modernization did not focus on religious reform but was linked instead to secularization, which expressed Jewishness in socialism and secular Jewish intellectualism via Hebrew or Yiddish. However, aside from Zionism, intensely Jewish forms of secularism were predominantly one-generation phenomena. Very few American Jews succeeded in passing their devotion to Jewish secular movements on to their children. Although there are certainly large numbers of secular Jews in America and especially in Israel, South America, Europe, and elsewhere, nineteenth- and twentieth-century secular ideological movements have exerted relatively little lasting influence on contemporary Jewish life. Perhaps counterintuitively, the descendents of East European Jews have been influenced far more by varieties of the Jewish experience that evolved from the German model, as is evidenced in the wings of American Judaism. Jews who were shaped by the Sephardi experience have brought yet another model of religious (but not necessarily ethnic) tolerance and inclusion into today's diverse American scene.

Today, the various types of American Jewishness each face their own challenges. The Reform movement has grown into the largest segment of American Judaism, and that growth itself has raised concerns. Reform leaders ask how the movement can accommodate both adherents who are inspired to become more deeply involved with traditional Jewish study and ceremonies, and those who resent activities they see as outside the purview of Reform lifestyles. The Conservative movement, losing some liberal adherents to Reform and some ritually observant adherents to Orthodoxy, struggles to define its boundaries and retain its own character without narrowing its scope. Orthodoxy, which does not have a single deliberating body as the other movements do, argues internally about the relationship between traditional Judaism and Western culture. Groups such as Reconstructionist Judaism, Jewish Renewal, Secular Jewish Humanism, and the Union for Traditional Judaism each present a vision of Jewishness, have an impact on American Jewish life, and often feel that their membership base does not reflect their true impact on American Jewish society.

American Jews frequently examine the extent to which their particular variety of Jewishness is thriving and devote considerable thought and energy to "branding" educational, philanthropic, and social ventures. Many religious and communal leaders evaluate their success by the extent to which their children grow up to be loyal to their stream of Judaism. However, in this closing chapter, we turn our attention to a common challenge faced by all American Jewish groups, and, indeed, by Jews around the world. An important renaissance of Jewish life is under way. That renaissance grows and flourishes where it is supported by the creation of Jewish social and ethnic capital—a process that takes concerted effort.[1] In these concluding pages we explore the ways the creation of ethnic capital can be accomplished, and argue that the community itself will determine whether renaissance or decline will win the day.

Social Networks and the Jewish Enterprise

Life Is With People, declared the title of a very popular book of Jewish social history in the 1950s.[2] Indeed, many observers of past Jewish communities and traditional Jewish communities today have suggested that Jewish life historically has been a social enterprise. Jewish societies valued the family as the primary social unit and placed a great deal of emphasis on communal responsibilities. Jews of all ages were urged toward marriage, and there was no comfortable social niche for unmarried adults. Having children was not the only reason for marriage—many rabbinic texts express enthusiastic respect for sexuality and companionship as good and powerful benefits of the married state—but couples unable to procreate were often looked on with pity.

Institutions that served the community and required communal support generally took priority. Jews moving to a new geographical area often began by purchasing land for a cemetery before they built a synagogue, feeling that a group could always pray together in someone's home, whereas the community could not compromise on communal institutions. Forced to live within walking distance of each other because of religious prohibitions against traveling on the Sabbath, Jews formed social networks that could exert considerable formal and informal control over the behavior of community members. Group norms were reinforced not only through religious proscriptions but also through social sanctions.

By contrast, contemporary American Jews have very much meshed American individualism into their Jewish values and activities.[3] Personalized, individual spiritual needs—*The Jew Within*, as a recent book has it—take precedence in the minds of many contemporary Jews over family and community.[4] Especially for the youngest adult Jews, this individualism profoundly affects life in every arena, including personal decisions, cultural and religious expressions, and affiliation patterns. Physically scattered over the suburban and exurban neighborhoods of their choice, American Jews literally and figuratively prize their own personal space. Many have never experienced anything but small social groupings and have little experiential knowledge of community. Except for a very few geographical locations, only segments of the Orthodox community voluntarily choose the kind of proximity that once was characteristic of the Jewish experience.

The choice of physical location is both practical and ideological. Jews who opt to live near each other are not only choosing to be able to walk to the synagogue. They are also choosing to forfeit aspects of their individual freedom for the sake of community cohesiveness, expressed through communal norms and expectations. This prioritizing of individual freedoms and community is one of the most profound differences between strictly Sabbath-observing and non-Sabbath-observing Jews today. The fact that many American Jews value individual goals over family and community because their social networks and culture champion individualism marks a change from Judaisms of the past and from some other Jewish communities today.

Ironically, the pervasive influence of individualism is spread partly through social networks, which transmit and reinforce beliefs.

People's lives are framed by particular institutions—the family, the school, the workplace, for example. The various social networks in which we participate are draped loosely over these institutions—we may have friendship circles based on family relationships, friends from school, colleagues from work. Each network establishes the worthwhileness of activities such as reading, sports, hunting, painting, sewing, philanthropy, dressing well, or having a particular type of car. Our perceptions of the worthwhileness of particular activities are also affected by advertisements and media presentations. Because our society also prizes individualism, we may be unaware of these influences of social networks and outside culture and believe ourselves to have embraced these values independently. However, strategies for Jewish cultural transmission need to take the impact of social networks into account in order to be effective.

The Hyphenation of American-Jewish Values

Personal behavior is profoundly influenced by a perception of what other people are doing, as Malcolm Gladwell has convincingly argued. Certain behaviors can be considered transgressive or unacceptable for a very long period of time. However, once enough individuals in a particular social network perceive these behaviors to be widespread or popular, a threshold has been passed and societal expectations go over a "tipping point." From that time forward, the once-transgressive behavior is viewed as normative and people will be pulled toward the changed standards, all other things being equal. Indeed, once the threshold has been passed, previously normative behaviors are often viewed as socially undesirable.[5]

Hybridized American-Jewish values that define much of American-Jewish life are created through a process that I call *coalescence*. Coalescence is in certain ways the opposite of compartmentalization, which used to be considered the paradigmatic American-Jewish way of dealing with cognitive dissonance. The psychology of compartmentalization is triggered by a desire to avoid discomfort or embarrassment. By compartmentalizing Jewish and American/normal/secular non-Jewish pieces of their lives, American Jews were able to function comfortably in their non-Jewish work-places or social circles and reserve their more Jewish behaviors and attitudes for settings in which they felt "safe" to do so. Compartmentalization is still a frequently used strategy among Jews who live in areas of the United States that are not familiar with Jews and Judaism, especially rural regions and in the Deep South.

Although compartmentalization still exists, its use has declined. Instead, coalescence is a much more prevalent way of juggling the Jewish and secular pieces of life today. Many aspects of Jewish culture have been absorbed into American culture, and many aspects of American values have been absorbed into American Judaism. The boundaries defining Jewishness in the United States today are enormously permeable and fluid.

Instead of the cultural hegemony of middle-class, middle-American White Anglo Saxon Protestant (WASP) culture, which arguably provided most of the images and language for American culture from the turn of the twentieth century through the 1960s, Jewish images, language, and customs have become increasingly familiar to the American public, and seem increasingly popular. This is a peculiarly American phenomenon. Jews in many other countries report that their cultures have not been Judaized in this way. In some countries, cultural expressions are openly hostile to Jews and Judaism.

The world of music provides one good example of change from the melting pot to coalescence. While American-Jewish composers like Irving Berlin, Aaron Copland, and the Gershwin brothers gave voice to the songs of America during the early decades of the twentieth century, they paid little attention to the Jewish milieus and Jewish cultures that had nurtured them, partly because Jewish ethnic expression was not acceptable in the artistic world or in popular cultural venues. By contrast, Jewish music today is familiar to many Americans and enjoys popularity on high- and lowbrow levels. National Public Television has fund-raising broadcasts featuring Yitzhak Perlman playing klezmer music on the streets of Warsaw. Adam Sandler's "Hanukkah Song" is played by DJs across America. Serious composers frequently include Jewish motifs in their music. Jewish music has become part of the broader American "cultural toolbox."

Coalescence not only brings Judaic elements into broader American culture, it also brings American values and behaviors into Judaic activities. Values such as fairness and equality are frequently used as lenses through which to evaluate—and change— Jewish values, standards, and behaviors. For many Jews in every stream of American Judaism, values like individualism, free choice, reproductive choice, social justice, and ecological concerns are seen as being part of their Jewishness. These are markers of the Americanization of Jewishness, but they may not be sufficient in terms of the creation of Jewish ethnic capital.

Creating Ethnic Capital

Terms like *ethnic capital* provide a way of talking about social transformations and measuring levels of effective Jewish cultural transmission without using terms like *nice* person or *good* Jew. American Jews are a very accomplished group of people. They like to feel competent when they embark on activities. Feeling ignorant or incompetent is a very alienating experience. That feeling of alienation is often cited, for example, as the reason why many American Jews do not like the recent incorporation of Hebrew into their religious services: They cannot navigate comfortably in Hebrew. This is a matter of concern because social scientists rank using an ethnic language as a very important technique for building ethnic capital. Not surprisingly, research shows that ethnic groups that succeed at transmitting their culture teach members of the group how to perform religious, cultural, and other activities that the group has defined as worthwhile. The ethnic group builds social capital—distinctive activities involving social groups, such as singing in a Jewish chorale—and human capital—distinctive activities that primarily involve the individual, such as listening to Jewish CDs. Education is a very effective strategy for inculcating the group's values and its perceptions of worthwhile behaviors, as well as cultural literacy and competence.

Individual members of the ethnic group are then able to "spend" their human and social ethnic capital when they acquire the necessary competence to (1) understand an ethnic activity, (2) value that activity, (3) engage in that activity, or (4) teach that ethnic activity to someone else, thus participating in the creation of new ethnic capital.

Jewish Ethnic Capital and the Melting Pot

Immigrant groups typically bring with them high levels of ethnic capital. That is, they almost always come to America speaking a language other than English, and they frequently have an interwoven fabric of foods, customs, and social attitudes that differentiate them from American culture. In the long period when America expected its ethnic immigrants to assimilate into the American "melting pot," immigrants and their children felt pressured to jettison their ethnic capital as quickly as possible. Since the 1970s, America has putatively become more appreciative of the value of ethnic particularism. For the vast majority of American Jews, however, the natural, effortless transmission of ethnic capital vanished long ago.

An ethnic set of preferred values and activities is most stable when it is not challenged by the proximity of other preferences—when individuals don't have "ethnic options," as Harvard sociologist Mary Waters puts it.[6] Ethnic capital often becomes very vulnerable when it is challenged by competing social preferences. When demographers measure the erosion of ethnically distinctive values and behaviors after the immigrant generation, one of the things they trace is the dynamic of the successive loss of ethnic capital. No matter where they fall on the continuum of American Jewish experiences, those who are concerned about Jewish cultural transmission face a similar challenge.

The transmission of Jewish culture and the building of ethnic capital today require thoughtful and active communal policies and personal commitments. A series of related questions face American Jews:

1. What aspects of Jewishness are most significant?
2. How do these aspects of Jewishness embody Jewish ethnic capital?
3. How can Jewish individuals and societies be encouraged to regard these Jewish values and behaviors as worthwhile?
4. What strategies would enhance commitments to these values and behaviors, and make them normative in Jewish societies?
5. How can Jewish individuals acquire the competence so that they can actively participate in these activities, share them with their peers, and teach them to their children?

The answers to these questions may well differ across America's diverse Jewish experiential groups. Historical Jewish communities used Jewish law (*halakhah*) as a resource for determining Jewish significance, and traditionalists today still do. They have generally adopted the traditional Jewish concept of obligation (*khiyuv*) as a way of defining as worthwhile a dense fabric of distinctively Jewish activities, educating their members to carry out those activities, and enforcing social norms that support those activities. These societies have been relatively successful in terms of their Jewish cultural transmission not because they are "better

Jews" but because they have found more effective strategies for producing Jewish ethnic capital.

Segments of the community committed to liberal or progressive Jewish experiences face the challenge of finding modes of ethnic capital production that are consonant with their Judaic world views. Some liberal groups have been extremely successful in this regard. One inescapable conclusion of recent research is that a laissez-faire approach is not likely to succeed. Jews are a tiny minority group embedded in a large, predominantly Christian culture. In this context, the production of ethnic capital requires thoughtful, energetic follow-through, and perhaps some hard choices.

The need to produce ethnic capital is not widely recognized, partly because the Jewish community is mistakenly perceived by some American Jews as being powerfully monolithic. "I'm not typical," Jews who are deeply involved in non-Jewish enterprises—but scarcely involved in Jewish enterprises—often say. But the fact is that they *are* typical. Statistically, more American Jews volunteer time for and give money to nonsectarian causes than to Jewish causes. Educationally, American Jewish secular educational levels generally tower over their Jewish educational levels. American Jews are tied to American life in profound and multifaceted ways, many of which occur coincidentally or "through osmosis." In historical Jewish communities, where densely Jewish lives were surrounded by significant boundaries—usually not of their own choosing— ethnic capital was also created coincidentally. In America today, however, ties to Jewish values, causes, and behaviors—the production of ethnic capital—is a countercultural activity that requires conscious interventions.

Jewish Counterculturalism

Distinctiveness is a necessary attribute for the ethnoreligious survival of minorities, history suggests. The fate of minority groups living in open societies has often concluded with disappearance over time, largely through religious/cultural intermixing, including mixed marriage. Moreover, American culture today celebrates mixed marriage and religious syncretism. The plots *Northern Exposure, Thirtysomething, The O.C.,* and many other television programs and films provide examples.

Recent research reveals that the transmission of Jewish ethnicity from one generation to the next can be enhanced through several interrelated strategies. One of the most important strategies is Jewish education, beginning with early childhood and stretching across the life cycle to adult educational activities.[7] Early childhood education, for example, has an important impact not only on the children but also on their families. Families whose children are enrolled in Jewish early childhood education measurably increase their own Jewish activities, in comparison to families whose children of the same age are in other educational settings. Jewish education for school-age children up through bar/bat mitzvah is enhanced to the extent that it is multidimensional, and that informal education is part of the package. Children who belong to Jewish youth groups and attend Jewish summer camps in addition to supplementary (after-school) Jewish programs and, even more dramatically, children who are enrolled in Jewish day schools participate in the creation of Jewish ethnic capital not only for themselves but for their families as well. To an extent not previously realized, Jewish education is an interactive affair.[8]

What is not often recognized is that terminating Jewish education after bar/bat mitzvah interrupts and undermines this entire process. Recent research shows that Jewish education for teenagers exerts a dramatic, transformative effect. Data from the 1990 and 2000–2001 National Jewish Population Surveys (NJPS) showed that each additional year of formal Jewish schooling—including supplementary schools—past the bar/bat mitzvah year had more of a measurable effect on adult Jewish connections than the year before it. Thus, Jewish education during the ages of sixteen and seventeen had a more substantial impact on adult Jewish connections than Jewish education from fifteen to sixteen, and so on. This impact of Jewish education during the teen years occurs not only because of curriculum—the cognitive transmission of information about Jewish subjects—but also because of social factors: Weekly classes provide a setting for the creation of Jewish peer groups. NJPS showed that the number of Jewish friends in one's teenage years was one of the best predictors of the strength of Jewish engagements when one reaches adulthood. Formal Jewish education during the teen years creates a context both for constructing Jewish social networks and for producing Jewish ethnic social and human capital.

Moreover, as with early childhood and school-age education, teen Jewish education has a synergistic impact on the rest of the family. Not only does familial Jewish activity influence the maturing child, but the child's going or not going to Jewish school influences familial Jewish activity. Within a year of a child or teenager's terminating her formal Jewish education, the whole family's level of Jewish activities declines measurably.

Familial Jewish involvements are important not only in and of themselves, but also because adults who model Jewish involvement for their children have a significant effect. The Jewish activism of the home figures prominently in the creation of Jewishly connected and engaged adults. The parental Jewish connections that have the greatest impact on children and teens are those in which adults (1) are involved in Jewish activities on a regular basis; (2) care deeply about their Jewish activities; and (3) are able to articulate their engagement with Judaism sincerely and frequently. Creating family memories of rituals, ceremonies, and Jewish culture are a significant part of the package. Teens who were interviewed spoke about enjoying the experiential aspects of Jewish culture. Many of them talked in detail about their pleasure in Jewish holiday food.

However, research shows that if cultural transmission is the goal, it's not enough for parents to walk the walk—they also need to talk the talk! With a verbal population like American Jews, children often assume that subjects not spoken about are simply not important enough to discuss.

A Jewish Renaissance

American Jewish communities today are undergoing a remarkable Jewish renaissance. This may strike some as surprising, given this chapter's discussion of the decline in ethnic cultural capital. However, an important minority of the community has been engaged in the past few decades in the production of Jewish ethnic capital at levels that supersede those of previous generations. This renaissance defines Jewishness for many American Jews.

One striking aspect of this renaissance is the proliferation of venues for adult Jewish education and the diversity of Jews who participate in them. In many communities, adult Jewish education has acquired a kind of cachet. After more than half a century of struggling ventures, in which congregational rabbis taught a handful of exceptional adults who were committed to engaging in Jewish studies on a regular basis, the past decades have seen a dramatic rise in adult education, attracting large numbers of eager and enthusiastic participants. The flowering of adult education is due to several interwoven factors. First, the creation of exclusive, elite tier programs such as the Wexner Heritage Program (initiated in 1985) and other "by invitation only" programs created an "ingroup" of invitees and an "outgroup" of would-be-invitees who longed for an invitation. Almost simultaneously, the Florence Melton Adult Mini-School program was initiated in 1986, requiring commitment and seriousness from participants but operating otherwise on an open basis. In 1998 Hadassah, the Women's Zionist Foundation of America, launched a new Hadassah Leadership Academy program, for which would-be participants needed to formally apply, and only a limited number were accepted each year. These programs and others helped to create a new culture in which participating in adult education was an activity sought out by participants, rather than the reverse. These were followed in many communities by transdenominational adult Jewish educational programs, which featured serious exploration led by scholars in the field, such as Me'ah in Boston, Drisha in New York, the Spertus College Program for Adult Learners in Chicago, and others.

Rigorous adult educational programs were being established in the same American environment in which Jewish studies programs were being created and were growing on college campuses across America. Beginning in the late 1960s and early 1970s, as America began to celebrate ethnic diversity, various departments of ethnic studies were founded on college campuses. Many of the first professors in these departments had received European training, or in subsequent years Israeli training, because prior to the 1960s there were few American programs for someone seeking a rigorous, nonsectarian, academic program in Jewish studies. Other pioneering professors received their PhDs in nonsectarian disciplines, such as history, philosophy, literature, or the social sciences, and made their way into Jewish studies because of their own overriding interests. As university-based Jewish studies programs became more fully developed, it became more common for college and graduate students to take classes in Bible, Jewish history, Jewish thought and philosophy, and modern Jewish languages and literatures. The idea that one could study Jewish subjects at a sophisticated level percolated into the consciousness of the wider American Jewish population—many of whom had associated studying Jewish subjects with the level of their own supplementary school experiences.

Academics in proliferating Jewish studies programs and departments also wrote books, disseminating Jewish scholarship to a broad reading public. These academic books joined the already burgeoning numbers of novels and short story collections by hugely popular Jewish authors, such as Bernard Malamud, Saul Bellow, and Philip Roth. Chaim Potok took a chance and wrote a novel, *The Chosen,* which explained and explored traditional Jewish lifestyles in a modern setting in a most sympathetic and appealing way. The book was made into a film of the same name and opened the way for more books by Potok and others that popularized Jewish lifestyles and concerns. Israeli writer S. Y. Agnon and Yiddish writer Isaac Bashevis Singer received international, non-sectarian, highly prestigious prizes. Their prizes were followed by numerous publications of old and new Jewish books translated from other languages, especially from Yiddish and Hebrew. The combination of all these examples of Jewish creativity and erudition as a prestige activity had a profound (and often unrecognized) impact on the way in which American Jews thought about Jewish intellectual work.

Not least, many middle-aged American Jews were being asked hard questions about the salience of Jewishness by their teenage and adult children. They found themselves having difficulty articulating their relationships to the Jewish past and the Jewish future. Some found themselves having a kind of Jewish midlife crisis. When innovative new adult education programs began appearing, many Jews with previously thin Jewish backgrounds found themselves intrigued and interested in attending.

In addition to the growth of transdenominational programs, many synagogues and movement-based institutions responded to this new adult interest by creating programs of their own. In some cases, these programs were open to using concepts, materials, and/or teachers who came from other wings of Judaism. As noted earlier, one of the most striking examples is the creation of Reform *kolel*s, adult educational institutes, borrowing a concept from the right-wing Orthodox world and remaking it for a Reform milieu and educational style.

Learning from Each Other

The contemporary American Jewish renaissance is occurring partly because, to an extent not often noted, the wings of American Judaism have learned from and influenced each other. Feminism, for example, first felt in the more liberal wings of Judaism, spread into observant communities and has transformed all of American Judaism in a variety of ways. One impact of women's new involvement was a growing excitement at the prospect of gaining liturgical and intellectual skills. Women's new access to Jewish sacred texts was one galvanizing factor in the growing devotion to adult education. In a number of contexts, lay sacred text study, at one time found primarily among Orthodox elites, has now been imported into the most liberal American Judaisms and has become a social ideal for all the movements. The lively, interactive, fervent melodies of the Hasidic world now punctuate the decorum of Reform, Conservative, and modern Orthodox worship.

The renaissance in American Jewish life is real and is contributing to an impressive building of Jewish ethnic human and social capital for a large and important minority of American Jews. This minority, and their renaissance, is important, for from their midst the future of American Jewish leadership is likely to emerge. However, for the great majority of the American Jewish community, the renaissance has had little impact.

We have noted that as America has become more Judaized, Judaism has become more Americanized. America has changed and Jews have changed. These changes have social as well as cultural implications. Social scientists have long argued about whether the boundaries around ethnic groups are the most important defining characteristic of the group, or whether the nucleus, the cultural values and behaviors inside the group, are most significant to the group's survival through cultural transmission.[9] Many leaders and observers of the American Jewish community have focused in recent years on boundary issues: Who should and should not be considered a member of the Orthodox/Conservative/Reform Jewish community? Less attention has been paid to the revitalization of Jewish life itself than to who is "inside" and who is "outside" its boundaries.

However, contemporary American culture makes strict boundary maintenance distasteful to most American Jews, and it seems unlikely that maintaining boundaries will ultimately be the most effective strategy for Judaic transmission. Instead, because the boundaries around Jews and Judaism are so permeable and fluid, it is the nucleus of Jewish life—Jewish values and behaviors—that can more usefully take center stage. To the extent that American Jews are willing to be countercultural and foreground Jewish cultural "stuff" inside Jewish individual lives, families, and communities, Jews can transmit Jewish culture to each other and to their children. African American Jew by Choice Julius Lester, who identifies strongly with concepts of Jewish peoplehood and chosenness in his proud declaration, "The revelation of God as One enters history through the Jews," captures much about the texture of quotidian Judaism as a conveyer of Jewishness:

> Value is found in suffusing the daily with holiness, and that is the *via mistica*. What is unique about the *via mistica* in Judaism is that it is not an experience for the few. It is not an experience of grace but is integral to practicing the religion.

For Lester, quotidian Judaism is best expressed in the rich ceremonialism and social interactions of a traditional Jewish Sabbath. He comments that he will not know if he has succeeded in transmitting Jewish culture, however, until he attends the bar or bat mitzvah of his Jewish grandchildren.[10]

Among the countercultural Jewish concepts that have seemed sadly neglected of late, renewed emphases on the building of Jewish friendship groups and families deserve communal attention. In a profoundly individualistic culture in which the commodification of human relationships has come to seem normal, many young and older Jews find themselves isolated and inexplicably lonely. The same Jewish traditions that support social action—a responsibility that many American Jews take very seriously as part of their Jewish identity—also support warmth and concern in smaller social groupings. One symptom of the hegemony of individualism is the virtual epidemic of delayed marriage and unwanted infertility. Renewed Jewish concern about social networks, including but not limited to discussion of these issues, could support the *Life Is With People* approach for those who find it appealing.

Among the quintessentially Jewish activities that have potential for the building of ethnic social and human capital, some of the most promising cluster around the creation of Shabbat and holiday environments in Jewish homes and in worship fellowships on a regular basis. Crucial to giving Jews cultural competence, as well as intellectual pleasure, are opportunities for high-quality, lifelong formal and informal Jewish education, imparting Jewish knowledge and skills, including Hebrew language and texts. Not least, experiences of Jewish peoplehood, including trips to Israel and other Jewish communities, and meaningful interactions with both small, intimate, and larger, diverse Jewish groups are an intrinsic part of the picture.

Access to Jewish social networks, Jewish intellectual and artistic expressions, and personal Jewish spiritual opportunities are all crucial, because on some level Jews living in an open society will only see Jewishness as worthwhile if they can truthfully answer for themselves the following questions: "Why be Jewish?" and "Why does it matter if Jewish culture is transmitted to future generations?" Mordecai Kaplan assumed that Jews would have "the will to maintain and perpetuate Jewish life." As sociologist Charles Liebman noted, that will can no longer be assumed, and is mostly found among those Jews "who begin with a sense of peoplehood."[11] Some answers will be more meaningful to some people, in some stages of their life cycles, than others. In this goal, the very diversity of the Jewish experience, in which the streams of Judaism can teach and learn from each other, and individuals can each find their own places, may continue to be a source of strength for contemporary American Jewish life now and in the future.

Notes

Introduction

1. Philip Roth, *Operation Shylock: A Confession* (New York: Simon & Schuster, 1993), p. 334.
2. Henry James, *The Varieties of Religious Experience* (New York: Collier Books, 1961).

Chapter 1: Ancient Jews, Homeland, and Exiles

1. Shaye J. D. Cohen, *The Beginnings of Jewishness: Boundaries, Varieties, Uncertainties* (Berkeley and Los Angeles: University of California Press, 1999), p. 3.
2. Yosef Hayim Yerushalmi, *Zakhor: Jewish History and Jewish Memory* (Seattle and London: University of Washington Press, 1982), pp. xiii–vi, 5–6.
3. Ilana Pardes, "Imagining the Birth of an Ancient Israel: National Metaphors in the Bible," in *Cultures of the Jews: A New History*, ed. David Biale (New York: Schocken Books, 2002), pp. 9–41, pp. 10–13.
4. Ibid., pp. 10–11.
5. Carol Meyers, *Exodus* (Cambridge: Cambridge University Press, 2005), p. 5.
6. Marc Zvi Brettler, "Judaism in the Hebrew Bible? The Transition from Ancient Israelite Religion to Judaism," in *The Catholic Biblical Quarterly* 61, no. 3 (July 1999): 429–447, 438–439.
7. Carol Meyers, *Discovering Eve: Ancient Israelite Women in Context* (New York: Oxford University Press, 1988), pp. 52–53.
8. Ibid., p. 56. Meyers (p. 143) quotes anthropologist Marshall Sahlins, who calls this the "familial mode of production."
9. Ibid., pp. 150, 157.
10. Cohen, *The Beginnings of Jewishness,* p. 170.
11. Meyers, *Discovering Eve,* pp. 124–126.
12. Yair Hoffman, "The Judges and a First Monarchy," "The Beginnings of the Monarchy: Saul and David," and "The Kingdom of Solomon," in *A Historical Atlas of the Jewish People from the Time of the Patriarchs to the Present,* ed. Eli Barnavi (New York: Schocken Books, 1999; translated from the Hebrew, Tel Aviv Books: Hachette Literature).
13. Andre LeMaire, "The United Monarchy: Saul, David and Solomon," in *Ancient Israel: From Abraham to the Roman Destruction of the Temple,*

ed. Hershel Shanks (Upper Saddle River, N.J.: Prentice Hall, and The Biblical Archeological Society, 1999), pp. 91–128, p. 116.

14. Yehezkiel Kaufman, *The Religion of Israel: Beginnings to the Babylonian Exile* (1960; repr., New York: Schocken Books, 1972), pp. 153–211.

15. Yair Hoffman, "Jerusalem and Samaria," in Barnavi, ed., *A Historical Atlas*.

16. Marc Zvi Brettler, *How to Read the Bible* (Philadelphia: Jewish Publication Society, 2005), pp. 24–25.

17. Ibid., pp. 24–27.

18. Cohen, *The Beginnings of Jewishness*, pp. 70–71. Cohen explains that originally the Hebrew word *Yehudi* meant "from the tribe of Judah," but that meaning had disappeared by Hellenistic times.

19. Ibid., pp. 72–73.

20. Ronald S. Hendel, "Israel Among the Nations: Biblical Culture in the Ancient Near East," in Biale, ed., *Cultures of the Jews*, pp. 43–76, pp. 60–63.

21. Ibid., pp. 62–63.

22. Brettler, "Judaism in the Hebrew Bible?", p. 441.

23. Bruce Halpern, "Sybil, or the Two Nations? Archaism, Kinship, Alienation, and the Elite Redefinition of Traditional Culture of Judah in the 8th–7th Centuries B.C.E.," in *The Study of the Ancient Near East in the Twenty-First Century*, eds. J. S. Cooper and G. M. Schwartz (Winona Lake, Ind.: Eisenbrauns, 1979).

24. Hendel, "Israel Among the Nations," pp. 63–65.

25. Ibid., pp. 65–66.

26. Ibid., pp. 66–67.

27. Brettler, *How to Read the Bible*, pp. 207–208.

28. This discussion is indebted to the following entries in the *Encyclopedia Judaica*: "Hassideans," "Hasmoneans," "Hellenism and the Jews," 7, 8 (Jerusalem: Keter Publishing House).

29. Lee I. Levine, "The Age of Hellenism: Alexander the Great and the Rise and Fall of the Hasmonean Kingdom," in Shanks, ed., *Ancient Israel*, pp. 231–264, pp. 249–250.

30. Isaiah Gafni, "Babylonian Rabbinic Culture," in Biale, ed., *Cultures of the Jews*, pp. 223–265.

31. Cohen, *The Beginnings of Jewishness*, pp. 363–368.

32. Eric M. Meyers, "Jewish Culture in Greco-Roman Palestine," in Biale, ed., *Cultures of the Jews*, pp. 135–179, pp. 164–169.

33. Cohen, *The Beginnings of Jewishness*, p. 369.

34. Jacob Katz, *Out of the Ghetto: The Social Background of Jewish Emancipation, 1770–1870* (New York: Schocken Books, 1988), pp. 4–5.

35. Barry Dov Walfish, *Esther in Medieval Garb: Jewish Interpretation of Esther in the Middle Ages* (Albany: State University of New York Press, 1993), p. 309.

36. Ruth Messinger, Letter to the Editor, *New York Times* (June 2, 2006): A22.

37. James L. Kugel, *The Bible As It Was* (Cambridge, Mass. and London: The Belknap Press of Harvard University Press, 1997), pp. xiv–xv.

Chapter 2: The Wandering Jews

1. Katz, *Out of the Ghetto*, pp. 4–5.
2. Ibid., pp. 20–21.
3. Jacob Katz, *Tradition and Crisis: Jewish Society at the End of the Middle Ages*, trans. Bernard Dov Cooperman (New York: Schocken Books, Inc., 1993; originally published in Hebrew as *Masoret U-Mashber*, 1958), p. 214.
4. I am indebted to Rabbi Benjamin Samuels for this information on ancient bitter herbs.
5. *Shabbat* 62a.
6. Katz, *Tradition and Crisis*, p. 13.
7. Howard M. Sachar, *Farewell, Espana: The World of the Sephardim Remembered* (New York: Alfred A. Knopf, 1994), pp. 3–5, 19.
8. Ibid., pp. 14–18.
9. Ibid., pp. 19–22.
10. Ibid., p. 22.
11. David Biale, *Eros and the Jews: From Biblical Israel to Contemporary America* (Los Angeles: University of California Press, 1997), especially "Rabbinic Authority and Popular Culture in Medieval Europe," pp. 60–85.
12. Sachar, *Farewell, Espana*, pp. 23–26.
13. Ibid., p. 30.
14. Ibid., p. 33.
15. Biale, "Rabbinic Authority."
16. "The Ban of Solomon ben [ibn] Adret, 1305," in Jacob Marcus, *The Jew in the Medieval World: A Sourcebook* (New York: Atheneum, A Temple Book, 1981), pp. 189–191.
17. Sachar, *Farewell, Espana*, p. 51.
18. Ibid., p. 58–67.
19. Renee Levine Melammed, *Heretics or Daughters of Israel? The Crypto-Jewish Women of Castille* (New York: Oxford University Press, 1999).
20. Marcus, *The Jew in the Medieval World*, pp. 200–204.
21. Judith R. Baskin, "Jewish Women in the Middle Ages," in *Jewish Women in Historical Perspective*, ed. Judith R. Baskin (Detroit: Wayne State University Press, 1991), pp. 94–114, p. 106.
22. Avraham Grossman, *Pious and Rebellious: Jewish Women in Medieval Europe* (Hanover, N.H.: Brandeis University Press, 2004).
23. I. L. Rabinowitz, *The Social Life of the Jews of Northern France in the XII–XIV Centuries as Reflected in the Rabbinical Literature of the Period* (London: Edward Goldston, 1938).
24. Shoshana Zolty, *And All Your Daughters Shall Be Learned: Women in the Study of Torah and in Jewish Law and History* (New York: Jason Aaronson, 1993), pp. 214–215.
25. "Mordecai ben Hillel Ha-Kohen," in *Encyclopedia Judaica* 12, pp. 311–314.
26. Maurice Kriegel, "From the Black Death to the End of the Expulsions," Israel Bartal, "The Ashkenazi Mosaic," and Elchanan Reiner, "Jewish Printing," in Barnavi, ed., *A Historical Atlas*.

27. President of the Jewish Community of Venice, Dario Calimani, in the *Judaic Digest #2006–40* (April 30–May 1, 2006) (listserv@h-net.msu .edu).

28. Cecil Roth, *The Jews of the Renaissance* (New York: Harper and Row, Publishers, 1959), pp. 21–43, 50–53.

29. Katz, *Tradition and Crisis,* p. 41.

30. Ibid., p. 45.

31. Natalie Zemon Davis, *Women on the Margins: Three Seventeenth-Century Lives* (Boston: Harvard University Press, 1996), pp. 5–62.

32. "Baruch Spinoza," *Encyclopedia Judaica* 15, pp. 275–283.

33. Rebecca Newberger Goldstein, "Reasonable Doubt," *New York Times* (July 29, 2006): A27. Goldstein's recent *Betraying Spinoza: The Renegade Jew Who Gave Us Modernity* (New York: Nextbook Publications, 2006) examines the philosopher's influence more extensively.

34. Alon Gal, "The Beginning of American Jewry," in Barnavi, ed., *Historical Atlas.*

35. Katz, *Tradition and Crisis,* pp. 200–201.

36. I. L. Peretz, "Between Two Mountains" (1900), in *Classic Yiddish Stories of S. Y. Abramovitsch, Sholem Aleichem, and I. L. Peretz,* ed. Ken Frieden; translated by Ken Frieden, Ted Gorelick, and Michael Wex (Syracuse: Syracuse University Press, 2004).

37. Glenn Dynner, *Men of Silk: The Hasidic Conquest of Polish Jewish Society* (Oxford, UK: Oxford University Press, 2006).

Chapter 3: Emancipating into Modern Jewishness

1. Katz, *Tradition and Crisis,* p. 195.

2. Michael A. Meyer, *The Origins of the Modern Jew: Jewish Identity and European Culture in Germany, 1749–1824* (Detroit: Wayne State University Press, 1967), p. 14.

3. *Encyclopedia Judaica* 6, "Emancipation," p. 698.

4. Excerpted in Paul Mendes-Flohr and Jehuda Reinharz, eds., *The Jew in the Modern World: A Documentary History,* 2nd ed. (New York and Oxford: Oxford University Press, 1995), pp. 114–116.

5. Katz, *Tradition and Crisis,* p. 214.

6. Howard M. Sachar, *The Course of Modern Jewish History* (Cleveland and New York: The World Publishing Company, 1958), pp. 53–70.

7. David Ellenson, *After Emancipation: Jewish Religious Responses to Modernity* (Cincinnati: Hebrew Union College Press, 2004), pp. 110–117.

8. John Murray Cuddihy, *The Ordeal of Civility: Freud, Marx, Levi-Strauss, and the Jewish Struggle with Modernity* (1974; repr., Boston: Beacon Press, 1987), discussing the ideas of sociologist Talcott Parsons and how they apply to the modernization of Judaism, pp. 9–14.

9. Katz, *Out of the Ghetto,* pp. 46–47.

10. Meyer, *Origins of the Modern Jew,* pp. 18–39; Katz, *Tradition and Crisis,* pp. 222–223.

11. Emily D. Bilski and Emily Braun, *Jewish Women and Their Salons: The Power of Conversation* (New Haven and London: Yale University Press, 2005); Deborah Hertz, *Jewish High Society in Old Regime Berlin* (New

Haven and London: Yale University Press, 1988); Meyer, *Origins of the Modern Jew,* pp. 90–114.

12. Meyer, *Origins of the Modern Jew,* pp. 144–146.

13. Ibid., pp. 147–175.

14. Marion A. Kaplan, *The Making of the Jewish Middle Class: Women, Family, and Identity in Imperial German* (New York and Oxford: Oxford University Press, 1991), pp. viii, x, 8–9.

15. Meyer, *Origins of the Modern Jew,* pp. 180–181.

16. Jacob Katz, *A House Divided: Orthodoxy and Schism in Nineteenth-Century Central European Jewry,* translated by Ziporah Brody (Hanover, N.H.: Brandeis University Press, 1998), p. 7.

17. Ellenson, *After Emancipation,* pp. 244–246.

18. Katz, *Out of the Ghetto,* pp. 158–159.

19. Ellenson summarizes Jacob Katz's analysis of these commonalities, pp. 60–61.

20. Israel Bartal, "Modernization in Eastern Europe," in Barnavi, *Historical Atlas,* pp. 176–177.

21. Annie Kriegel, "Jews and Social Utopia," in Barnavi, *Historical Atlas,* pp. 196–197.

22. Iris Parush, *Reading Jewish Women: Marginality and Modernization in Nineteenth-Century Eastern European Jewish Society* (Hanover, N.H.: Brandeis University Press, 2005).

23. Menachem Brayer, *The Jewish Woman in Rabbinic Literature: A Psychohistorical Approach,* vol. 2 (Hoboken, N.J.: KTAV Publishing House, 1986) pp. 79–80.

24. Excerpted from Micha Josef Berdichevski's "Wrecking and Building" (1900–1903), in *The Zionist Idea: A Historical Analysis and Reader,* ed. Arthur Herzberg (Philadelphia: Jewish Publication Society, 1997), p. 293.

25. Margalit Shilo, *Princess or Prisoner? Jewish Women in Jerusalem, 1840–1914* (Hanover, N.H.: Brandeis University Press, 2005), pp. 1–34, 108–142.

26. Sander Gillman, *The Jew's Body* (New York and London: Routledge, 1991).

27. Philip Roth, *The Counterlife* (New York: Farrar, Strauss & Giroux, 1986), pp. 53–54.

28. Jonathan Sarna, *American Judaism: A History* (New Haven, Conn.: Yale University Press, 2004), pp. 36–39.

29. Ibid., p. 63.

30. William B. Helmreich, *Against All Odds: Holocaust Survivors and the Successful Lives They Made in America* (New York: Simon & Schuster, 1992), pp. 40–42.

Chapter 4: Reforming American Judaism

1. Eugene Borowitz, "The Second Phase of Reform Jewish Piety," in *The Chronicle, HUC-JIR,* 2006, no. 67:7–9.

2. Marc Lee Raphael, *Judaism in America* (New York: Columbia University Press, 2003), p. 105.

3. Sarna, *American Judaism,* pp. 97–99.
4. Leon A. Jick, "The Reform Synagogue," in *The American Synagogue: A Sanctuary Transformed,* ed. Jack Wertheimer (Hanover, N.H.: Brandeis University Press, 1987), pp. 85–110, pp. 88–89.
5. "A Statement of Principles for Reform Judaism Adopted at the 1999 Pittsburgh Convention Central Conference of American Rabbis" (http://ccarnet.org/Articles/index.cfm?id=44&pge_id=1606).
6. *Yearbook of the Central Conference of American Rabbis* 45 (1935), pp. 198–200; reprinted with permission in *The Jew in the Modern World: A Documentary History,* 2nd ed., ed. Paul Mendes-Flohr and Jehuda Reinharz (New York and Oxford: Oxford University Press, 1995), pp. 468–469.
7. Jick, "The Reform Synagogue," p. 94.
8. Ibid., p. 92.
9. Ibid., p. 94.
10. Ibid., p. 97.
11. Mendes-Flohr and Reinharz, *The Jew in the Modern World,* pp. 517–518.
12. Jick, "The Reform Synagogue," pp. 101–102.
13. Manfred Jonas, "A German-Jewish Legacy," in *The German-Jewish Legacy in America, 1938–1988,* ed. Abraham J. Peck (Detroit: Wayne State University Press, 1989), pp. 51–56, p. 55.
14. George Mosse, "The End Is Not Yet: A Personal Memoir of the German-Jewish Legacy in America," in Peck, *The German-Jewish Legacy.*
15. Jick, "The Reform Synagogue," p. 98.
16. Ibid., pp. 103–104.
17. Marshall Sklare, "The Image of the Good Jew in Lakeville," in Jonathan Sarna, ed., *Observing America's Jews* (Hanover, N.H.: Brandeis University Press, 1993), pp. 205–214.
18. Philip Roth, "Eli the Fanatic," in *Goodbye, Columbus* (New York: Random House, 1959).
19. Kaplan, *The Making of the Jewish Middle Class.*
20. Sarna, *American Judaism,* p. 314. See also *The Jewish 1960s: An American Sourcebook,* ed., Michael E. Staub (Waltham, Mass.: Brandeis University Press, 2004).
21. "A Statement of Principles for Reform Judaism Adopted at the 1999 Pittsburgh Convention Central Conference of American Rabbis" (http://ccarnet.org/Articles/index.cfm?id=44&pge_prg_id=3032&pge_id =1656).

Chapter 5: Shades of American Orthodoxy

1. Noel Murray, reviewer, "Matisyahu," *The A.V. Club* (http://avclub.com /content/node/46284), accessed March 14, 2006.
2. YCT advertisement in *New Voices: Students with Jews on the Mind* 14, issue 5 (May/June 2004):6.
3. Jeffrey S. Gurock, "Resisters and Accommodators: Varieties of Orthodox Rabbis in America, 1886–1983," in *The History of Judaism in America: Transplantations, Transformations, and Reconciliations,* vol. 5, ed.

Jeffrey S. Gurock (New York and London: Routledge, 1998), pp. 1–88, p. 109.

4. Ibid., p. 164.

5. Jack Wertheimer, "The American Synagogue: Recent Issues and Trends," in *American Jewish Year Book 2005* (New York: The American Jewish Committee, 2005), pp. 3–83, p. 47.

6. Jim Schwartz, Jeffrey Scheckner, and Lawrence Kotler-Berkowitz, "Census of U.S. Synagogues," pp. 117–118; cited in Wertheimer, "The American Synagogue," p. 46.

7. Personal interview with Rabbi Professor David Berger on the impact of feminism on Orthodoxy, in which he discussed the approach he and others take toward Chabad/Lubavitch (April 19, 1999).

8. Gurock, "Resisters and Accommodators," pp. 104–106.

9. Sarna, *American Judaism,* pp. 175–191.

10. Gurock, "Resisters and Accommodators," pp. 110–114.

11. Ibid.

12. Samuel C. Heilman and Steven M. Cohen, *Cosmopolitans and Parochials: Modern Orthodox Jews in America* (Chicago and London: The University of Chicago Press, 1989), pp. 21–25.

13. Jenna Weissman Joselit, *New York's Jewish Jews* (Bloomington: Indiana University Press, 1990), pp. 18–22.

14. Jenna Weissman Joselit, p. 22, quoting Trude Weiss-Rosmarin, "Where Orthodox Jewry Has Failed," *Jewish Spectator* (June 1944):7; and p. 23, quoting Mordecai M. Kaplan Diaries, April 10, 1915, and September 13, 1914.

15. Wertheimer, "The American Synagogue," p. 21.

16. Haim Soloveitchik, "Rupture and Reconstruction: The Transformation of Contemporary Orthodoxy," *Tradition* 28, no. 4 (Summer 1994): 64–130.

17. Marvin Schick, *A Census of Jewish Day Schools in the United States, 2003-2004* (New York: The Avi Chai Foundation, 2005).

18. Yossi Prager, "The Tuition Squeeze: Paying the Price of Jewish Education," in *Jewish Action* (Fall 2005), pp. 13–18, discussing Schick, *A Census of Jewish Day Schools.*

19. Jack Wertheimer, "The Orthodox Moment," *Commentary* 107 (1999): 18–25.

20. Steven Bayme, "Real Modern Orthodoxy Must Stand Up," in The *New York Jewish Week* (November 6, 1998).

21. Jonathan Sarna, "The Future of American Orthodoxy," in *Sh'ma* 31, no. 579 (February 2001):1–3.

Chapter 6: Conservative Judaism at the Crossroads

1. Charles Liebman, "Reconstructionism in American Jewish Life," *American Jewish Year Book* 71 (New York and Philadelphia: American Jewish Committee and Jewish Publication Society of America, 1970), pp. 3–99. Reprinted in *Understanding American Judaism: Toward the Description of a Modern Religion,* II, ed. Jacob Neusner (New York: Ktav Publishing House, Inc., 1975), pp. 219–246, pp. 236–239.

2. Ibid.
3. Samuel Heilman, "Holding Firmly With an Open Hand: Life in Two Conservative Synagogues," in *Jews in the Center: Conservative Synagogues and Their Members,* ed. Jack Wertheimer (New Brunswick, N.J.: Rutgers University Press, 2000), pp. 95–196, p. 109. The terms *folk* and *elite* for Conservative Jews were coined by Charles A. Liebman, "American Jews Still a Distinctive Group," *Commentary* 64, no. 2 (August 1977): 57–60.
4. Arthur A. Cohen, *The Carpenter* (New York: New American Library, 1967).
5. Steven M. Cohen, "Assessing the Vitality of Conservative Judaism in North America: Evidence from a Survey of Synagogue Members," in Wertheimer, *Jews in the Center,* pp. 13–65, p. 25; Sidney Goldstein and Alice Goldstein, *Conservative Jews in the United States: A Sociodemographic Profile* (New York: The Jewish Theological Seminary of the United States, 1998), pp. 133–135.
6. Committee on Laws and Standards, 1950 ruling on driving to synagogue on Shabbat, originally issued for use "in special circumstances," later became the norm.
7. Mordecai Waxman, "Ideology of the Conservative Movement," in Neusner, ed., *Understanding American Judaism,* pp. 247–257, traces the influence of European ideas on American religious leaders such as Lesser, Morais, and Kohut.
8. Moshe Davis, *The Emergence of Conservative Judaism: The Historical School in 19th Century America* (Philadelphia: Jewish Publication Society, 1963), notes the writings of Nahman Krochmal, Leopold Zunz, and Zecharais Frankel in particular, pp. 13, 14. See also Waxman, "Ideology of the Conservative Movement."
9. Marshall Sklare, *Conservative Judaism: An American Religious Movement* (1955; repr., New York: Schocken Books, 1972).
10. Waxman, "Ideology of the Conservative Movement."
11. *Encyclopedia Judaica* 14, p. 948.
12. Sarna, *American Judaism,* pp. 188–189.
13. Waxman, "Ideology of the Conservative Movement," pp. 248–249.
14. Sklare, *Conservative Judaism.*
15. Ibid., p. 203.
16. Ibid., p. 210.
17. Abraham Joshua Heschel, "Religion and Race," in *The Insecurity of Freedom* (1966), pp. 85–100; Reprinted in Staub, ed., *The Jewish 1960s,* pp. 105–107.
18. Statements made in a panel discussion at Limmud, New York, January 12–16, 2006, at Kutcher's Country Club in the Catskills, New York. The same statements appear in a more scholarly and formal fashion in a "37-page, heavily footnoted paper for the Committee on Jewish Law and Standards of the Rabbinical Assembly," according to Gary Rosenblatt, "All Eyes on Rabbi Tucker at Panel," *The New York Jewish Week* (January 20, 2006):9, 18.

19. Wertheimer, "The American Synagogue," pp. 44–45.
20. Steven M. Cohen, "Change in a Very Conservative Movement," in *Sh'ma* 36, no. 628 (February 2006):6.
21. Mel Scult, *Judaism Faces the Twentieth Century: A Biography of Mordecai M. Kaplan* (Detroit: Wayne State University Press, 1993), p. 246.
22. This is the major thesis of Steven M. Cohen and Arnold Eisen, *The Jew Within: Self, Family and Community in America* (Bloomington: Indiana University Press, 2000).

Chapter 7: An American Kaleidoscope
1. Sarna, *American Judaism,* pp. 243–245.
2. Mordecai Kaplan, *Judaism as a Civilization: Toward a Reconstruction of American Jewish Life* (1934; repr., Philadelphia: Jewish Publication Society, 1994).
3. Sarna, *American Judaism,* p. 246.
4. Liebman, "Reconstructionism."
5. Rebecca T. Alpert and Jacob J. Staub, *Exploring Judaism: A Reconstructionist Approach* (Philadelphia: The Reconstructionist Press, 2000), pp. 135–137.
6. Wertheimer, "The American Synagogue," pp. 56–57.
7. Meredith Woocher, "Radical Tradition: The Ideological Underpinnings of the Early Havurah Movement" (seminar paper, Brandeis University, 1997).
8. Marshall Sklare, "The Greening of Judaism," in *Observing America's Jews,* ed. Jonathan Sarna (Hanover, N.H.: Brandeis University Press, 1993), pp. 75–86.
9. Bill Novak, "The Making of a Jewish Counter Culture," in Staub, ed., *The Jewish 1960s,* pp. 282–283.
10. David Colman, "Hanging by a Chain, A Young Man's Secret Self," in *The New York Times* (July 20, 2006):E5.
11. See, for example, Zalman Schachter-Shalomi and Joel Segel, *Jewish with Feeling: A Guide to Meaningful Jewish Practice* (New York: Riverhead Books, 2005); Zalman Schachter-Shalomi and Nataniel M. Miles-Yepez, eds., *Wrapped in a Holy Flame: Teachings and Tales of the Hasidic Masters* (San Francisco: Jossey-Bass, 2003); and Zalman Schachter-Shalomi and Donald Gropman, *First Steps to a New Jewish Spirit: Reb Zalman's Guide to Recapturing the Intimacy and Ecstasy in Your Relationship with God* (Woodstock, Vt.: Jewish Lights Publishing, 2003).
12. Wertheimer, "The American Synagogue," pp. 59–60.
13. Isaac Deutscher, "Message of the Non-Jewish Jew," in *The Non-Jewish Jew and Other Essays,* ed. Tamara Deutscher (London and New York: Oxford University Press, 1968), pp. 25–41.
14. Amoz Oz, "A Full Wagon, An Empty Wagon," in *Contemplate: The International Journal of Cultural Jewish Thought* 3 (Winter 2005–Spring 2006), pp. 60–72, p. 72.

15. Herb Silverman, "Is Jewish Atheist an Oxymoron?" in *Humanistic Judaism* 34, no. 2 (Spring 2006), pp. 27–32.

16. A. B. Yehoshua, "The Future of the Past: What Will Become of the Jewish People?" Keynote symposium (with Cynthia Ozick, Rabbi Adin Steinsaltz, and Leon Wieseltier) at American Jewish Committee Annual Convention, Washington, D.C.: Capital Hilton, May 1, 2006.

17. Deutscher, "Message of the Non-Jewish Jew."

18. Alfred Kazin, *Walker in the City* (New York: Harcourt, Brace and Company, 1951); Susan Glenn, *Daughters of the Shtetl: Life and Labor in the Immigrant Generation* (Ithaca, N.Y., and London: Cornell University Press, 1990); Irving Howe and Kenneth Libo, *World of Our Fathers: The Journey of East European Jews to America and the Life They Found and Made* (New York: Simon & Schuster, 1976), p. 172.

19. Jonathan Woocher, "'Sacred Survival' Revisited: American Jewish Civil Religion," in Dana Evan Kaplan, ed., *The Cambridge Companion to American Judaism* (Cambridge, UK, and New York: Cambridge University Press, 2005), pp. 283–297, p. 293.

20. Ben Hecht, *A Child of the Century* (New York: Donald I. Fine, Inc., 1985; rpt. 1954).

21. The entire issue of *Humanistic Judaism* 34, no. 2 (Spring 2006), was devoted to exploring these issues.

22. Bonnie Cousens, "With Benefits Come Responsibilities," in *Humanora: The Newsletter of the Society for Humanistic Judaism, affiliated with the International Federation of Secular Humanistic Jews* 28, no. 3 (Spring 2006), p. 11.

23. *JTA*, Miami, May 21, 2006, "Project Feeds Secular Culture into Universities' Jewish Studies."

Chapter 8: Jews by Choice

1. A more extensive report on this original interview research appears in Sylvia Barack Fishman, *Choosing Jewish: Conversations About Conversion* (New York: American Jewish Committee, 2006).

2. Bernard Lazerwitz, J. Alan Winter, Arnold Dashefsky, and Ephraim Tabory, *Jewish Choices: American Jewish Denominationalism* (Albany: State University of New York Press, 1998), p. 189. Within marriages performed in the two decades from 1970 to 1990, 12 percent of the born non-Jewish wives of Jewish men and 5 percent of the born non-Jewish husbands of Jewish wives converted to Judaism; as of 1990, about 16 percent of intermarriages had resulted in conversion to Judaism. The Lazerwitz et al. study's analysis uses data from the 1990 National Jewish Population Survey conducted by the Council of Jewish Federations.

3. Benjamin Phillips and Shaul Kellner, "Reconceptualizing Religious Change: Ethno-apostasy and Change in Religion Among American Jews," in *Sociology of Religion*, Special Issue on the 2000–01 National Jewish Population Survey, ed. Moshe and Harriet Hartman, 2006, Vol. 67, no. 4: 507–524.

4. Lazerwitz et al., *Jewish Choices*, p. 189. In 1990, data indicated that "98 percent of Jewish-Convert couples report they are raising their children as Jews, and 38 percent of mixed married couples report they are doing so."

5. *The National Jewish Population Survey 2000–01: Strength, Challenge and Diversity in the American Jewish Population* (New York: Mandell L. Berman Institute-North American Jewish Data Bank, 2003), p. 55. The United Jewish Community's analysis of NJPS 2000–01, a study conducted by the UJC, suggested that 33 percent of the children of intermarriages were being raised as Jews.

6. Gabriele Glaser, "Can a Gentile Wife Raise Jewish Kids?" *Moment* 24, no. 2 (April 1999):58–61, 59.

7. Harvey Cox, *Common Prayers: Faith, Family, and a Christian's Journey Through the Jewish Year* (New York: Houghton Mifflin, 2001), p. 83.

8. Phillips and Kellner, "Reconceptualizing Religious Change."

9. NJPS 2000–01 data, analyzed by Benjamin Phillips and Sylvia Barack Fishman. Unless otherwise specified, data cited from NJPS 2000–01 was evaluated by Phillips and Fishman.

10. B. Forster and J. Tabachnick, *Jews by Choice: A Study of Converts to Reform and Conservative Judaism* (Hoboken, N.J.: KTAV Publishing House, Inc., 1991). Forster and Tabachnik's Chicago-based study of Jews by Choice also found that 15 percent of their primarily female married conversionary population converted before they met a Jewish partner, out of attraction to Judaism itself.

11. Forster and Tabachnik, *Jews by Choice*, pp. 81–82.

12. Exodus 12:47–49, translated in *Etz Hayim: Torah and Commentary* (New York: Rabbinical Assembly, 2001).

13. See also the prescriptive materials in Deuteronomy 21:10–14 and Numbers 31:17–18.

14. Cohen, *The Beginnings of Jewishness*, pp. 261–265.

15. Lawrence H. Schiffman, *From Text to Tradition: A History of Second Temple and Rabbinic Judaism* (Hoboken, N.J.: KTAV Publishing House, Inc., 1991), p. 46.

16. Cohen, *The Beginnings of Jewishness*, pp. 110–111.

17. Ibid., pp. 198–211. Cohen puts tractate *Gerim,* which describes the process of proselytizing, as "almost certainly" post-talmudic (i.e., post–500 C.E.) and "first attested explicitly about 1300."

18. Ibid., pp. 211–233.

19. Ibid.

20. "By the Numbers: Understanding American Jewry," Brandeis University conference launching the Steinhardt Social Research Institute (November 3, 2005). Barry A. Kosmin, Egon Mayer, and Ariela Keysar, who conducted the *American Religious Identification Survey* 2001 (ARIS) (New York: The Graduate Center of the City University of New York, 2001) and the *American Jewish Identity Survey* 2001 (AJIS) (New York: The Graduate Center of the City University of New York, 2001; reissued by

The Center for Cultural Judaism, New York, 2003) assert that secularism has grown dramatically among white Americans, and that "the proportion of the population that can be classified as Christian has declined from 86 percent in 1990 to 77 percent in 2001" (ARIS, p. 10). Kosmin et al. also calculate that about 7.7 million Americans report having some Jewish ancestry, and that "nearly 4 percent of America's 105 million residential households have at least one member who is Jewish by religion or is of Jewish parentage or upbringing or considers him/herself Jewish" (AJIS, p. 6).

21. Benjamin T. Phillips and Sylvia Barack Fishman, "Ethnic Capital and Intermarriage: A Case Study of American Jews," in *Sociology of Religion*, Special Issue on the 2000–01 National Jewish Population Survey, eds. Moshe and Harriet Hartman, 2006, Vol. 67, no. 4: 487–505.

22. One typical example of the high standards characteristic of Orthodox rabbinic authorities in the contemporary period can be found in Rabbi Moses Feinstein's *Iggrot Moshe, Yoreh Deah* 3, no. 106 (Tamuz 1969). In this case, Rabbi Feinstein declines to convert a woman who wishes to become Jewish because of marriage but rejects the standards of modesty required of Orthodox women in their clothing and head coverings; Rabbi Feinstein declares that the woman is not motivated "for the sake of heaven."

23. Hayim Nahman Bialik and Yehoshua Hana Ravnitsky, *The Book of Legends: Sefer Ha-Aggadah, Legends from the Talmud and Midrash*, translated by William G. Braude (New York: Schocken Books, 1992), p. 350. *Sefer Ha-Aggadah* was originally published in Hebrew in Odessa, 1908–1911.

24. Cited by Daniel Schiff, Rappaport Center for the Study of Assimilation, Bar Ilan University, Neve Ilan Conference Center, July 22, 2005; "Rabbi Officiating at Mixed Marriages," in *American Reform Responsa*, Item 148, 39 (1919):75–76.

25. Schiff, "Baptism and Jewish Status," CCAR Responsa, 5759.2.

26. David Landau, *Who Is A Jew? A Case Study of American Jewish Influence on Israeli Policy* (New York: American Jewish Committee, 1996).

Conclusion

1. Phillips and Fishman, "Ethnic Capital and Intermarriage," explores this issue in detail, with extensive statistical evidence.

2. Mark Zborowski and Elizabeth Herzog, *Life Is With People: The Culture of the Shtetl* (1952; repr., New York: Schocken Books, 1995).

3. See Sylvia Barack Fishman, *Jewish Life and American Culture* (Hanover, N.H.: Brandeis University Press, 1999), pp. 15–32, for a fuller discussion of this phenomenon.

4. Cohen and Eisen, *The Jew Within*.

5. Malcolm Gladwell, *The Tipping Point: How Little Things Can Make a Big Difference* (New York: Little, Brown & Company, 2000).

6. Mary C. Waters, *Ethnic Options: Choosing Identities in America* (Berkeley: University of California Press, 1990).
7. Jack Wertheimer, ed., *Family Matters: Jewish Education in an Age of Choice* (Hanover, N.H.: Brandeis University Press, forthcoming, 2006).
8. Jack Wertheimer, *Linking the Silos: How to Accelerate the Momentum in Jewish Education Today* (New York: Avi Chai Foundation, 2005).
9. For discussions of boundaries and cultural "stuff" as definers of ethnic particularism, see Frederik Barth, *Ethnic Groups and Boundaries* (Boston: Little, Brown and Company, 1968), p. 38, and Joanne Nagel, "Constructing Ethnicity: Creating and Recreating Ethnic Identity and Culture," *Social Problems* 41, no. 1 (February 1994): 152–176.
10. Julius Lester, *Lovesong: Becoming a Jew* (New York: Arcade Publishing, 1988), p. 170.
11. Liebman, "Reconstructionism," p. 221.

Glossary

This glossary includes terms from Hebrew, Yiddish, and other foreign-language and culture-specific sources. The comments reflect the way many Jews use these words, not just the technically correct versions. When two pronunciations of a Hebrew word are listed, the first is the way the word is sounded in contemporary Israeli Hebrew, and the second is the way it is sometimes heard in common speech, often under the influence of Yiddish, the folk language of the Jews of northern and eastern Europe. "Kh" is used to represent a guttural sound, similar to the German "ch" (as in "sprach").

agunah (ah-goo-NAH): Hebrew: tied or chained woman. A woman who wants a divorce but is unable to attain one from her husband, because he has disappeared, is disabled, or is unwilling to grant her one.

Agudath Israel: An organization of ultra-Orthodox Jews that was first established in nineteenth-century Germany. The founders originally included diverse Orthodox leaders—**Hasidic, Mitnagdic, Modern Orthodox**, and **ultra-Orthodox**. It quickly became exclusively ultra-Orthodox in its orientation.

Amidah (ah-mee-DAH, ah-MEE-dah): Hebrew: "standing." One of the three commonly used titles for the second of the three central units in the worship service, the first being the *Shema* and Its Blessings and the third being the reading of the Torah. It is composed of a series of blessings, many of which are petitionary (except for the Sabbath and holidays, when the petitions are removed out of deference to the holiness of the day). Also called *ha-tefillah* ("the prayer") and *shemoneh esrei* ("eighteen"). The term *amidah* refers to the fact that the prayer is said standing up. It is traditionally recited in a whisper.

am Yisrael (ahm yees-rah-AYL, ahm yees-ROH-ayl): Hebrew, "the people (or nation) of Israel." Refers to the totality of the Jewish people, however widely dispersed.

anusim (ah-new-SEEM): Hebrew, "the forced (or compelled) ones." Jews who were forced to convert to Christianity (or Islam), especially during the Middle Ages. Also called **crypto-Jews**.

Ashkenaz (noun), **Ashkenazi** (adj.), **Ashkenazic** (adj.). Noun: Biblical term used in medieval times to denote German Jews, and later expanded to mean the wider European and Russian communities that have been home to large portions of the world's Jews. The adjectives refer to anything pertaining to those communities. Often used in contrast to Sepharad, Sephardi, **Sephardic**, Jews who once made their home on the Iberian Peninsula.

avodah zarah (ah-voe-DAH zah-RAH, ah-VOE-dah ZOH-rah): Hebrew, "worship of foreign gods, idolatry." Also the name of a tractate of the Mishnah, Tosefta, and Talmud discussing laws governing Jews' interactions with idolaters.

Babylonian Talmud: See Talmud.

bar/bat mitzvah: Hebrew, "son/daughter of the commandment." When a girl reaches the age of twelve or a boy reaches the age of thirteen, they are each responsible for their own religious and moral behavior, according to Jewish law. Boys have traditionally marked this occasion by being called up to make a blessing on the Torah, an honor that is now extended to girls as well in many Reform and Conservative congregations. In the United States, the attainment of this status is often the occasion for elaborate celebrations. Additionally, today women and sometimes men who did not have the opportunity to mark their bar/bat mitzvah status at the usual ages have festive adult ceremonies.

beit knesset (BAYT k'NEH-set): Hebrew, "house of assembly." One of the Hebrew names for a synagogue.

beit midrash (BAYT meed-RAHSH, BASE MEHD-resh): Hebrew, "house of study" or "house of interpretation." One of the Hebrew names for a synagogue or study hall.

beit tefillah (BAYT teh-fee-LAH): Hebrew, "house of prayer." One of the Hebrew names for a synagogue.

Bildung (BILL-dung): German, concept describing the process of continuously building and perfecting admirable character traits, including education, culture, and refinement.

brit milah (BREET mee-LAH): Hebrew, "covenant of circumcision." The circumcision of a Jewish boy on his eighth day of life (or thereafter if health reasons require a postponement), together with prescribed blessings and the naming of the child, to mark his entry into the covenant of Abraham and of Israel. See Genesis 17:10–14; Leviticus 12:3. Commonly referred to as a *bris*, meaning "covenant."

Canaan: One name used in biblical times for what we now call the Land of Israel.

Catholic Israel: A phrase, utilized by Rabbi Solomon Schechter, referring to the whole entity of the Jewish people, in all their variations and locations.

Centrist Orthodox: A modern but traditionalist segment of the American Orthodox Jewish community that promotes high levels of Jewish education and strict loyalty to rabbinic law (*halakhah*), while acknowledging—with some guardedness and concerns—the importance of a secular education and involvement in the modern world.

Chabad: See **Lubavitch Hasidim.**

challah (Kha-LAH, KHAH-leh); pl. *challot* (kha-LOT): Special bread, customarily served in two whole loaves on Sabbaths and Jewish holidays. Among Ashkenazim its usually egg bread, sometimes braided.

chesed (KHEH-sed): Hebrew, "loyalty" (to God and to a fellow human being), with secondary meanings of piety and loving-kindness.

Chumash (khoo-MAHSH, KHUH-m'sh): Hebrew, "Five." The first part of the Bible, which is read in the synagogue on Mondays, Thursdays, the Sabbath, and holidays. Also called the **Pentateuch**, Five Books of Moses, or the **Torah**, it contains the books *B'reishit* (In the Beginning), *Shemot* (Names), *Vayikra* (And [God] Called), *Bamidbar* (In the Desert), and *Devarim* (Words or Commandments). These names are the first key words mentioned in each book, but they allude to the content of each one. The English names for the five books of the Torah—Genesis, Exodus, Leviticus, Numbers, and Deuteronomy—are based on the titles in the Latin Bible, which were drawn from the Greek translations of the Hebrew names.

chuppah (khoo-PAH, KHOO-pah): Hebrew, "canopy." In a traditional Jewish wedding service the ceremony is performed under a canopy, which can be as simple or elaborate as desired. Sometimes a **tallit** (prayer shawl) is used for this purpose.

Conservative Judaism: A movement of Judaism often considered to occupy a religious position between the **Orthodox** and **Reform** movements. Conservative Jewish thinkers describe the movement as guided by Jewish law, while also teaching that Jewish religious culture has developed organically over time. The term *Conservative* is primarily used by American Jews, while the Hebrew term *Masorti* (mah-sawr-TEE, literally, "traditional") is used for the same movement in Israel and elsewhere.

converso: Spanish, "converted person." In our discussion, Jews who have converted into Christianity.

covenant: *brit*, in Hebrew. Refers to the marriage, as it were, between God and the people of Israel, beginning with Abraham and lasting to our own day. The terms of the covenant are spelled out in Jewish law, beginning with the revelation at Mount Sinai, described in chapters 19–24 of the biblical book of Exodus, and continuing in Jewish legal interpretations and decisions throughout the ages, including contemporary rabbinic rulings. The essence of the covenant is the ongoing relationship between God and the Jewish people, a relationship shaped by Jewish law, prayer, religious thought, questioning God, other forms of spirituality, and a complex network of communal and social action responsibilities *(tikkun olam).*

crypto-Jew: Secret Jews who converted into Christianity under duress, especially during the times of the Catholic inquisitions. Also referred to as *anusim* or marranos, a derogatory Spanish expression meaning "pigs."

day school: Jewish elementary or high school, all-day school incorporating both Jewish and general subjects.

derech eretz (DEH-rekh EH-retz): Hebrew, "the ways of the land." Politeness and appropriate behavior, as defined by the wider society.

Diaspora: Communities living outside their homeland. When used in connection to Jews, refers to Jewish communities located outside of the Land of Israel. Can be used as an adjective to describe particular communities, or as a noun, i.e. "the Jewish Diaspora."

Emancipation: Refers to the political process of formally granting Jewish populations of particular countries (especially those of Europe) the status and rights of citizens.

Essenes: Ascetic Jewish sect of the Second Temple period that continued into the first century of the Common Era.

ethnic capital: A term used by sociologists to describe a cluster of distinctive values, behaviors, and activities that define a group's ethnoreligious identity. Ethnic behaviors include such concrete activities as cooking ethnic dishes, speaking an ethnic language, and celebrating ethnic festivals. Ethnic social capital is the extent and nature of an individual's ties to members of a given ethnic group. Ethnic capital can be built up and increased, and transmitted to the next generation, or it can decline.

Gemara (Geh-mah-RAH): see **Talmud**.

ger (GEHR): Hebrew, "stranger" or "convert" [into Judaism]. The term in biblical texts often refers to non-Jews living among Israelites who adopted some early Jewish customs. Rabbinical interpretations generally understand the term to mean proselytes.

halakhah (hah-lah-KHAH, hah-LOH-kheh): Hebrew, "walking" or "going." The term for rabbinic or Jewish law. Used as an anglicized adjective, halakhic (hah-LAH-khic), meaning "legal." Denotes the way a Jew should "walk" through life.

Hanukkah (KHAH-noo-kah): Hebrew, "dedication." Eight-day holiday commemorating the Maccabee family's defeat of the Syrian Greeks who attempted to prevent Jewish religious observances. Name refers to the cleansing and rededication of the Jerusalem Temple, which had been deliberately defiled by Syrian Greek soldiers as part of their campaign.

haredi (khah-ray-DEE, khah-RAY-dee): Hebrew, literally "shaking" or "trembling" before God. Very pious. This Hebrew term is often used to refer to **ultra-Orthodox** Jewish individuals or societies who see Jewish texts, laws, and lifestyles as containing all truth, and reject the independent worth of secular culture, except for its utilitarian value, such as technical or medical usages.

Hasidic (khah-SIH-dihk): Hebrew, "pious." Pertains to the doctrine generally traced to an eighteenth-century Polish Jewish mystic and spiritual leader known as the Baal Shem Tov (called also the BeSHT, an acronym composed of the initials of his name). Followers are called Hasidim (khah-see-DEEM or khah-SIH-dim); sing., Hasid (khah-SEED or, commonly, KHOH-sihd) from the Hebrew word *chesed*.

Haskalah (hah-skah-LAH, has-KOH-leh): Hebrew, "Enlightenment." The Jewish Enlightenment consisted of waves of intellectual and cultural awakenings that opened the world of Western arts and sciences to the

Jews of Western Europe in the late eighteenth and nineteenth centuries, and to Eastern European Jewry in the nineteenth and early twentieth centuries.

Hasmoneans: A dynasty of kings and high priests who ruled the Land of Israel and achieved military triumphs in the period following Mattathias and Judah Maccabee.

Hassideans: Hebrew, "pietists." During the time of the **Hasmonean** dynasty, these devout Jews promoted religious purity and disparaged military might.

hatan (khah-TAN, KHOH-sen): Hebrew, "bridegroom."

havdalah (hahv-dah-LAH, hahv-DOH-leh). Hebrew, "making a distinction." A ceremony dividing the holiness of the Sabbath from the work-a-day week; performed with a multi-wicked candle, wine, and spices. The liturgy emphasizes the traditional Jewish view of binary divisions, including that which divides the Jews from "the other nations of the world."

havurah (khah-voo-RAH): Hebrew, "association." An egalitarian Jewish worship and study group that typically emphasizes peer group activities and does not have paid religious leaders. These personalized groups rebelled against huge congregations, and grew out of the **Reconstructionist** movement in the 1960s and 1970s, but have attained popularity across the wings of American Judaism.

High Holy Days: Also known as High Holidays. Rosh Hashanah (the New Year) and Yom Kippur (the Day of Atonement), ten days later. The period between these two days is known as the Ten Days of Repentance. Set by the Jewish lunar calendar, this sacred season occurs in the fall. Traditionally, it focuses on the process through which God reviews the behavior of individual human beings and charts their destiny during the coming year. Human beings, for their part, have the opportunity to repent of their misdeeds, correct the damage they have done to other persons, and pledge not to repeat these misdeeds.

inmarriage: Sociological term, endogamy. Marriage between two individuals who share an ethnoreligious heritage.

intermarriage: See **mixed marriage**.

Jerusalem Talmud: See **Talmud**.

Jew by Choice: A person who chooses to go through a process of formal conversion into the Jewish religion. After conversion Jewish law considers a Jew by Choice to be a full Jew.

Jewish Renewal: Contemporary Jewish religious movement.

Judaea; pl. Judaeans: Originally refers only to the members of the tribe of Judah who settled in the ancient Land of Israel. Later a variant of this word is used to indicate Jews as a people: Jews were people who came from Judaea.

Judaizers: Persons who adopted some Jewish behaviors.

Kabbalah (kah-bah-LAH, kah-BOH-lah): Hebrew, "receive," or "welcome." Understood as "tradition," implying the receiving of tradition. A general term for Jewish mysticism, but used properly for a specific mystical doctrine that was recorded in the Zohar in the thirteenth century, and then was further elaborated, especially in the Land of Israel (in Safed), in the sixteenth century.

Kaddish (kah-DEESH, KAH-dish): Hebrew, "sanctification." Prayer glorifying God's name that is traditionally recited by mourners during their period of mourning and on the anniversaries of their bereavement.

kallah (kah-LAH, KAH-leh): Hebrew, "bride."

Karaites: Medieval group of Jews who accepted only biblical law and rejected the authority of rabbinic law and traditions.

kashrut (kahsh-ROOT, KAHSH-res): Hebrew, "ritually appropriate or correct." Usually used in regard to food, to indicate food that is acceptable for Jews to eat according to biblical and rabbinic law.

kehillah (keh-hee-LAH, keh-HEE-lah): Hebrew, "congregation," or "group." In European Jewish communities, the name given to the organized Jewish community. In some rabbinic texts that discuss prayer, the *kehillah* refers to the group of worshipers. In its Hebrew possessive form, frequently a prefix to a congregational name: e.g., Kehillat Jeshurun.

ketubah (keh-too-BAH, K'SOO-bah): Hebrew, wedding contract.

Kiddush (kee-DOOSH, KIH-dush): Hebrew: "sanctification." Blessing over wine on Jewish Sabbath and holidays.

kol ishah (kohl ee-SHAH, kol EE-shah): Hebrew, "the voice of a woman." Refers to a group of rabbinic laws prohibiting pious Jewish men from listening to women's voices because those voices might arouse them sexually. Most commonly understood to mean a woman singing seductively, but at its most extreme expanded by some to mean the voices of women in many contexts.

lashon ha-ra (lah-SHOWN hah-RAH, LOH-shen HOH-reh): Hebrew, "bad language," or gossip. Forbidden by Jewish law.

Lubavitch Hasidim: A Hasidic group attached to the leadership of the Lubavitch rabbinical dynasty, often called **Chabad.** Unlike **Satmar Hasidim** and other more insular Hasidic groups that avoid contact with outsiders, Lubavitch Hasidim reach out to less affiliated Jews, sending Lubavitch religious emissaries (*shlichim*, "messengers") to far-flung international locations to service and build up Jewish communities. Some Lubavitch Hasidim regard the late Lubavitcher Rebbe (religious leader) Rabbi Menachem Mendel Schneerson as a messianic figure, a controversial belief.

mahkatonim (mah-khah-TAWN-eem): Yiddish adapted from the Hebrew and pronounced by Israelis *mekhutanim* (meh-KHU-tah-NEEM), "the parents of one's son- or daughter-in-law." Western cultures typically do not have a word designating this quasi-familial relationship.

maskilim (mahs-key-LEEM, mahs-KEY-lim): Hebrew, "enlightenened persons." Thinkers, writers, and creative artists connected to the **Jewish Enlightenment** (*Haskalah*) movements, first in Western Europe and then in Eastern Europe.

matzah (mah-TZAH, commonly MAH-tzah): Unleavened bread. Flat, cracker-like bread eaten on Passover when Jewish law prohibits the ownership, use, and consumption of leavened grain products.

megillah (meh-gee-lah, m'gill-ah); pl. *megillot* (meh-gee-LOTE): Hebrew, "scroll." Five *megillot* are read during the Jewish liturgical year: Ecclesiastes *(Kohelet)* on Sukkot, Esther on Purim, Song of Songs *(Shir ha-Shirim)* on Passover, Ruth on Shavuot, and Lamentations *(Eicha)*on the Ninth of Av. Used in a colloquial expression, "The whole *megillah*!"

meshumad (meh-shoo-MAHD, Yiddish: meh-SHOO-m'd): Hebrew, "apostate," convert out of Judaism into another religion.

midrash (meed-RAHSH, MED-rihsh); pl. midrashim (mid-rah-SHEEM): Hebrew: From the word *darash,* "to seek, search, or demand [meaning from the biblical text]." A literary genre focused upon the explication of the Bible. Midrash refers to a body of rabbinic literature, some parts very ancient, that offer interpretations of the Bible. Today often used to refer to narratives from diverse sources, including contemporary readers, that expand the meaning of or provide materials to fill the lacunae in biblical stories.

mikveh (meek-VEH; Yiddish, MIK-veh): Hebrew, "ritual bath." A pool that must contain a specified amount of water from natural sources, which is used in ritual observances for purification of a Jewish woman after completion of her monthly menstrual cycle, by Jewish men before their weddings and before the **High Holy Days**, and by some **Hasidic** men after sexual intercourse. Immersion in a *mikveh* is also a step in the process of conversion into Judaism. Feminists and **Jewish Renewal** groups have created diverse new rituals that utilize the waters of the *mikveh.*

minyan (min-YAN, MIN-yen): A quorum of ten adult Jews, that is, ten Jews beyond their thirteenth birthday. Orthodox and a few Conservative synagogues require males in counting a *minyan,* but the vast majority of Conservative synagogues and all Reform and Reconstructionist synagogues include women as well. In such contexts, girls may be counted after their bat mitzvah, which may occur as early as age twelve. Colloquially used to mean prayer services, as in, "Did you go to *minyan* this morning?"

Mishnah (meesh-NAH, MISH-nah): After the compilations of laws in several sections of the **Torah** (e.g., Exodus 20–24; Leviticus 18–27; Deuteronomy 20–25), the Mishnah is the first written summary of "the Oral Law," that is, the laws and customs communicated through example and speech from generation to generation, from approximately the fifth century B.C.E. to the end of the second century C.E. The Mishnah was compiled by Rabbi Judah, the president of the Sanhedrin, in the Land of Israel about the year 200 C.E., based on the earlier work of Rabbi Akiva and his students throughout the second century. The Mishnah is divided into six parts, or orders (*sedarim* [seh-dah-REEM]; sing. *seder* [SAY-dehr]), organized by topic. It treats a whole range of legal subjects, including civil law (e.g., contracts, landlord-tenant relationships, property ownership, lost objects), criminal law (e.g., personal injuries, types of theft and murder), penalties for infringement of the law, court procedures, family law (e.g., marriage, divorce), agricultural law dealing with the Land of Israel, laws governing the ancient Temple's sacrifices, and the first written description of the structure of Jewish prayer.

Mishneh Torah (meesh-NAY toh-RAH, MISH-nah TOH-rah): The title of Maimonides' Code of Jewish Law, completed in 1177 C.E.

Mitnagdim (meet-nahg-DEEM, miss-NAHG-dim): Hebrew, "those who oppose," or non-Hasidic Jews. The meaning of this term was coined in response to the rise of **Hasidic** Judaism, and refers to religious Jews who oppose Hasidic doctrines and behaviors.

mitzvah (meetz-VAH, MITZ-vah); pl. *mitzvot* (meetz-VOTE): Hebrew, "commandment." Used commonly to mean "good deed," but in the more technical sense, denoting any commandment from God, and therefore, by extension, what God wants us to do. Reciting the *Shema* morning and evening, for instance, is a mitzvah, and helping the poor is a mitzvah.

mixed marriage: Sociological term, exogamy. Marriage between two individuals with differing ethnoreligious heritages.

Modern Orthodox: A segment of the Orthodox Jewish religious movement that embraces Western arts and culture while upholding Orthodox beliefs and practices. Modern Orthodox synagogues, for example, are distinguished from most **Conservative** synagogues in that they maintain a physical separation (*mekhitzah*) between male and female worshipers. They are distinguished from most **Centrist Orthodox** synagogues in that they try to expand the roles of women within the boundaries of rabbinic law (*halakhah*).

Oral Law, Oral Torah: In Hebrew, *Torah she'b'al peh* (toe-RAH sheh-bih-ahl-PEH). The commentaries, interpretations, legal writings, and legends that students and teachers have woven around the Written Torah, or *Torah she-bikhtav* (toe-RAH sheh-BIKH-tahv), that were thought to have been originally transmitted out loud rather than in writing. Some of these materials are quite ancient, and the process of biblical interpretation is reported even in the Hebrew Bible itself.

Orthodox Judaism: These most traditional forms of Judaic practice were first considered "Orthodox" in response to the changes called for by reformers in nineteenth-century Germany and Hungary. In other words, Orthodoxy was defined as a self-conscious variety of Jewishness by the creation of non-Orthodoxy.

Palestinian Talmud: See **Talmud.**

Passover: See **Pesach.**

Pentateuch: Greek: "Five-volumed book." Refers to the Hebrew Bible because the five parts of the Torah were transcribed on separate scrolls. The Hebrew equivalent is *hamishah humshei Torah* (khah-mee-shah khoom-shay toe-RAH), or, in abbreviated form, the **Chumash.**

Pesach (PAY-sakh): Hebrew, "paschal sacrifice." Most commonly refers to Passover, the spring holiday that commemorates the Exodus of the Israelites from Egypt. The name Passover derives from the biblical narrative that recounts the Angel of Death "passing over" the homes of the Israelites as the tenth plague, the death of the firstborn sons, was implemented. This is the Jewish festival most commonly observed by Jews around the world.

Pharisees: Hebrew, *perushim* (peh-roo-SHEEM, peh-ROO-shim). A group of Jewish leaders prominent during the Second Temple period who emphasized Torah study and individual prayer rather than cultic sacrifices. Pharisees believed in the immortality of the soul, and in human free will to implement good or bad actions that would be rewarded or punished by God's divine providence. Considered a precursor to rabbinic Judaism, and influenced Christian doctrines as well. Often contrasted with the **Sadducees.**

priests: Hebrew, *kohen* (koe-HAYN, KOE-hayn); pl. *kohanim* (koe-HAHN-eem). Jews descended from the Tribe of Aaron/Levi who had responsibility and authority for the sacrificial cult that was the context for early Jewish prayer. Priests could not hold private property, but were instead supported by required donations from the community. After the destruction of the Temple, membership in the priestly class continued to be passed on from father to son, but any real power was dissipated, although they retained certain honors in traditional synagogue worship services, such as being called first to the Torah and blessing the congregation on festivals and special occasions.

rabbi: Hebrew, *rav* (RAHV, ROHV). "Teacher," or "master of the tradition." The first people called by that title lived in the first century C.E., and the classical "rabbinic period" lasts from then until the close of the Talmud c. 500 C.E. When one speaks of "the Rabbis," one is referring to the rabbis of that period, the ones whose interpretations, opinions, and actions are described in the **Mishnah**, Tosefta, **Midrash**, and **Talmud**. The title continues from then to our own day, however, to describe those who are themselves committed to the Jewish tradition in their own lives and have learned the tradition well enough to teach it, having been duly authorized to do so, either by a degree-granting institution or by a learned individual who is him- or herself a rabbi.

Rabbinic Judaism: The dominant form of Judaism that developed during and after the Second Temple period in Jerusalem, characterized by an emphasis on individual piety, prayer, and study of sacred texts, and guided by the discussions and rulings of rabbinic interpretation. The defining texts of rabbinic Judaism were the **Mishnah**, completed in 200 C.E., and the **Gemara**, completed in 600 C.E., often referred to as the **Talmud**.

rebbe (REH-bee): Dynastic rabbinic leader within a **Hasidic** community. Now also used for one's rabbinic authority outside the Hasidic world, especially in a *yeshiva*.

Reconstructionist Judaism: An approach to Judaism that was shaped in twentieth-century America by Rabbi Mordecai Kaplan. Emphasizes egalitarianism and Jewish civilization as it is lived by the people. A small movement numerically, but very influential—many of its ideas have been adopted by other wings of Judaism.

Reform Judaism: An approach to Judaism that was shaped in eighteenth- and nineteenth-century Germany by lay leaders and Judaic scholars who wanted to modernize Jewish doctrine and practice. Reformers empha-sized those aspects of historical Jewish texts and cultures that were dig-nified, rational, and consonant with Western ideas and practices, and rejected those that were not. Promoted worship in the vernacular lan-guage of the country. Became even more Western in its American settings in the nineteenth and twentieth centuries. A plurality of American Jews consider themselves to be Reform. In the past few decades the movement has re-incorporated more Hebrew and traditional rituals and practices.

Sabbateans: Followers of Sabbatai Tzvi, a seventeenth-century "false mes-siah," who was regarded by numerous Jews as their true redeemer until he succumbed to pressure and converted into Islam in Turkey. Most gave up their belief in him at this point, but the experience had a devastating effect on Jewish societies.

Sadducees: Hebrew, *tzedukim* (tzeh-doo-KEEM, tzeh-DOO-keem). Elite class including **priests**, members of the **Sanhedrin**, and some property owners during the Second Temple period (third century B.C.E. to first century C.E.), who opposed the **Pharisees** and rejected the religious authority of rabbis and the **Oral Law.**

Sanhedrin (san-HEHD-rin): Term used for any Jewish court, but especially "the Sanhedrin," which was the Supreme Court that existed in Israel from the first century B.C.E. to 361 C.E. Also the tractate of the **Mishnah** and **Talmud** dealing mainly with legal procedures and the court system.

Satmar Hasidim: A highly insular ultra-Orthodox Hasidic sect that developed in Satmar, Hungary, and currently is primarily located in enclaves in and around New York and Jerusalem, with smaller groups elsewhere.

Secular Jewish Humanists: An international movement of Jews who are prin-cipled non-theists. Secular Jewish Humanists run educational programs that teach Jewish history, culture, and values from a secular vantage point, and have developed secular Jewish life-cycle celebrations and cer-emonies.

secular socialist Jewishness: During the late nineteenth and early twentieth centuries many Jews were attracted to secular socialist and Communist ideologies and movements, which promised to create a world in which ethnoreligious divisions no longer precipitated enmity and persecution. Some were involved in groups with specifically Jewish orientations, such as the secular Labor Zionist movement or the anti-Zionist, Yiddish-cultural Bund, or Jewish Workman's Circle.

Sepharad (noun), **Sephardi** (adj.), **Sephardic** (adj.): Jews who lived or whose ancestors lived on the Iberian Peninsula, which was the great medieval center of Jewish culture. Often used in contradistinction to **Ashkenaz,** European Jewry. After the Catholic Inquisition and the expulsions from Spain and Portugal, large numbers of Sephardic Jews migrated and set-tled across the Ottoman Empire, in Western Europe, and in the Americas, as well as other locales. These communities experienced particularistic histories, and as a result developed diverse cultures.

Shabbat (shah-BAHT, SHAH-bess): Hebrew, "Sabbath." From a word mean-ing "to desist [from work]" and thus "to rest." "Remembering the

Sabbath" by resting on the seventh day is one of the Ten Commandments, and the weekly cessation of quotidian life is one of the central organizing events of traditional Jewish families and communities. On the Jewish Sabbath human appetites are given sanctified expression, with commandments to enjoy food, drink, sex and song, as well as prayer and study. The holiness of **Yom Kippur** is expressed by calling it the "Sabbath of Sabbaths." Also the name of the tractate of the **Mishnah**, Tosefta, and **Talmud** devoted primarily to the laws of the Sabbath.

Shavuot (shah-voo-OHT, shah-VOO-iss): Hebrew, "weeks." One of the three agricultural-historical festivals described in the Hebrew Bible, along with Sukkot and **Passover (Pesach)**. An early summer holiday celebrating the first seasonal harvest each year in the Land of Israel, given the additional meaning of commemorating the giving of the Torah at Mount Sinai. Comes seven weeks after Passover—hence its name—and traditionally celebrated by all-night Torah study and the eating of sweet dairy foods in Ashkenazi communities.

Shema (sh'-MAH): Hebrew, "hear." The central prayer in the first of the three central units in the worship service, the second being the *Amidah* and the third being the reading of the Torah. The *Shema* comprises three citations from the Bible: Deuteronomy 6:4–9, Deuteronomy 11:13–21, and Numbers 15:37–41. The larger liturgical unit in which it is embedded (called the *Shema* and Its Blessings) contains a formal call to prayer *(bar'khu)* and a series of blessings on the theological themes that, together with the *Shema*, constitute a liturgical creed of faith. *Shema* is the first word of the first line of the first biblical citation, "Hear, O Israel, Adonai is our God, Adonai is One," which is the paradigmatic statement of Jewish faith, the Jews' absolute commitment to the presence of a single and unique God in time and space.

Shemoneh Esrei (sh'moh-NEH es-RAY, sh'-MOH-neh ES-ray): Hebrew, "eighteen." A name given to the *Amidah,* the second of the two main units in the worship service. This central prayer once had eighteen benedictions in it for the weekday service (it now has nineteen).

shtetl: Any little town in a pre-modern Eastern European setting. Jews were often prohibited from settling in major metropolitan areas, so they tended to live in provincial communities that lacked bucolic or pastoral dimensions.

Shulchan Arukh (shool-KHAN ah-ROOKH, SHOOL-khan OHR-rekh): Hebrew, "the set table." The title of the code of Jewish law by Joseph Karo, completed in 1563 C.E. Shortly thereafter Moses Isserles added glosses to indicate where the practice of Northern and Eastern European Jews (**Ashkenazim**) differed from those of Mediterranean Jews (**Sephardim**) that Karo had articulated in his code.

siddur (see-DOOER, SIH-dehr): Hebrew, "order." A Hebrew prayer book, with the prayers for each service arranged in order of recitation.

sukkah (soo-KAH, SOOK-ah); pl. *sukkot* (soo-KOTE): The hut that the Torah commands Jews to construct during the harvest festival that follows the **High Holy Days** in the fall (see Leviticus 23:42–43); also, the book of the **Mishnah,** Tosefta, and **Talmud** that deals with the laws of the Sukkot holiday.

tallit (tal-LEET, TAH-liss): Hebrew, "prayer shawl." Worn traditionally by men and now by many women during prayer.

Talmud (tahl-MOOD, TAHL-m'd): The name given to each of two great compendia of Jewish law and lore compiled from the first to the sixth centuries C.E., and ever since, the literary core of the rabbinic heritage. The Talmud Yerushalmi (y'-roo-SHAHL-mee), the "Jerusalem Talmud" or "the Palestinian Talmud," is the earlier one, a product of the Land of Israel generally dated about 400 C.E. The better-known Talmud Bavli (BAHV-lee), or "Babylonian Talmud," took shape in Babylonia (present-day Iraq) and is traditionally dated about 550 C.E. When people say "the Talmud" without specifying which one they mean, they are referring to the Babylonian version. The word *talmud* comes from the Hebrew root meaning "to learn" and, in a different form, "to teach." Sometimes called the Gemara.

Talmud Torah: Supplementary Jewish religious school for elementary and middle-school-age children, typically meeting after school and/or on Sunday mornings.

TaNaKh: An acronym that is derived from the initial letters of the three divisions of the Hebrew Bible: **Torah** (the Five Books of Moses), *Nevi'im* (Prophets), and *Ketuvim* (Writings).

Temple, First and Second: In ancient times, a central building for the worship of God in Israel. The First Temple was built by Solomon, and its construction is described in the first book of Kings. In 586 B.C.E., King Nebuchadnezzar and the Babylonians conquered Judaea and destroyed the Temple, sending the Jews into exile in Babylonia. In 538 B.C.E., the Persians conquered the Babylonians, and a small remnant of the Jews returned to Palestine, where they rebuilt the Temple and reinstated the sacrificial cult. The Temple was destroyed again by the Romans in 70 C.E. The building was razed, but the retaining wall of the Temple Mount remains to this day and is known as the "Western Wall."

tikkun olam (tee-KOON oh-LAHM): Hebrew, "repairing the world." In traditional Hebrew texts it often refers to God's amelioration of problems. Today, however, this term is commonly used to characterize Jewish forms of human social action.

Tisha B'av (tee-SHAH be-AHV, TIH-shah BOHV): Hebrew, "the ninth (day) of Av." A day of mourning commemorating numerous catastrophes that affected the Jewish people, beginning with the destruction of the **First Temple** in 586 B.C.E. A twenty-four-hour fast in which all forms of creature comfort are traditionally prohibited, and the book of Lamentations (*Eicha*) is read while sitting on low stools or on the floor.

Torah (toe-RAH, TOE-rah; variants: TAY-rah, TOI-rah): Hebrew, "teaching," or "direction." In its narrowest meaning, Torah refers to the first five books of the Bible, also called the "Five Books of Moses," or the *Chumash* (khoo-MAHSH or, commonly, KHUH-m'sh), which is read in the synagogue on Monday, Thursday, the Sabbath, and holidays. In this sense, "the Torah" is sometimes used to refer to the parchment scroll on which these books are written for public reading in the synagogue. Later, during rabbinic times (approximately the first to the sixth centuries C.E.), the Five Books of Moses are referred to as the Written Torah *(Torah she-bikhtav)*, in contrast to the Oral Torah *(Torah she'-b'al peh)*, which consists of ongoing interpretations and expansions of the meaning of the Written Torah as well as the customs that evolved over time among the Jewish people and ultimately got written down, in large measure, in the **Mishnah**, Tosefta, and **Talmud**. The term *Torah* is used by extension to mean all Jewish sacred literature, including books written in the Middle Ages, the modern period, and even contemporary times, and including not only topics of Jewish law but also Jewish literature, thought, history, and ethics. Thus, in this extended meaning, one is "learning Torah" when one is studying these texts as well as classical Jewish literature (the Bible, Mishnah, Talmud, **Midrash**).

tractate: The term commonly used for a book of the **Mishnah**, Tosefta, or **Talmud**, so called because each tractate is a treatise on a specific area of Jewish law.

tzedek (TZEH-dek); *tzedakah* (tzeh-dah-KAH, tzeh-DAH-kah): Hebrew, "justice," with a very widespread secondary meaning of acts of supporting the poor.

ultra-Orthodox: See *Haredi*.

Wissenschaft des Judentums (VEE-zehn-shahft days YOO-dehn-tuhms): German, "the scientific study of Jewishness" (Jewish history and culture). This approach grew out of the *Wissenschaft* movement, prominent in nineteenth-century German universities, which used modern intellectual tools to critically examine the development of various cultures.

yahrzeit (YAHR-tzite): Yiddish, "time of year." The day of the anniversary of the death of a loved one. On that anniversary day the bereaved person traditionally recites the Mourner's *Kaddish* at synagogue services.

yekke (YEH-keh): A German Jew.

yeshiva (yeh-shee-VAH, yeh-SHEE-vah): Hebrew, "sitting." Rabbinical seminary or higher educational institution that focuses on the study of Hebrew and Aramaic sacred texts, especially the **Talmud** and other rabbinic literature. Sometimes colloquially used to refer to any Jewish day school, especially within the ultra-Orthodox sphere.

yeshivish: A slang expression describing styles of speaking, dressing, and behaving that are associated with ultra-Orthodox but non-Hasidic families.

Yizkor (YIHZ-kor): Hebrew, "remember." A prayer for departed Jews said in synagogues on major holidays.

yetzer (YAY-tzehr): Hebrew, "inclination." Can refer to the inclination to do good *(yetzer ha-TOV)* or to do evil *(yetzer ha-RAH, yetzer HOH-roh)*.

Yom Kippur (yohm kee-POOR, YOHM KIH-pehr): Hebrew, "day of atonement." The tenth day of the month of Tishre, a twenty-four-hour fast day that is considered the holiest day of the Jewish year. Jews historically have believed that on Yom Kippur God seals divine judgment of each human being for the year ahead. The day also has a joyous aspect (unlike other fast days) in anticipation of success in attaining individual and communal forgiveness, and thus observant Jews dress in festive, holiday attire—albeit avoiding leather footwear.

Zionism: A modern nationalist movement founded primarily by nineteenth-century secular European Jewish thinkers that had as its goal the creation of a Jewish State, as an antidote to the historical vulnerability of the Jews as a wandering, stateless people.

Suggestions for Further Reading

Among the hundreds of wonderful new and old books dealing with aspects of Jewish diversity, I recommend the following fifteen books as a start:

Early Jews

Cohen, Shaye D. *The Beginnings of Jewishness: Boundaries, Varieties, Uncertainties.* Berkeley: University of California Press, 1999.

Shanks, Hershel, ed. *Ancient Israel: From Abraham to the Roman Destruction of the Temple.* Revised and expanded. Upper Saddle River, N.J.: Prentice Hall and the Biblical Archaeological Society, 1999.

Pre-Modern Jewish Societies and Cultures

Biale, David ed. *Cultures of the Jews: A New History.* New York: Schocken Books, 2002.

Boyarin, Daniel. *Carnal Israel: Reading Sex in Talmudic Culture.* Berkeley and Los Angeles: University of California Press, 1993.

Gerber, Jane. *The Jews of Spain: A History of the Sephardic Experience.* New York: Free Press, 1992.

Katz, Jacob. *Tradition and Crisis: Jewish Society at the End of the Middle Ages.* Translated by Bernard Dov Cooperman. New York: Schocken Books, 1993.

Emancipation and Modernity

Ellenson, David. *After Emancipation: Jewish Religious Responses to Modernity.* Cincinnati: Hebrew Union College Press, 2004.

Hyman, Paula. *Gender and Assimilation in Modern Jewish History: The Roles and Representations of Women.* Seattle: University of Washington Press, 1995.

Kaplan, Marion. *The Making of the Jewish Middle Class: Women, Family, and Identity in Imperial Germany.* New York: Oxford University Press, 1991.

Meyer, Michael. *The Origins of the Modern Jew: Jewish Identity and European Culture in Germany.* Detroit: Wayne State University Press, 1967.

Pearl, Judea and Ruth. *I Am Jewish: Personal Reflections Inspired by the Last Words of Daniel Pearl.* Woodstock, VT: Jewish Lights Publishing, 2005.

Jewishness in America

Fishman, Sylvia Barack. *Jewish Life and American Culture*. Albany: State University of New York Press, 2000.

Glenn, Susan. *Daughters of the Shtetl: Life and Labor in the Immigrant Generation*. Ithaca: Cornell University Press, 1990.

Howe, Irving, Kenneth Libo, and Morris Dickstein. *The World of Our Fathers: The Journey of the East European Jews to America and the Life They Found and Made*. New York: New York University Press, 2005.

Joselit, Jenna Wiseman. *The Wonders of America: Reinventing Jewish Culture, 1880–1950*. New York: Hill and Wang, 1994.

Sarna, Jonathan D. *American Judaism: A History*. New Haven: Yale University Press, 2004.

Index

Bar/Bat Mitzvah

The JGirl's Guide: The Young Jewish Woman's Handbook for Coming of Age
By Penina Adelman, Ali Feldman, and Shulamit Reinharz
An inspirational, interactive guidebook designed to help pre-teen Jewish girls
address the spiritual, educational, and psychological issues surrounding coming of
age in today's society.   6 x 9, 240 pp, Quality PB, 978-1-58023-215-9 **$14.99**
   Also Available: **The JGirl's Teacher's and Parent's Guide**
8½ x 11, 56 pp, PB, 978-1-58023-225-8 **$8.99**

Bar/Bat Mitzvah Basics: A Practical Family Guide to Coming of Age Together
Edited by Cantor Helen Leneman   6 x 9, 240 pp, Quality PB, 978-1-58023-151-0 **$18.95**
The Bar/Bat Mitzvah Memory Book, 2nd Edition: An Album for Treasuring the
Spiritual Celebration *By Rabbi Jeffrey K. Salkin and Nina Salkin*
8 x 10, 48 pp, Deluxe HC, 2-color text, ribbon marker, 978-1-58023-263-0 **$19.99**
For Kids—Putting God on Your Guest List: How to Claim the Spiritual Meaning
of Your Bar or Bat Mitzvah *By Rabbi Jeffrey K. Salkin*
6 x 9, 144 pp, Quality PB, 978-1-58023-015-5 **$14.99** *For ages 11–13*

Putting God on the Guest List, 3rd Edition: How to Reclaim the Spiritual
Meaning of Your Child's Bar or Bat Mitzvah *By Rabbi Jeffrey K. Salkin*
6 x 9, 224 pp, Quality PB, 978-1-58023-222-7 **$16.99**; HC, 978-1-58023-260-9 **$24.99**
Also Available: **Putting God on the Guest List Teacher's Guide**
8½ x 11, 48 pp, PB, 978-1-58023-226-5 **$8.99**
Tough Questions Jews Ask: A Young Adult's Guide to Building a Jewish Life
By Rabbi Edward Feinstein 6 x 9, 160 pp, Quality PB, 978-1-58023-139-8 **$14.99** *For ages 12 & up*
Also Available: **Tough Questions Jews Ask Teacher's Guide**
8½ x 11, 72 pp, PB, 978-1-58023-187-9 **$8.95**

Bible Study/Midrash

**Abraham's Bind & Other Bible Tales of Trickery, Folly, Mercy
and Love** *By Michael J. Caduto*
Re-imagines many biblical characters, retelling their stories and highlighting their
foibles and strengths, their struggles and joys. Readers will learn that God has a
way of working for them and through them, even today.
6 x 9, 224 pp, HC, 978-1-59473-186-0 **$19.99** *(A SkyLight Paths book)*
Ancient Secrets: Using the Stories of the Bible to Improve Our Everyday Lives
By Rabbi Levi Meier, PhD 5½ x 8½, 288 pp, Quality PB, 978-1-58023-064-3 **$16.95**

The Genesis of Leadership: What the Bible Teaches Us about Vision,
Values and Leading Change *By Rabbi Nathan Laufer; Foreword by Senator Joseph I. Lieberman*
Unlike other books on leadership, this one is rooted in the stories of the Bible, and
teaches the values that the Bible believes are prerequisites for true leadership.
6 x 9, 288 pp, HC, 978-1-58023-241-8 **$24.99**

Hineini in Our Lives: Learning How to Respond to Others through 14 Biblical Texts and
Personal Stories *By Norman J. Cohen* 6 x 9, 240 pp, Quality PB, 978-1-58023-274-6 **$16.99**
Moses and the Journey to Leadership: Timeless Lessons of Effective Management from
the Bible and Today's Leaders *By Dr. Norman J. Cohen* 6 x 9, 240 pp, HC, 978-1-58023-227-2 **$21.99**
Self, Struggle & Change: Family Conflict Stories in Genesis and Their Healing Insights for
Our Lives *By Norman J. Cohen* 6 x 9, 224 pp, Quality PB, 978-1-879045-66-8 **$18.99**
The Triumph of Eve & Other Subversive Bible Tales *By Matt Biers-Ariel*
5½ x 8½, 192 pp, HC, 978-1-59473-040-5 **$19.99** *(A SkyLight Paths book)*
Voices from Genesis: Guiding Us through the Stages of Life *By Norman J. Cohen*
6 x 9, 192 pp, Quality PB, 978-1-58023-118-3 **$16.95**

Or phone, fax, mail or e-mail to: **JEWISH LIGHTS** Publishing
Sunset Farm Offices, Route 4 • P.O. Box 237 • Woodstock, Vermont 05091
Tel: (802) 457-4000 • Fax: (802) 457-4004 • www.jewishlights.com
Credit card orders: **(800) 962-4544** (8:30AM–5:30PM ET Monday–Friday)
Generous discounts on quantity orders. SATISFACTION GUARANTEED. Prices subject to change.

Congregation Resources

The Art of Public Prayer, 2nd Edition: Not for Clergy Only *By Lawrence A. Hoffman*
6 x 9, 272 pp, Quality PB, 978-1-893361-06-5 **$19.99** *(A SkyLight Paths book)*

Becoming a Congregation of Learners: Learning as a Key to Revitalizing
Congregational Life *By Isa Aron, PhD; Foreword by Rabbi Lawrence A. Hoffman*
6 x 9, 304 pp, Quality PB, 978-1-58023-089-6 **$19.95**

Finding a Spiritual Home: How a New Generation of Jews Can Transform the
American Synagogue *By Rabbi Sidney Schwarz*
6 x 9, 352 pp, Quality PB, 978-1-58023-185-5 **$19.95**

Jewish Pastoral Care, 2nd Edition: A Practical Handbook from Traditional &
Contemporary Sources *Edited by Rabbi Dayle A. Friedman*
6 x 9, 528 pp, HC, 978-1-58023-221-0 **$40.00**

Jewish Spiritual Direction: An Innovative Guide from Traditional and Contemporary
Sources *Edited by Rabbi Howard A. Addison and Barbara Eve Breitman*
6 x 9, 368 pp, HC, 978-1-58023-230-2 **$30.00**

The Self-Renewing Congregation: Organizational Strategies for Revitalizing
Congregational Life *By Isa Aron, PhD; Foreword by Dr. Ron Wolfson*
6 x 9, 304 pp, Quality PB, 978-1-58023-166-4 **$19.95**

Spiritual Community: The Power to Restore Hope, Commitment and Joy
By Rabbi David A. Teutsch, PhD 5½ x 8¼, 144 pp, HC, 978-1-58023-270-8 **$19.99**

The Spirituality of Welcoming: How to Transform Your Congregation into a
Sacred Community *By Dr. Ron Wolfson* 6 x 9, 224 pp, Quality PB, 978-1-58023-244-9 **$19.99**

Rethinking Synagogues: A New Vocabulary for Congregational Life
By Rabbi Lawrence A. Hoffman 6 x 9, 240 pp, Quality PB, 978-1-58023-248-7 **$19.99**

Children's Books

What You Will See Inside a Synagogue
By Rabbi Lawrence A. Hoffman and Dr. Ron Wolfson; Full-color photos by Bill Aron
A colorful, fun-to-read introduction that explains the ways and whys of Jewish
worship and religious life.
8½ x 10½, 32 pp, Full-color photos, HC, 978-1-59473-012-2 **$17.99** *For ages 6 & up (A SkyLight Paths book)*

The Kids' Fun Book of Jewish Time
By Emily Sper 9 x 7½, 24 pp, Full-color illus., HC, 978-1-58023-311-8 **$16.99**

In God's Hands
By Lawrence Kushner and Gary Schmidt 9 x 12, 32 pp, HC, 978-1-58023-224-1 **$16.99**

Because Nothing Looks Like God
By Lawrence and Karen Kushner
Introduces children to the possibilities of spiritual life.
11 x 8½, 32 pp, Full-color illus., HC, 978-1-58023-092-6 **$16.95** *For ages 4 & up*

Also Available: **Because Nothing Looks Like God Teacher's Guide**
8½ x 11, 22 pp, PB, 978-1-58023-140-4 **$6.95** *For ages 5–8*

Board Book Companions to *Because Nothing Looks Like God*
5 x 5, 24 pp, Full-color illus., SkyLight Paths Board Books *For ages 0–4*

What Does God Look Like? 978-1-893361-23-2 **$7.99**

How Does God Make Things Happen? 978-1-893361-24-9 **$7.95**

Where Is God? 978-1-893361-17-1 **$7.99**

The Book of Miracles: A Young Person's Guide to Jewish Spiritual Awareness
By Lawrence Kushner. All-new illustrations by the author
6 x 9, 96 pp, 2-color illus., HC, 978-1-879045-78-1 **$16.95** *For ages 9 and up*

In Our Image: God's First Creatures
By Nancy Sohn Swartz 9 x 12, 32 pp, Full-color illus., HC, 978-1-879045-99-6 **$16.95** *For ages 4 & up*

Also Available as a Board Book: **How Did the Animals Help God?**
5 x 5, 24 pp, Board, Full-color illus., 978-1-59473-044-3 **$7.99** *For ages 0–4 (A SkyLight Paths book)*

Holidays/Holy Days

Rosh Hashanah Readings: Inspiration, Information and Contemplation
Yom Kippur Readings: Inspiration, Information and Contemplation
Edited by Rabbi Dov Peretz Elkins with Section Introductions from Arthur Green's These Are the Words
An extraordinary collection of readings, prayers and insights that enable the modern worshiper to enter into the spirit of the High Holy Days in a personal and powerful way, permitting the meaning of the Jewish New Year to enter the heart.
RHR: 6 x 9, 400 pp, HC, 978-1-58023-239-5 **$24.99**
YKR: 6 x 9, 368 pp, HC, 978-1-58023-271-5 **$24.99**

Jewish Holidays: A Brief Introduction for Christians
By Rabbi Kerry M. Olitzky and Rabbi Daniel Judson
5½ x 8½, 144 pp, Quality PB, 978-1-58023-302-6 **$16.99**

Leading the Passover Journey: The Seder's Meaning Revealed, the Haggadah's Story Retold *By Rabbi Nathan Laufer*
Uncovers the hidden meaning of the Seder's rituals and customs.
6 x 9, 224 pp, HC, 978-1-58023-211-1 **$24.99**

Reclaiming Judaism as a Spiritual Practice: Holy Days and Shabbat
By Rabbi Goldie Milgram
7 x 9, 272 pp, Quality PB, 978-1-58023-205-0 **$19.99**

7th Heaven: Celebrating Shabbat with Rebbe Nachman of Breslov
By Moshe Mykoff with the Breslov Research Institute
5⅛ x 8¼, 224 pp, Deluxe PB w/flaps, 978-1-58023-175-6 **$18.95**

The Women's Passover Companion: Women's Reflections on the Festival of Freedom *Edited by Rabbi Sharon Cohen Anisfeld, Tara Mohr, and Catherine Spector*
Groundbreaking. A provocative conversation about women's relationships to Passover as well as the roots and meanings of women's seders.
6 x 9, 352 pp, Quality PB, 978-1-58023-231-9 **$19.99**

The Women's Seder Sourcebook: Rituals & Readings for Use at the Passover Seder *Edited by Rabbi Sharon Cohen Anisfeld, Tara Mohr, and Catherine Spector*
Gathers the voices of more than one hundred women in readings, personal and creative reflections, commentaries, blessings, and ritual suggestions that can be incorporated into your Passover celebration.
6 x 9, 384 pp, Quality PB, 978-1-58023-232-6 **$19.99**

Creating Lively Passover Seders: A Sourcebook of Engaging Tales, Texts & Activities
By David Arnow, PhD 7 x 9, 416 pp, Quality PB, 978-1-58023-184-8 **$24.99**

Hanukkah, 2nd Edition: The Family Guide to Spiritual Celebration
By Dr. Ron Wolfson. Edited by Joel Lurie Grishaver.
7 x 9, 240 pp, illus., Quality PB, 978-1-58023-122-0 **$18.95**

The Jewish Family Fun Book: Holiday Projects, Everyday Activities, and Travel Ideas
with Jewish Themes *By Danielle Dardashti and Roni Sarig. Illus. by Avi Katz.*
6 x 9, 288 pp, 70+ b/w illus. & diagrams, Quality PB, 978-1-58023-171-8 **$18.95**

The Jewish Gardening Cookbook: Growing Plants & Cooking for Holidays
& Festivals *By Michael Brown* 6 x 9, 224 pp, 30+ b/w illus., Quality PB, 978-1-58023-116-9 **$16.95**

The Jewish Lights Book of Fun Classroom Activities: Simple and Seasonal
Projects for Teachers and Students *By Danielle Dardashti and Roni Sarig*
6 x 9, 240 pp, Quality PB, 978-1-58023-206-7 **$19.99**

Passover, 2nd Edition: The Family Guide to Spiritual Celebration
By Dr. Ron Wolfson with Joel Lurie Grishaver 7 x 9, 352 pp, Quality PB, 978-1-58023-174-9 **$19.95**

Shabbat, 2nd Edition: The Family Guide to Preparing for and Celebrating the Sabbath
By Dr. Ron Wolfson 7 x 9, 320 pp, illus., Quality PB, 978-1-58023-164-0 **$19.99**

Sharing Blessings: Children's Stories for Exploring the Spirit of the Jewish Holidays
By Rahel Musleah and Rabbi Michael Klayman
8½ x 11, 64 pp, Full-color illus., HC, 978-1-879045-71-2 **$18.95** *For ages 6 & up*

Inspiration

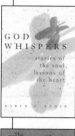

God's To-Do List: 103 Ways to Be an Angel and Do God's Work on Earth
By Dr. Ron Wolfson 6 x 9, 144 pp, Quality PB, 978-1-58023-301-9 **$15.99**

God in All Moments: Mystical & Practical Spiritual Wisdom from Hasidic Masters
Edited and translated by Or N. Rose with Ebn D. Leader
5½ x 8½, 192 pp, Quality PB, 978-1-58023-186-2 **$16.95**

Our Dance with God: Finding Prayer, Perspective and Meaning in the Stories of Our
Lives By Karyn D. Kedar 6 x 9, 176 pp, Quality PB, 978-1-58023-202-9 **$16.99**

Also Available: **The Dance of the Dolphin** (HC edition of Our Dance with God)
6 x 9, 176 pp, HC, 978-1-58023-154-1 **$19.95**

The Empty Chair: Finding Hope and Joy—Timeless Wisdom from a Hasidic Master,
Rebbe Nachman of Breslov Adapted by Moshe Mykoff and the Breslov Research Institute
4 x 6, 128 pp, 2-color text, Deluxe PB w/flaps, 978-1-879045-67-5 **$9.95**

The Gentle Weapon: Prayers for Everyday and Not-So-Everyday Moments—
Timeless Wisdom from the Teachings of the Hasidic Master, Rebbe Nachman of Breslov
Adapted by Moshe Mykoff and S. C. Mizrahi, together with the Breslov Research Institute
4 x 6, 144 pp, 2-color text, Deluxe PB w/flaps, 978-1-58023-022-3 **$9.99**

God Whispers: Stories of the Soul, Lessons of the Heart By Karyn D. Kedar
6 x 9, 176 pp, Quality PB, 978-1-58023-088-9 **$15.95**

An Orphan in History: One Man's Triumphant Search for His Jewish Roots
By Paul Cowan; Afterword by Rachel Cowan. 6 x 9, 288 pp, Quality PB, 978-1-58023-135-0 **$16.95**

Restful Reflections: Nighttime Inspiration to Calm the Soul, Based on Jewish Wisdom
By Rabbi Kerry M. Olitzky & Rabbi Lori Forman 4½ x 6½, 448 pp, Quality PB, 978-1-58023-091-9 **$15.95**

Sacred Intentions: Daily Inspiration to Strengthen the Spirit, Based on Jewish Wisdom
By Rabbi Kerry M. Olitzky and Rabbi Lori Forman 4½ x 6½, 448 pp, Quality PB, 978-1-58023-061-2 **$15.95**

Kabbalah/Mysticism/Enneagram

Awakening to Kabbalah: The Guiding Light of Spiritual Fulfillment
By Rav Michael Laitman, PhD 6 x 9, 192 pp, HC, 978-1-58023-264-7 **$21.99**

Seek My Face: A Jewish Mystical Theology By Arthur Green
6 x 9, 304 pp, Quality PB, 978-1-58023-130-5 **$19.95**

Zohar: Annotated & Explained
Translation and annotation by Daniel C. Matt; Foreword by Andrew Harvey
5½ x 8½, 176 pp, Quality PB, 978-1-893361-51-5 **$15.99** (A SkyLight Paths book)

Cast in God's Image: Discover Your Personality Type Using the Enneagram and Kabbalah
By Rabbi Howard A. Addison
7 x 9, 176 pp, Quality PB, Layflat binding, 20+ journaling exercises, 978-1-58023-124-4 **$16.95**

Ehyeh: A Kabbalah for Tomorrow
By Arthur Green 6 x 9, 224 pp, Quality PB, 978-1-58023-213-5 **$16.99**

The Enneagram and Kabbalah, 2nd Edition: Reading Your Soul
By Rabbi Howard A. Addison 6 x 9, 192 pp, Quality PB, 978-1-58023-229-6 **$16.99**

Finding Joy: A Practical Spiritual Guide to Happiness By Dannel I. Schwartz with Mark Hass
6 x 9, 192 pp, Quality PB, 978-1-58023-009-4 **$14.95**

The Flame of the Heart: Prayers of a Chasidic Mystic By Reb Noson of Breslov. Translated by
David Sears with the Breslov Research Institute 5 x 7¼, 160 pp, Quality PB, 978-1-58023-246-3 **$15.99**

The Gift of Kabbalah: Discovering the Secrets of Heaven, Renewing Your Life on Earth
By Tamar Frankiel, PhD 6 x 9, 256 pp, Quality PB, 978-1-58023-141-1 **$16.95;**
HC, 978-1-58023-108-4 **$21.95**

Kabbalah: A Brief Introduction for Christians
By Tamar Frankiel, PhD 5½ x 8½, 208 pp, Quality PB, 978-1-58023-303-3 **$16.99**

The Lost Princess and Other Kabbalistic Tales of Rebbe Nachman of Breslov
The Seven Beggars and Other Kabbalistic Tales of Rebbe Nachman of Breslov
Translated by Rabbi Aryeh Kaplan; Preface by Rabbi Chaim Kramer
Lost Princess: 6 x 9, 400 pp, Quality PB, 978-1-58023-217-3 **$18.99**
Seven Beggars: 6 x 9, 192 pp, Quality PB, 978-1-58023-250-0 **$16.99**

See also *The Way Into Jewish Mystical Tradition* in Spirituality / The Way Into... Series

Life Cycle
Marriage / Parenting / Family / Aging

Jewish Fathers: A Legacy of Love
Photographs by Lloyd Wolf. Essays by Paula Wolfson. Foreword by Rabbi Harold Kushner.
Honors the role of contemporary Jewish fathers in America. Each father tells in his own words what it means to be a parent and Jewish, and what he learned from his own father. Insightful photos.
10¾ x 9⅞, 144 pp with 100+ duotone photos, HC, 978-1-58023-204-3 **$30.00**

The New Jewish Baby Album: Creating and Celebrating the Beginning of a Spiritual Life—A Jewish Lights Companion
By the Editors at Jewish Lights. Foreword by Anita Diamant. Preface by Rabbi Sandy Eisenberg Sasso.
A spiritual keepsake that will be treasured for generations. More than just a memory book, *shows you how—and why it's important*—to create a Jewish home and a Jewish life. 8 x 10, 64 pp, Deluxe Padded HC, Full-color illus., 978-1-58023-138-1 **$19.95**

The Jewish Pregnancy Book: A Resource for the Soul, Body & Mind during Pregnancy, Birth & the First Three Months
By Sandy Falk, MD, and Rabbi Daniel Judson, with Steven A. Rapp
Includes medical information, prayers and rituals for each stage of pregnancy, from a liberal Jewish perspective. 7 x 10, 208 pp, Quality PB, b/w photos, 978-1-58023-178-7 **$16.95**

Celebrating Your New Jewish Daughter: Creating Jewish Ways to Welcome Baby Girls into the Covenant—New and Traditional Ceremonies *By Debra Nussbaum Cohen; Foreword by Rabbi Sandy Eisenberg Sasso* 6 x 9, 272 pp, Quality PB, 978-1-58023-090-2 **$18.95**

The New Jewish Baby Book, 2nd Edition: Names, Ceremonies & Customs—A Guide for Today's Families *By Anita Diamant* 6 x 9, 336 pp, Quality PB, 978-1-58023-251-7 **$19.99**

Parenting As a Spiritual Journey: Deepening Ordinary and Extraordinary Events into Sacred Occasions *By Rabbi Nancy Fuchs-Kreimer*
6 x 9, 224 pp, Quality PB, 978-1-58023-016-2 **$16.95**

Parenting Jewish Teens: A Guide for the Perplexed
By Joanne Doades 6 x 9, 200 pp, Quality PB, 978-1-58023-305-7 **$16.99**

Judaism for Two: A Spiritual Guide for Strengthening and Celebrating Your Loving Relationship *By Rabbi Nancy Fuchs-Kreimer and Rabbi Nancy H. Wiener; Foreword by Rabbi Elliot N. Dorff* Addresses the ways Jewish teachings can enhance and strengthen committed relationships. 6 x 9, 224 pp, Quality PB, 978-1-58023-254-8 **$16.99**

Embracing the Covenant: Converts to Judaism Talk About Why & How
By Rabbi Allan Berkowitz and Patti Moskovitz 6 x 9, 192 pp, Quality PB, 978-1-879045-50-7 **$16.95**

The Guide to Jewish Interfaith Family Life: An InterfaithFamily.com Handbook
Edited by Ronnie Friedland and Edmund Case 6 x 9, 384 pp, Quality PB, 978-1-58023-153-4 **$18.95**

Introducing My Faith and My Community
The Jewish Outreach Institute Guide for the Christian in a Jewish Interfaith Relationship
By Rabbi Kerry M. Olitzky 6 x 9, 176 pp, Quality PB, 978-1-58023-192-3 **$16.99**

Making a Successful Jewish Interfaith Marriage: The Jewish Outreach Institute Guide to Opportunities, Challenges and Resources *By Rabbi Kerry M. Olitzky with Joan Peterson Littman*
6 x 9, 176 pp, Quality PB, 978-1-58023-170-1 **$16.95**

The Creative Jewish Wedding Book: A Hands-On Guide to New & Old Traditions, Ceremonies & Celebrations *By Gabrielle Kaplan-Mayer*
9 x 9, 288 pp, b/w photos, Quality PB, 978-1-58023-194-7 **$19.99**

Divorce Is a Mitzvah: A Practical Guide to Finding Wholeness and Holiness When Your Marriage Dies *By Rabbi Perry Netter; Afterword by Rabbi Laura Geller.*
6 x 9, 224 pp, Quality PB, 978-1-58023-172-5 **$16.95**

A Heart of Wisdom: Making the Jewish Journey from Midlife through the Elder Years
Edited by Susan Berrin; Foreword by Harold Kushner
6 x 9, 384 pp, Quality PB, 978-1-58023-051-3 **$18.95**

So That Your Values Live On: Ethical Wills and How to Prepare Them
Edited by Jack Riemer and Nathaniel Stampfer
6 x 9, 272 pp, Quality PB, 978-1-879045-34-7 **$18.99**

Meditation

The Handbook of Jewish Meditation Practices

A Guide for Enriching the Sabbath and Other Days of Your Life
By Rabbi David A. Cooper Easy-to-learn meditation techniques.
6 x 9, 208 pp, Quality PB, 978-1-58023-102-2 **$16.95**

Discovering Jewish Meditation: Instruction & Guidance for Learning an Ancient
Spiritual Practice By Nan Fink Gefen
6 x 9, 208 pp, Quality PB, 978-1-58023-067-4 **$16.95**

A Heart of Stillness: A Complete Guide to Learning the Art of Meditation
By David A. Cooper 5½ x 8½, 272 pp, Quality PB, 978-1-893361-03-4 **$16.95** (A SkyLight Paths book)

Meditation from the Heart of Judaism: Today's Teachers Share Their
Practices, Techniques, and Faith Edited by Avram Davis
6 x 9, 256 pp, Quality PB, 978-1-58023-049-0 **$16.95**

Silence, Simplicity & Solitude: A Complete Guide to Spiritual Retreat at Home
By David A. Cooper 5½ x 8½, 336 pp, Quality PB, 978-1-893361-04-1 **$16.95**
(A SkyLight Paths book)

The Way of Flame: A Guide to the Forgotten Mystical Tradition of Jewish
Meditation By Avram Davis 4½ x 8, 176 pp, Quality PB, 978-1-58023-060-5 **$15.95**

Ritual/Sacred Practice/Journaling

The Jewish Dream Book: The Key to Opening the Inner Meaning of
Your Dreams By Vanessa L. Ochs with Elizabeth Ochs; Full-color illus. by Kristina Swarner
Instructions for how modern people can perform ancient Jewish dream practices
and dream interpretations drawn from the Jewish wisdom tradition.
8 x 8, 128 pp, Full-color illus., Deluxe PB w/flaps, 978-1-58023-132-9 **$16.95**

The Jewish Journaling Book: How to Use Jewish Tradition to Write
Your Life & Explore Your Soul By Janet Ruth Falon
Details the history of Jewish journaling throughout biblical and modern times, and
teaches specific journaling techniques to help you create and maintain a vital journal,
from a Jewish perspective. 8 x 8, 304 pp, Deluxe PB w/flaps, 978-1-58023-203-6 **$18.99**

The Book of Jewish Sacred Practices: CLAL's Guide to Everyday & Holiday
Rituals & Blessings Edited by Rabbi Irwin Kula and Vanessa L. Ochs, PhD
6 x 9, 368 pp, Quality PB, 978-1-58023-152-7 **$18.95**

Jewish Ritual: A Brief Introduction for Christians
By Rabbi Kerry M. Olitzky and Rabbi Daniel Judson
5½ x 8½, 144 pp, Quality PB, 978-1-58023-210-4 **$14.99**

The Rituals & Practices of a Jewish Life: A Handbook for Personal Spiritual
Renewal Edited by Rabbi Kerry M. Olitzky and Rabbi Daniel Judson
6 x 9, 272 pp, illus., Quality PB, 978-1-58023-169-5 **$18.95**

The Sacred Art of Lovingkindness: Preparing to Practice
By Rabbi Rami Shapiro 5½ x 8½, 176 pp, Quality PB, 978-1-59473-151-8 **$16.99**
(A SkyLight Paths book)

Science Fiction/Mystery & Detective Fiction

Mystery Midrash: An Anthology of Jewish Mystery & Detective Fiction
Edited by Lawrence W. Raphael; Preface by Joel Siegel
6 x 9, 304 pp, Quality PB, 978-1-58023-055-1 **$16.95**

Criminal Kabbalah: An Intriguing Anthology of Jewish Mystery & Detective Fiction
Edited by Lawrence W. Raphael; Foreword by Laurie R. King
6 x 9, 256 pp, Quality PB, 978-1-58023-109-1 **$16.95**

Wandering Stars: An Anthology of Jewish Fantasy & Science Fiction
Edited by Jack Dann; Introduction by Isaac Asimov
6 x 9, 272 pp, Quality PB, 978-1-58023-005-6 **$16.95**

More Wandering Stars: An Anthology of Outstanding Stories of Jewish Fantasy and
Science Fiction Edited by Jack Dann; Introduction by Isaac Asimov
6 x 9, 192 pp, Quality PB, 978-1-58023-063-6 **$16.95**

Spirituality

The Adventures of Rabbi Harvey: A Graphic Novel of Jewish Wisdom and Wit in the Wild West *By Steve Sheinkin*
Jewish and American folktales combine in this witty and original graphic novel collection. Creatively retold and set on the western frontier of the 1870s.
6 x 9, 144 pp, Full-color illus., Quality PB, 978-1-58023-310-1 **$16.99**
Also Available: **The Adventures of Rabbi Harvey Teacher's Guide**
8½ x 11, 32 pp, PB, 978-1-58023-326-2 **$8.99**

Ethics of the Sages: *Pirke Avot*—Annotated & Explained
Translation and Annotation by Rabbi Rami Shapiro
5½ x 8½, 192 pp, Quality PB, 978-1-59473-207-2 **$16.99** *(A SkyLight Paths book)*

A Book of Life: Embracing Judaism as a Spiritual Practice
By Michael Strassfeld 6 x 9, 528 pp, Quality PB, 978-1-58023-247-0 **$19.99**

Meaning and Mitzvah: Daily Practices for Reclaiming Judaism through Prayer, God, Torah, Hebrew, Mitzvot and Peoplehood *By Rabbi Goldie Milgram*
7 x 9, 336 pp, Quality PB, 978-1-58023-256-2 **$19.99**

The Soul of the Story: Meetings with Remarkable People
By Rabbi David Zeller 6 x 9, 288 pp, HC, 978-1-58023-272-2 **$21.99**

Aleph-Bet Yoga: Embodying the Hebrew Letters for Physical and Spiritual Well-Being
By Steven A. Rapp. Foreword by Tamar Frankiel, PhD and Judy Greenfeld. Preface by Hart Lazer.
7 x 10, 128 pp, b/w photos, Quality PB, Layflat binding, 978-1-58023-162-6 **$16.95**

Entering the Temple of Dreams: Jewish Prayers, Movements, and Meditations for the End of the Day *By Tamar Frankiel, PhD, and Judy Greenfeld*
7 x 10, 192 pp, illus., Quality PB, 978-1-58023-079-7 **$16.95**

Does the Soul Survive? A Jewish Journey to Belief in Afterlife, Past Lives & Living with Purpose *By Rabbi Elie Kaplan Spitz; Foreword by Brian L. Weiss, MD*
6 x 9, 288 pp, Quality PB, 978-1-58023-165-7 **$16.99**

First Steps to a New Jewish Spirit: Reb Zalman's Guide to Recapturing the Intimacy & Ecstasy in Your Relationship with God *By Rabbi Zalman M. Schachter-Shalomi with Donald Gropman* 6 x 9, 144 pp, Quality PB, 978-1-58023-182-4 **$16.95**

God in Our Relationships: Spirituality between People from the Teachings of Martin Buber *By Rabbi Dennis S. Ross* 5½ x 8½, 160 pp, Quality PB, 978-1-58023-147-3 **$16.95**

Judaism, Physics and God: Searching for Sacred Metaphors in a Post-Einstein World
By Rabbi David W. Nelson 6 x 9, 368 pp, Quality PB, inc. reader's discussion guide, 978-1-58023-306-4 **$18.99**;
HC, 352 pp, 978-1-58023-252-4 **$24.99**

The Jewish Lights Spirituality Handbook: A Guide to Understanding, Exploring & Living a Spiritual Life *Edited by Stuart M. Matlins*
What exactly is "Jewish" about spirituality? How do I make it a part of my life? Fifty of today's foremost spiritual leaders share their ideas and experience with us.
6 x 9, 456 pp, Quality PB, 978-1-58023-093-3 **$19.99**

Bringing the Psalms to Life: How to Understand and Use the Book of Psalms
By Daniel F. Polish 6 x 9, 208 pp, Quality PB, 978-1-58023-157-2 **$16.95**;
HC, 978-1-58023-077-3 **$21.95**

God & the Big Bang: Discovering Harmony between Science & Spirituality
By Daniel C. Matt 6 x 9, 216 pp, Quality PB, 978-1-879045-89-7 **$16.99**

Minding the Temple of the Soul: Balancing Body, Mind, and Spirit through Traditional Jewish Prayer, Movement, and Meditation *By Tamar Frankiel, PhD, and Judy Greenfeld*
7 x 10, 184 pp, illus., Quality PB, 978-1-879045-64-4 **$16.95**
Audiotape of the Blessings and Meditations: 60 min. **$9.95**
Videotape of the Movements and Meditations: 46 min. **$20.00**

One God Clapping: The Spiritual Path of a Zen Rabbi *By Alan Lew with Sherril Jaffe*
5½ x 8½, 336 pp, Quality PB, 978-1-58023-115-2 **$16.95**

There Is No Messiah ... and You're It: The Stunning Transformation of Judaism's Most Provocative Idea *By Rabbi Robert N. Levine, DD*
6 x 9, 192 pp, Quality PB, 978-1-58023-255-5 **$16.99**

These Are the Words: A Vocabulary of Jewish Spiritual Life
By Arthur Green 6 x 9, 304 pp, Quality PB, 978-1-58023-107-7 **$18.95**

Spirituality/Lawrence Kushner

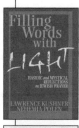

Filling Words with Light: Hasidic and Mystical Reflections on Jewish Prayer
By Lawrence Kushner and Nehemia Polen
5½ x 8½, 176 pp, HC, 978-1-58023-216-6 **$21.99**

The Book of Letters: A Mystical Hebrew Alphabet
Popular HC Edition, 6 x 9, 80 pp, 2-color text, 978-1-879045-00-2 **$24.95**
Collector's Limited Edition, 9 x 12, 80 pp, gold foil embossed pages, w/limited edition silkscreened
print, 978-1-879045-04-0 **$349.00**

The Book of Miracles: A Young Person's Guide to Jewish Spiritual Awareness
6 x 9, 96 pp, 2-color illus., HC, 978-1-879045-78-1 **$16.95** *For ages 9 and up*

The Book of Words: Talking Spiritual Life, Living Spiritual Talk
6 x 9, 160 pp, Quality PB, 978-1-58023-020-9 **$16.95**

Eyes Remade for Wonder: A Lawrence Kushner Reader *Introduction by Thomas Moore*
6 x 9, 240 pp, Quality PB, 978-1-58023-042-1 **$18.95**

God Was in This Place & I, i Did Not Know: Finding Self, Spirituality and Ultimate
Meaning   6 x 9, 192 pp, Quality PB, 978-1-879045-33-0 **$16.95**

Honey from the Rock: An Introduction to Jewish Mysticism
6 x 9, 176 pp, Quality PB, 978-1-58023-073-5 **$16.95**

Invisible Lines of Connection: Sacred Stories of the Ordinary
5½ x 8½, 160 pp, Quality PB, 978-1-879045-98-9 **$15.95**

Jewish Spirituality—A Brief Introduction for Christians
5½ x 8½, 112 pp, Quality PB, 978-1-58023-150-3 **$12.95**

The River of Light: Jewish Mystical Awareness
6 x 9, 192 pp, Quality PB, 978-1-58023-096-4 **$16.95**

The Way Into Jewish Mystical Tradition
6 x 9, 224 pp, Quality PB, 978-1-58023-200-5 **$18.99**; HC, 978-1-58023-029-2 **$21.95**

Spirituality/Prayer

Pray Tell: A Hadassah Guide to Jewish Prayer
By Rabbi Jules Harlow, with contributions from many others
8½ x 11, 400 pp, Quality PB, 978-1-58023-163-3 **$29.95**

Witnesses to the One: The Spiritual History of the *Sh'ma By Rabbi Joseph B. Meszler;*
Foreword by Rabbi Elyse Goldstein 6 x 9, 176 pp, HC, 978-1-58023-309-5 **$19.99**

My People's Prayer Book Series

Traditional Prayers, Modern Commentaries   *Edited by Rabbi Lawrence A. Hoffman*
Provides diverse and exciting commentary to the traditional liturgy, helping modern
men and women find new wisdom in Jewish prayer, and bring liturgy into their lives.
Each book includes Hebrew text, modern translation, and commentaries from all
perspectives of the Jewish world.

Vol. 1—The *Sh'ma* and Its Blessings
7 x 10, 168 pp, HC, 978-1-879045-79-8 **$24.99**
Vol. 2—The *Amidah*
7 x 10, 240 pp, HC, 978-1-879045-80-4 **$24.95**
Vol. 3—*P'sukei D'zimrah* (Morning Psalms)
7 x 10, 240 pp, HC, 978-1-879045-81-1 **$24.95**
Vol. 4—*Seder K'riat Hatorah* (The Torah Service)
7 x 10, 264 pp, HC, 978-1-879045-82-8 **$23.95**
Vol. 5—*Birkhot Hashachar* (Morning Blessings)
7 x 10, 240 pp, HC, 978-1-879045-83-5 **$24.95**
Vol. 6—*Tachanun* and Concluding Prayers
7 x 10, 240 pp, HC, 978-1-879045-84-2 **$24.95**
Vol. 7—Shabbat at Home
7 x 10, 240 pp, HC, 978-1-879045-85-9 **$24.95**
Vol. 8—*Kabbalat Shabbat* (Welcoming Shabbat in the Synagogue)
7 x 10, 240 pp, HC, 978-1-58023-121-3 **$24.99**
Vol. 9—Welcoming the Night: *Minchah* and *Ma'ariv* (Afternoon and
Evening Prayer) 7 x 10, 272 pp, HC, 978-1-58023-262-3 **$24.99**
Vol. 10—Shabbat Morning: *Shacharit* and *Musaf* (Morning and
Additional Services) 7 x 10, 240 pp, HC, 978-1-58023-240-1 **$24.99**

Spirituality/Women's Interest

The Quotable Jewish Woman: Wisdom, Inspiration & Humor from the Mind & Heart
Edited and compiled by Elaine Bernstein Partnow
6 x 9, 496 pp, HC, 978-1-58023-193-0 **$29.99**

The Knitting Way: A Guide to Spiritual Self-Discovery *By Linda Skolnick and Janice MacDaniels* 7 x 9, 240 pp, Quality PB, 978-1-59473-079-5 **$16.99** *(A SkyLight Paths book)*

The Quilting Path: A Guide to Spiritual Self-Discovery through Fabric, Thread and Kabbalah
By Louise Silk 7 x 9, 192 pp, Quality PB, 978-1-59473-206-5 **$16.99** *(A SkyLight Paths book)*

The Divine Feminine in Biblical Wisdom Literature: Selections Annotated &
Explained *Translated and Annotated by Rabbi Rami Shapiro*
5½ x 8½, 240 pp, Quality PB, 978-1-59473-109-9 **$16.99** *(A SkyLight Paths book)*

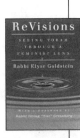

Lifecycles, Vol. 1: Jewish Women on Life Passages & Personal Milestones
Edited and with Introductions by Rabbi Debra Orenstein
6 x 9, 480 pp, Quality PB, 978-1-58023-018-6 **$19.95**

Lifecycles, Vol. 2: Jewish Women on Biblical Themes in Contemporary Life
Edited and with Introductions by Rabbi Debra Orenstein and Rabbi Jane Rachel Litman
6 x 9, 464 pp, Quality PB, 978-1-58023-019-3 **$19.95**

Moonbeams: A Hadassah Rosh Hodesh Guide *Edited by Carol Diament, PhD*
8½ x 11, 240 pp, Quality PB, 978-1-58023-099-5 **$20.00**

ReVisions: Seeing Torah through a Feminist Lens *By Rabbi Elyse Goldstein*
5½ x 8½, 224 pp, Quality PB, 978-1-58023-117-6 **$16.95**

The Women's Haftarah Commentary: New Insights from Women Rabbis on the
54 Weekly Haftarah Portions, the 5 Megillot & Special Shabbatot
Edited by Rabbi Elyse Goldstein 6 x 9, 560 pp, HC, 978-1-58023-133-6 **$39.99**

The Women's Torah Commentary: New Insights from Women Rabbis on the 54
Weekly Torah Portions *Edited by Rabbi Elyse Goldstein*
6 x 9, 496 pp, HC, 978-1-58023-076-6 **$34.95**

The Year Mom Got Religion: One Woman's Midlife Journey into Judaism
By Lee Meyerhoff Hendler 6 x 9, 208 pp, Quality PB, 978-1-58023-070-4 **$15.95**

See Holidays for *The Women's Passover Companion: Women's Reflections on the Festival of Freedom* and *The Women's Seder Sourcebook: Rituals & Readings for Use at the Passover Seder.* Also see Bar/Bat Mitzvah for *The JGirl's Guide: The Young Jewish Woman's Handbook for Coming of Age.*

Travel

Israel—A Spiritual Travel Guide, 2nd Edition
A Companion for the Modern Jewish Pilgrim
By Rabbi Lawrence A. Hoffman 4¾ x 10, 256 pp, Quality PB, illus., 978-1-58023-261-6 **$18.99**
Also Available: **The Israel Mission Leader's Guide** 978-1-58023-085-8 **$4.95**

12-Step

100 Blessings Every Day: Daily Twelve Step Recovery Affirmations, Exercises for
Personal Growth & Renewal Reflecting Seasons of the Jewish Year
By Rabbi Kerry M. Olitzky; Foreword by Rabbi Neil Gillman
4½ x 6¼, 432 pp, Quality PB, 978-1-879045-30-9 **$15.99**

Recovery from Codependence: A Jewish Twelve Steps Guide to Healing Your Soul
By Rabbi Kerry M. Olitzky 6 x 9, 160 pp, Quality PB, 978-1-879045-32-3 **$13.95**

Renewed Each Day: Daily Twelve Step Recovery Meditations Based on the Bible
By Rabbi Kerry M. Olitzky and Aaron Z.
Vol. 1—Genesis & Exodus: 6 x 9, 224 pp, Quality PB, 978-1-879045-12-5 **$14.95**
Vol. 2—Leviticus, Numbers & Deuteronomy: 6 x 9, 280 pp, Quality PB, 978-1-879045-13-2 **$18.99**

Twelve Jewish Steps to Recovery: A Personal Guide to Turning from Alcoholism &
Other Addictions—Drugs, Food, Gambling, Sex ...
By Rabbi Kerry M. Olitzky and Stuart A. Copans, MD; Preface by Abraham J. Twerski, MD
6 x 9, 144 pp, Quality PB, 978-1-879045-09-5 **$14.95**

Theology/Philosophy

Christians and Jews in Dialogue: Learning in the Presence of the Other
By Mary C. Boys and Sara S. Lee; Foreword by Dr. Dorothy Bass
6 x 9, 240 pp, HC, 978-1-59473-144-0 **$21.99** (A SkyLight Paths book)

The Death of Death: Resurrection and Immortality in Jewish Thought
By Neil Gillman 6 x 9, 336 pp, Quality PB, 978-1-58023-081-0 **$18.95**

Ethics of the Sages: Pirke Avot—Annotated & Explained
Translation & Annotation by Rabbi Rami Shapiro
5½ x 8½, 208 pp, Quality PB, 978-1-59473-207-2 **$16.99** (A SkyLight Paths book)

Evolving Halakhah: A Progressive Approach to Traditional Jewish Law
By Rabbi Dr. Moshe Zemer 6 x 9, 480 pp, Quality PB, 978-1-58023-127-5 **$29.95**;
HC, 978-1-58023-002-5 **$40.00**

Hasidic Tales: Annotated & Explained
By Rabbi Rami Shapiro; Foreword by Andrew Harvey
5½ x 8½, 240 pp, Quality PB, 978-1-893361-86-7 **$16.95** (A SkyLight Paths Book)

Healing the Jewish-Christian Rift: Growing Beyond our Wounded History
By Ron Miller and Laura Bernstein; Foreword by Dr. Beatrice Bruteau
6 x 9, 288 pp, Quality PB, 978-1-59473-139-6 **$18.99** (A SkyLight Paths book)

A Heart of Many Rooms: Celebrating the Many Voices within Judaism
By David Hartman 6 x 9, 352 pp, Quality PB, 978-1-58023-156-5 **$19.95**

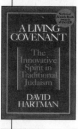

The Hebrew Prophets: Selections Annotated & Explained
Translation & Annotation by Rabbi Rami Shapiro; Foreword by Zalman M. Schachter-Shalomi
5½ x 8½, 224 pp, Quality PB, 978-1-59473-037-5 **$16.99** (A SkyLight Paths book)

A Jewish Understanding of the New Testament
By Rabbi Samuel Sandmel; Preface by Rabbi David Sandmel
5½ x 8½, 368 pp, Quality PB, 978-1-59473-048-1 **$19.99** (A SkyLight Paths book)

Keeping Faith with the Psalms: Deepen Your Relationship with God Using the Book
of Psalms By Daniel F. Polish 6 x 9, 320 pp, Quality PB, 978-1-58023-300-2 **$18.99**;
HC, 978-1-58023-179-4 **$24.95**

A Living Covenant: The Innovative Spirit in Traditional Judaism
By David Hartman 6 x 9, 368 pp, Quality PB, 978-1-58023-011-7 **$20.00**

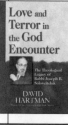

Love and Terror in the God Encounter
The Theological Legacy of Rabbi Joseph B. Soloveitchik
By David Hartman 6 x 9, 240 pp, Quality PB, 978-1-58023-176-3 **$19.95**;
HC, 978-1-58023-112-1 **$25.00**

The Personhood of God: Biblical Theology, Human Faith and the Divine Image
By Dr. Yochanan Muffs; Foreword by Dr. David Hartman
6 x 9, 240 pp, HC, 978-1-58023-265-4 **$24.99**

Tormented Master: The Life and Spiritual Quest of Rabbi Nahman of Bratslav
By Arthur Green 6 x 9, 416 pp, Quality PB, 978-1-879045-11-8 **$19.99**

Traces of God: Seeing God in Torah, History and Everyday Life
By Neil Gillman 6 x 9, 240 pp, HC, 978-1-58023-249-4 **$21.99**

We Jews and Jesus: Exploring Theological Differences for Mutual Understanding
By Rabbi Samuel Sandmel; Preface by Rabbi David Sandmel
6 x 9, 176 pp, Quality PB, 978-1-59473-208-9 **$16.99** (A SkyLight Paths book)

Your Word Is Fire: The Hasidic Masters on Contemplative Prayer
Edited and translated by Arthur Green and Barry W. Holtz
6 x 9, 160 pp, Quality PB, 978-1-879045-25-5 **$15.95**

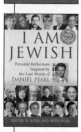

I Am Jewish

Personal Reflections Inspired by the Last Words of Daniel Pearl

Almost 150 Jews—both famous and not—from all walks of life, from all around
the world, write about Identity, Heritage, Covenant / Chosenness and Faith,
Humanity and Ethnicity, and *Tikkun Olam* and Justice.
Edited by Judea and Ruth Pearl
6 x 9, 304 pp, Deluxe PB w/flaps, 978-1-58023-259-3 **$18.99**; HC, 978-1-58023-183-1 **$24.99**
Download a free copy of the *I Am Jewish Teacher's Guide* at our website:
www.jewishlights.com

Theology/Philosophy/The Way Into... Series

The Way Into... series offers an accessible and highly usable "guided tour" of the Jewish faith, people, history and beliefs—in total, an introduction to Judaism that will enable you to understand and interact with the sacred texts of the Jewish tradition. Each volume is written by a leading contemporary scholar and teacher, and explores one key aspect of Judaism. *The Way Into...* series enables all readers to achieve a real sense of Jewish cultural literacy through guided study.

The Way Into Encountering God in Judaism
By Neil Gillman
For everyone who wants to understand how Jews have encountered God throughout history and today.
6 x 9, 240 pp, Quality PB, 978-1-58023-199-2 **$18.99**; HC, 978-1-58023-025-4 **$21.95**
Also Available: **The Jewish Approach to God:** A Brief Introduction for Christians
By Neil Gillman
5½ x 8¼, 192 pp, Quality PB, 978-1-58023-190-9 **$16.95**

The Way Into Jewish Mystical Tradition
By Lawrence Kushner
Allows readers to interact directly with the sacred mystical text of the Jewish tradition. An accessible introduction to the concepts of Jewish mysticism, their religious and spiritual significance and how they relate to life today.
6 x 9, 224 pp, Quality PB, 978-1-58023-200-5 **$18.99**; HC, 978-1-58023-029-2 **$21.95**

The Way Into Jewish Prayer
By Lawrence A. Hoffman
Opens the door to 3,000 years of Jewish prayer, making available all anyone needs to feel at home in the Jewish way of communicating with God.
6 x 9, 224 pp, Quality PB, 978-1-58023-201-2 **$18.99**

The Way Into Judaism and the Environment
By Jeremy Benstein
Explores the ways in which Judaism contributes to contemporary social-environmental issues, the extent to which Judaism is part of the problem and how it can be part of the solution.
6 x 9, 288 pp, HC, 978-1-58023-268-5 **$24.99**

The Way Into *Tikkun Olam* (Repairing the World)
By Elliot N. Dorff
An accessible introduction to the Jewish concept of the individual's responsibility to care for others and repair the world.
6 x 9, 320 pp, HC, 978-1-58023-269-2 **$24.99**

The Way Into Torah
By Norman J. Cohen
Helps guide in the exploration of the origins and development of Torah, explains why it should be studied and how to do it.
6 x 9, 176 pp, Quality PB, 978-1-58023-198-5 **$16.99**; HC, 978-1-58023-028-5 **$21.95**

The Way Into the Varieties of Jewishness
By Sylvia Barack Fishman, PhD
Explores the religious and historical understanding of what it has meant to be Jewish from ancient times to the present controversy over "Who is a Jew?"
6 x 9, 288 pp, HC, 978-1-58023-030-8 **$24.99**

About Jewish Lights

People of all faiths and backgrounds yearn for books that attract, engage, educate, and spiritually inspire.

Our principal goal is to stimulate thought and help all people learn about who the Jewish People are, where they come from, and what the future can be made to hold. While people of our diverse Jewish heritage are the primary audience, our books speak to people in the Christian world as well and will broaden their understanding of Judaism and the roots of their own faith.

We bring to you authors who are at the forefront of spiritual thought and experience. While each has something different to say, they all say it in a voice that you can hear.

Our books are designed to welcome you and then to engage, stimulate, and inspire. We judge our success not only by whether or not our books are beautiful and commercially successful, but by whether or not they make a difference in your life.

For your information and convenience, at the back of this book we have provided a list of other Jewish Lights books you might find interesting and useful. They cover all the categories of your life:

Bar/Bat Mitzvah	Life Cycle
Bible Study / Midrash	Meditation
Children's Books	Parenting
Congregation Resources	Prayer
Current Events / History	Ritual / Sacred Practice
Ecology	Spirituality
Fiction: Mystery, Science Fiction	Theology / Philosophy
Grief / Healing	Travel
Holidays / Holy Days	12-Step
Inspiration	Women's Interest
Kabbalah / Mysticism / Enneagram	

Stuart M. Matlins, Publisher

Or phone, fax, mail or e-mail to: **JEWISH LIGHTS** Publishing
Sunset Farm Offices, Route 4 • P.O. Box 237 • Woodstock, Vermont 05091
Tel: (802) 457-4000 • Fax: (802) 457-4004 • www.jewishlights.com
Credit card orders: **(800) 962-4544** (8:30AM–5:30PM ET Monday–Friday)
Generous discounts on quantity orders. SATISFACTION GUARANTEED. Prices subject to change.